HYMNS IN CHRISTIAN WORSHIP

I SIR PHILIP SIDNEY, Elizabethan poet and courtier who, together with his sister, the Countess of Pembroke, made some notable paraphrases of the Psalms.

HYMNS
in Christian
WORSHIP

I will sing with the spirit, and I will sing with the understanding also.

ST. PAUL

By H. A. L.
JEFFERSON

7837

ROCKLIFF
SALISBURY SQUARE · LONDON

IN
GRATITUDE
FOR THE
PIONEER WORK
OF
W. GARRETT HORDER

COPYRIGHT 1950
BY ROCKLIFF PUBLISHING CORPORATION LTD
MADE AND PRINTED IN GREAT BRITAIN BY
WILLIAM CLOWES & SONS LTD
LONDON AND BECCLES

Author's Acknowledgements

I AM deeply indebted to those who have given me permission to make use of copyright material, and to other friends who have placed at my disposal valuable data concerning the subject of this book. I have to thank the Oxford University Press for enabling me to quote the following hymns:

The Maker of the sun and moon (Laurence Housman)
    from *The English Hymnal*

Rise up, O men of God (W. P. Merrill)
    from Enlarged *Songs of Praise*

Jesus, good above all other (Percy Dearmer, 1867–1936)
    from Enlarged *Songs of Praise*

also for permission to quote from the prefaces of *The English Hymnal* and *Songs of Praise* (original edition):

The Clarendon Press, Oxford for permission to reproduce the two hymns by Robert Bridges:

Rejoice, O land, in God thy might

Thee will I love, my God and King :

And the National Society for allowing me to quote the hymn:

When lamps are lighted in the town (M. M. Penstone):

Messrs. J. Curwen & Sons Ltd., for sanction to reproduce *All creatures of our God and King* (W. H. Draper): Messrs. Eyre & Spottiswoode Ltd., for permission to make the quotations (which appear in the last chapter of this book) by Dr. Walford Davies, and Dr. Harvey Grace, from *Music and Worship* and Mrs. Charter Piggott, for allowing me to reproduce *In our work and in our play* (W. Charter Piggott). Further, I have to thank most cordially the Hymn Society of America, and especially its

v

Executive Secretary, Dr. R. L. McAll, for approval to quote two recent American hymns, namely:

God, who hast set us in this time (Hermann Hagedorn)

God of all peoples everywhere (R. S. & R. E. Cushman):

also for Dr. McAll's helpful courtesy in giving me important data concerning recent American developments in hymnody, and for his sympathetic interest in the preparation of this book. No one studying the subject can afford to neglect the really fine work which is being done on the other side of the Atlantic.

I am obliged to various correspondents who have shown interest in this enterprise, and for helpful information and material. I should thank especially Lady Sykes, the Reverend Dr. John Stevens, the Reverend Wilson H. Geller, Mr. W. H. Carpenter, Mrs. Beatrice Price, and the Epworth Press.

But above all I am indebted to Miss C. Morley Horder who freely placed at my disposal a wealth of important material relating to the work of Dr. W. Garrett Horder. This has been of the greatest help, together with the kindly interest and encouragement she has shown. By her kindness I have been allowed to quote freely from *Worship Song*, the book compiled by her father, which marked a new era in English hymnody.

I trust indulgence and pardon will be granted if I have omitted thanks to anyone to whom it is due, and if, in error, any copyright has been overlooked in relation to hymns which have been quoted. I am sure those concerned will accept my assurance that any such oversight is not intentional.

H.A.L.J.

Contents

Illustrations

viii

Introduction

HYMNS and worship are inseparably linked, but the manner in which hymns are used has greatly varied. It is the distinction of the Hebrew and Christian religions that they use hymns as a constant and integral part of worship.

Yet it is surprising to reflect that hymn singing, now so widespread and popular, so far as it enters into congregational worship, is a quite recent development. It is easy to overlook this fact when account is taken of the existing abundance of hymnody in Great Britain and America, and the rapidly increasing collection of hymns throughout the English-speaking world.

It is not easy for us to understand the opposition once offered by good Christian folk to the singing of hymns. Not only is it almost impossible to think of Christian worship now without this feature, but it has become a much-favoured and popular practice, even apart from organized religious worship.

It is significant how frequently community hymn singing is included in radio programmes, and it is undoubtedly enjoyed by scores of people who have not been to church. Those of us who had experience of religious services for the troops during the war will remember that the most popular feature was the hymns. Men and women who were lost in trying to find their way through the offices of the Prayer Book, were quite at home in the singing of hymns, which they enjoyed to the full. Critics may urge that this was because the hymns provided an easy form of emotional expression, but this is no discredit, for emotion is the driving force of life, and true worship is emotion purified by reason.

It is this purification by reason which is so important. Although hymn singing is popular, few elements in public worship can at times be less intelligent. This may occasion no surprise when the singers form part of the heterogeneous crowd at a Cup Final, but it cannot be condoned when it is a failure in the corporate worship of a Christian congregation. Yet those with experience and knowledge of the subject cannot feel satisfied with the average use which church congregations make of their hymn books, nor, very frequently, with the contents of the hymn books.

One illustration of this unsatisfactory use is the surprising lack of familiarity with many fine and worthy hymns, and a placid contentment with some of inferior worth. Most of the hymnals now in general use contain anything up to a thousand hymns. Yet it is likely that if the average worshipper made a list of the hymns with which he is familiar, a postcard would contain the total, and some of these would not be the best.

This is the more remarkable when we remember that England and America have the richest and most varied collection of hymnody in the world. If there is much dross there is also a wealth of purest gold. In more recent years Americans have added greatly to this store of good material, and they have greatly enriched our modern English hymnals, with much more available for inclusion in future editions.

One purpose of the following pages is to help and encourage the reader to understand and enjoy hymns more readily, and contribute to the growing movement for a better congregational standard.

There has been in recent years much more literature on the subject, and a number of books have appeared dealing with it from various angles. These works range from what are mere collections of anecdotes concerning popular hymns, to more substantial outlines of the development of English hymnody. Above all the serious student will remain indebted to the comprehensive and truly encyclopædic work of Dr. Julian in his now-famous *Dictionary of Hymnology*. One of the existing difficulties is that books of real value are out of print, while others are either too elementary to give the reader a deeper insight and more critical understanding, or are too technical except for the student who seeks a more or less specialized knowledge of the subject.

The aim here is to help the general reader who wants something more than an assembly of anecdotes, but has neither time nor inclination for exhaustive historical surveys in this vast field. How vast it is may be measured by the fact that Dr. Julian, in his *Dictionary*, was obliged to examine some 400,000 hymns in various languages when he prepared the first edition of his work in 1891, and this did not by any means include all the hymn books in existence.

During the nineteenth century an immense number of different hymn books appeared, sponsored by all the denominations, and even the most remote and eccentric sects felt it necessary to produce their own collections. The moving impulse responsible for this prolific stream was the desire to make the hymn the medium of theological dogma and opinion. This was not a new impulse. In earlier centuries, when the theological disputes were intense and bitter, hymns had been written and sung as a means of doctrinal propaganda. It has been said that the Reformation was more the work of the choir than of the pulpit. In later times, when religious sects became numerous, it was small wonder that they should have reverted to this ancient practice. Hymn books were compiled with a careful eye, not so much to the quality of the contents, but rather to the value of the hymns included in setting forth doctrinal view points. The result was disastrous for two reasons. (1) It encouraged the inclusion, and survival, of inferior hymns, because they were held to serve a particular school of doctrine, and (2) it tended to exclude and ignore hymns of merit which did not appear to contain sufficient dogmatic material. Furthermore, this method tended to make the hymn book the servant of sectarian division and dispute, and so lost one of the most valuable effects of a good hymn, which is to reveal and express the universal elements in religious experience, and so foster the unity of the Spirit in the bond of peace. It is a consummation devoutly to be wished that one day there will appear a hymn book which can be the common treasure of all Churches. The hymns contained in such a book will be fewer in number, but vastly superior in quality to many of those now retained.

The following pages will frequently express strongly critical views. This is done with no wish to encourage a "battle of the books", but with the sincere desire to foster better standards, and more intelligent understanding of many of the hymns employed in our acts of worship. A hymn, unlike a comic song or a popular ballad, is not simply something sung for the enjoyment of the singer, or the audience. *It is an offering to God.* It is an act of worship. It is above all else an expression of adoration, praise, supplication, or mystic communion. It is not a theological discourse uttered in rhyme, nor is it merely a pretty jingle pleasing to the ear. Nor is it an ingenious device to excite human emotions for a particular end, which is the bane and weakness of most 'revivalist' hymns. Let it be repeated, it is an offering to God in worship and communion. It will be insisted here that this must always be applied as the test of a good and worthy hymn.

It should be remembered that inferior hymns are often retained and used because they are linked with tunes, familiar and appreciated. It would be an excellent corrective if the reader would make a practice of meditating upon the words and thoughts of a hymn, without reference to its tune, and without singing it. Make the hymn book a private manual of devotion. Do not restrict its use to public worship. This personal use will be found a more exacting test of value. It will be much easier to detect and feel what is insincere, merely florid, exaggerated, or crude.

It will be easier, also, to sense and appreciate what is beautiful and good.

Crudity in hymns is not confined to a remote past. Recent examples are not far to seek. It was about 1890 when the following found expression:

> Good Elijah went to heaven
>   In a chariot of fire;
> Bright and warm to Glory driven,
>   Fiery horses drew him higher.

Up God's deathless way to glory,
　　Where God's holy seraphs burn,
Enoch travelled by translation,
　　With no ticket to return.

On the other hand, there has been in more recent years
the emergence of a number of hymns of real excellence which
are, as yet, too little known. For this reason attention is given
in the following pages to some of these lesser known writers
as well as to others whose hymns are more familiar. It can be
assumed that every member of a Christian congregation
knows, more or less, the hymns of Watts and Wesley preserved
in our existing books. But he may have little knowledge,
if any, of the hymns linked with the names of J. G. Whittier,
T. T. Lynch, Harriet Beecher Stowe, Anna Waring, F. L.
Hosmer, Lucy Larcom, J. S. B. Monsell, Alice Cary and
Adelaide Proctor, to mention only a very few English and
American writers whose hymns are marked by the highest
devotional beauty and insight.

An effort has been made to guide the reader through the
natural course of English hymn development. This begins
with the Tudor background and the effect of the Reformation,
as a result of which for two centuries congregational singing
was confined to the narrow limits of the Psalter. Certain
seventeenth-century hymn writers are mentioned, and the way
is seen to the real foundation of English congregational hymn
singing, through the pioneer work of Isaac Watts; gathering
increasing momentum by the influence of the Methodist
Revival. Then comes the era of development in the Anglican
Church, and the progress of hymnody that marked the nineteenth century. Reference is made to our debt to other than
English sources, for the store has been greatly enriched by the
hymns from Germany, translated by John Wesley and others,
and the adaptation to our use of the treasures contained
in Greek and Latin hymnody. Reference is made to the
inclusion in recent English hymn books of hymns of outstanding merit contributed by American writers, paying
attention particularly to recent American work not yet known

in England. Another later development of which mention is made is the enrichment derived from the poets. Something is also said of the work of leading English hymnologists, to whom we owe a great debt for a new era in our hymnody, which began over half a century ago. Expression is given to some critical views regarding leading hymn books now in general use, with a brief section dealing with tunes and the music of hymns. Full treatment of this latter theme would demand a separate work, but it is a subject which has an important bearing on our use of hymns, and is not one we can afford to neglect.

In dealing with English hymns one must be eclectic and comprehensive. Here, if anywhere, sectarian boundaries should be transcended. In some recent Anglican books I have felt a lack of adequate regard for the work done by Nonconformist hymn writers, and, on the other hand, a surprising lack of Catholic sympathy on the part of some Free Church compilers.

The purpose of the present volume will be served if it helps the reader to sing, not only with the spirit, but with the understanding also.

Come, O come, in pious lays
Sound we God Almighty's praise:
Hither bring, in one consent,
Heart and voice and instrument.
Let those things which do not live
In still music praises give,
Nor a creature dumb be found,
That hath either voice or sound.

Come, ye sons of human race,
In this chorus take your place:
And amid the mortal throng
Be ye masters of the song.
Let, in praise of God, the sound
Run a never-ending round,
That our song of praise may be
Everlasting, as is He.

So this huge, wide orb we see
Shall one choir, one temple be,
And our song shall overclimb
All the bounds of space and time,
And ascend from sphere to sphere
To the great Almighty's ear.
Then, O come, in pious lays
Sound we God Almighty's praise.

George Wither (1588-1667)

"Slow Singers and Quick Singers"

IN the middle of the eighteenth century, troops under General Wolfe were stationed in Aberdeen. They held a church parade in the cathedral, during which they sang hymns very heartily. It was much of a novelty and innovation, for there was acute division between those who sought to make hymn singing an essential part of public worship, and others who contended to preserve the prevailing practice of restricting singing to the psalms.

However, the good folk of Aberdeen were so impressed on this occasion that they secured one of the troopers, Thomas Channon by name, to be their choirmaster. He was a success. So much so that the Synod of Aberdeen obtained his discharge from the Army in order that he could become the singing-master for the parishes of the city.

The students of the university, who attended the cathedral, joined in the hymns with fervour, and the singing became increasingly popular. All would have been well but for the fact that one section of the people preferred the old solemn method of psalm singing. They resolved to silence the enthusiastic hymn singers. To this end they hired three young urchins with shrill voices to sit on the pulpit steps, and sing lustily out of tune. In this discordant enterprise they were assisted by a young man named Gideon Duncan. It is not surprising to learn that the service ended in an uproar, as the "slow singers" and the "quick singers" contended with each other. But the dominant party was that of the university, who

A   1

favoured the new way. The unruly boys were given a sound thrashing, while the unfortunate Duncan was hauled before the magistrate for singing out of tune, being fined £50 and imprisoned until it was paid. It may sound surprising to learn that at this period it was possible to be fined for singing out of tune in church, just as it was possible, also, to be fined for not attending.

This story illustrates the fact that only two centuries ago the singing of hymns in public worship was a novelty, and an occasion of violent dispute. But the Aberdonians were not the first to find hymn singing a bone of contention. There was a memorable instance at an earlier date, for it is on record that at the beginning of 1693 a group of twenty-two aggrieved persons from a Baptist church in Southwark, which was under the ministry of the Rev. Benjamin Keach, sought fellowship with a neighbouring community on the ground that they were "dissatisfied with the setting up of common set form singing after it had been exploded by the Baptised churches as a human invention".

It is said that the good Benjamin Keach was the first to introduce hymns into the regular worship of an English congregation. He prepared a book of three hundred hymns, called *Spiritual Melody*, published in 1691, although he had published hymns for children as early as 1664. When we ponder a few examples of his verses we wonder if the split in the church was provoked by the objection to hymn singing in general, or because of the particular quality of the good pastor's hymns.

Here are one or two typical verses:

> Here meets them now that worm that gnaws,
> And plucks their vitals out;
> The pit, too, on them shuts her jaws,
> This dreadful is, no doubt.

Here is another:

> Repentance like a bucket is
> To pump the water out;

> For leaky is our ship, alas,
> Which makes us look about.

We may sympathize with the feelings of a congregation invited to sing the following:

> Our wounds do stink and are corrupt,
> Hard swellings do we see;
> We want a little ointment, Lord,
> Let us more humble be.

Religious verse of this character was not likely to lift the soul to the heavenly places. Nor can we imagine that some of the verse designed for the moral instruction of youth was any more cheering. A young maiden who may have found pleasure in her mirror's reflection was duly admonished in the words of another verse maker of the period:

> When by Spectators I am told
> What beauty doth adorn me,
> Or in a glass when I behold
> How sweetly God did form me:
> Hath God such comeliness display'd
> And on me made to dwell,
> What pitty such a pretty Maid
> As I should go to Hell.

Mr. Keach seems to have supported his efforts to introduce congregational hymn singing by an ingenious appeal to Scripture; an exercise by no means confined to his own time. A favourite proof text he cited for the purpose was Exodus xxxii. 18, "the noise of them that sing do I hear", claiming that one man's voice could not have made such a noise, and, therefore, the singing must have been congregational. His critics pointed out, however, that the congregational act in question was in praise of the Golden Calf! These opponents of hymn singing also argued that, furthermore, some people cannot sing, not having tunable voices, and women ought anyhow to keep silence in the churches. So the wrangles and disputes continued, but the "slow singers", or supporters of singing restricted to the Psalms, dominated the position, and England had long to wait before hymn singing became not only tolerated, but popular.

Undoubtedly the efforts of those who sought to promote congregational singing were weakened by the almost ludicrous nature of many of the doggerels of the time. Mr. Keach's effusions did not stand alone, as the following verse indicates. It is from a Scottish hymn descriptive of Jonah's plight:

> Ah Me! this is an awesome place,
> Without e'er coal or candle,
> Nothing but fishes tripes to eat,
> And fishes tripes to handle.

It would, however, be quite wrong to assume that no acceptable and worthy hymns in English had been written at this period. It is not surprising that the volume was not large, small encouragement being given in a period when hymn singing was frowned upon by authority; disallowed in the Established Church, and banned by the vast majority of Dissenters. But for private devotion, and possibly, in a very few places, for congregational use, verses of enduring merit had been written. Some of these now find a place in our more recent hymn books. For an early example we must look to an Elizabethan courtier, George Gascoigne, who in 1557 represented Bedford in Parliament, and was a lawyer and playwright. He wrote the original of the following morning hymn:

> You that have spent the silent night
>   In sleep and quiet rest,
> And joy to see the cheerful light
>   That riseth in the east,
> Now clear your voice, now cheer your heart,
>   Come, help me now to sing;
> Each willing wight, come, bear a part,
>   To praise the heavenly King.

For, as the darksome night did last
  But for a little space,
And heavenly day, now night is past,
  Doth show his pleasant face,
So must we hope to see God's face,
  At last, in heaven on high,
When we have changed this mortal place
  For immortality.

Unto which joy for to attain,
  God grant us all His grace,
And send us, after worldly pain,
  In heaven to have a place;
Where we may still enjoy that light
  Which never shall decay;
Lord, for Thy mercy, lend us might
  To see that joyful day.

Another example from the Elizabethan court may be found
in the work of the Sidneys, brother and sister. Sir Philip,
in common with others of the time, including the Queen,
found pleasure in compiling metrical psalms. He undertook
the production of a complete metrical psalter, in which work
his sister, the Lady Mary, Countess of Pembroke, proved a
skilled and gifted collaborator. It is a pleasant flight of
imagination to picture these two poetic Elizabethans sitting
on a summer's day in the gardens of the Countess at Wilton,
musing on the Psalms, and composing verses of devotion.
One such production has found inclusion in recent hymn
books.

O Lord, in me there lieth nought
But to Thy search revealed lies;
      For when I sit
      Thou markest it;
No less Thou notest when I rise:
Yea, closest closet of my thought
Hath open windows to Thine eyes.

5

Thou walkest with me when I walk;
When to my bed for rest I go,
    I find Thee there,
    And everywhere;
Not youngest thought in me doth grow,
No, not one word I cast to talk
But yet, unuttered, Thou dost know.

If forth I march, Thou goest before;
If back I turn, Thou com'st behind;
    So forth nor back
    Thy guard I lack;
Nay, on me too Thy hand I find.
Well I Thy wisdom may adore,
But never reach with earthly mind.

Do thou thy best, O secret night,
In sable veil to cover me;
    Thy sable veil
    Shall vainly fall;
With day unmasked my night shall be;
For night is day and darkness light,
O Father of all lights, to Thee.

It should be repeated that such lines were not written originally for congregational singing. Rather, they were religious odes designed for private meditation and devotion. This should be borne in mind when comparing them with the hymns of a later period intended for public worship. In our more recent hymn books, particularly *Songs of Praise*, a number of these earlier religious poems, of varying degrees of suitability and merit, have been adapted and employed as hymns for congregational worship. Others will be considered more fully later when we deal with the modern use of poetry in the service of hymnody. The purpose here is to give some examples of the devotional poetry which was already providing possible material for hymns during the long period when congregational singing was narrowly restricted to metrical versions of the psalter.

Some of the writers of this early period wrote in a form and metre more definitely suitable for later congregational use. This is in evidence in what may now be regarded as the oldest English hymn to be found in any of our books. This was written, so far as we know, by the Rev. John Marckant, who became Rector of Great Clacton in the second year of Elizabeth. The modern version is a revision made by Bishop Reginald Heber. The original is as follows:

O Lord turn not Thy face from me,
    Who lie in woeful state,
Lamenting all my woeful life,
    Before Thy mercy-gate;

A gate which opens wide to those
    That do lament their sin;
Shut not that gate against me, Lord,
    But let me enter in.

And call me not to strict account,
    How I have sojourned here,
For then my guilty conscience knows
    How vile I shall appear.

So come I to Thy mercy gate,
    Where mercy doth abound;
Imploring pardon for my sin,
    To heal my deadly wound.

Mercy, good Lord, mercy I ask,
    This is the total sum;
For mercy, Lord, is all my suit,
    O let Thy mercy come.

Judged by later and more mature standards this hymn is probably not of the highest merit. Its interest lies in the fact that it was included with versions of the Psalms, and so appears to have enjoyed something in the way of official sanction. It is also of interest because it expresses so clearly a deep sense of sin and contrition, which was a feature in earlier hymnody, both Evangelical and Catholic. The latter type of religion also retained a delicate and sensitive appreciation of the Divine element in Nature, reflected in some of the Elizabethan poets, and echoing the joyful note found in St. Francis, and in his beautiful *Canticle to the Creatures*. It was a note destined to be silenced for a while by the prevailing doctrine of Calvinism, though even there, as we shall see, it found later a certain type of expression in many of the hymns of Isaac Watts.

One gentle Catholic spirit of the period was Robert Southwell, a Jesuit poet. As a reminder that religious intolerance, in that age of intolerance, was not confined to the Romanist, we may recall that Southwell endured martyrdom, together with many other Jesuit Fathers, at the hands of the Elizabethan Government. He wrote a few of his poems in prison. Here are two verses to indicate the quality of his thought:

> Yet God's must I remain,
>   By death, by wrong, by shame;
> I cannot blot out of my heart
>   That grace wrought in His name.
>
> I cannot set at naught
>   Whom I have held so dear;
> I cannot make Him seem afar
>   That is indeed so near.

A hymn well known to most congregations to-day, for it will be found in all the standard hymn books, is *Jerusalem, my happy home*. The version common now is one of six verses, over the name of Joseph Bromehead, although variations will be found in different books. In *Songs of Praise* it is given in two versions; one version giving twenty-six verses, divided into four parts. This closely reflects the original. It has sometimes appeared with the initials "F.B.P." attached, at one time assumed to stand for Francis Baker, Priest, but this was pure conjecture. The authorship is really unknown. It is contained in a MS. quarto volume, number 15,225, in the British Museum, and from internal evidence it would seem that the date is near to 1616. The hymn itself is probably of the time of Queen Elizabeth, and in its original form is an excellent example of the style and thought of the period. As the hymn, in the modern version, is so well known and popular, readers may like to see the original. It is as follows:

> Hierusalem! my happie Home!
>   When shall I come to thee?
> When shall my sorrows have an end?
>   Thy ioyes when shall I see?
>
> O happie harbor of the saints,
>   O sweete and pleasant soyle,
> In thee no sorrow may be found,
>   Noe greefe, noe care, noe toyle!
>
> In thee noe sicknesse may be seene,
>   Noe hurt, noe ache, noe sore;
> There is no death, nor ugly devill,
>   But Life for evermore.
>
> Noe dampish mist is seene in thee
>   Noe cold nor darksome night;
> There everie soule shines as the sun;
>   There God Himselfe gives light.
>
> There lust and lucre cannot dwell,
>   There envy bears no sway;
> There is no hunger, heate nor colde,
>   But pleasure everie way.
>
> Hierusalem! Hierusalem!
>   God grant I once may see
> Thy endless ioyes, and of the same
>   Partaker aye to bee!

Thy walls are made of pretious stones,
 Thy bulwarkes diamondes square,
Thy gates are of right orient pearle,
 Exceedinge riche and rare.

Thy turrettes and thy pinnacles
 With carbuncles doe shine;
Thy verrie streets are paved with gould,
 Surpassinge clear and fine.

Thy houses are of yvorie,
 Thy windows crystal cleare;
Thy tyles are made of beaten gould;
 O God, that I were there!

Within thy gates nothinge doth come
 That is not passinge cleane;
Noe spider's web, no durt, no dust,
 Noe filthe may there be seen.

Ah! my sweete Home, Hierusalem,
 Would God I were in thee!
Would God my woes were at an end,
 Thy ioyes that I might see!

Thy saints are crowned with glorie great,
 They see God face to face;
They triumph still, they still reioyce;
 Most happie is their case.

Wee that are heere in banishment
 Continuallie doe moane;
We sigh and sob, we weepe and waile,
 Perpetuallie we groane.

Our sweete is mixed with bitter gaule,
 Our pleasure is but paine;
Our ioyes scarce last the lookeing on,
 Our sorrowes still remaine.

10

But there they live in such delight,
   Such pleasure and such play,
As that to them a thousand yeares
   Doth seeme as yesterday.

Thy vineyardes and thy orchardes are
   Most beautifull and faire,
Full furnished with trees and fruits,
   Most wonderfull and rare.

Thy gardens and thy gallant walkes
   Continually are greene;
There growe such sweet and pleasant flowers
   As noe where else are seene.

There's nectar and ambrosia made
   There's muske and civette sweete;
There manie a fair and daintie drugge
   Are trodden under feete.

There cinnamon, there sugar grows,
   There narde and balm abound.
What tounge can telle or harte conceive
   The ioyes that there are found?

Quyt through the streetes with silver sound,
   The Flood of Life do flowe;
Upon whose bankes on everie syde,
   The Wood of Life doth growe.

There trees for evermore bear fruite,
   And evermore doe springe;
There evermore the angels sit,
   And evermore doe singe.

There David stands with harpe in hands,
   As master of the queere;
Tenne thousand times that man were blest,
   That might this musicke heare!

11

Our Ladie singes *Magnificat*,
  With tune surpassinge sweete;
And all the Virginns beare their parte,
  Sitting aboute her feete.

Te Deum doth Saint Ambrose singe,
  Saint Austine doth the like;
Ould Simeon and Zacharie
  Have not their songes to seeke.

There Magdalene hath left her mone,
  And cheerfullie doth singe
With blessed Saints, whose harmonie
  In everie street doth ringe.

Hierusalem! my happie Home!
  Would God I were in thee!
Would God my woes were at an end,
  Thy ioyes that I might see!

This hymn is interesting for several reasons. It reflects the prominence given in earlier religious thought to the life beyond death. The rich and varied imagery is derived, as will be noted, from the vision of the Heavenly Jerusalem in the Apocalypse, with the addition of features reproduced from medieval theology. Such a graphic and literal protrayal of the delights of heaven stands in significant contrast to the thought of our more earth-bound epoch, in which the delights of the mundane utopia inspire hymns more readily than any vision of Jerusalem above. But seen thus in full, there is a charm and beauty in the thought, clothed as it is in opulent metaphor, which keeps its freshness of appeal. The hymn is found to-day in the most Evangelical of Protestant hymn books, and by the omission of certain stanzas the uninstructed may remain quite ignorant of its Catholic origin. It is a clear instance of the satisfying manner in which a hymn can find a home in the common treasury of mystical devotion. The poet in his vision transcends sectarian boundaries. We can find many examples of this, illustrating the welcome fact that in the dialect of devotion we have the language of unity.

12

2

The Seventeenth Century Prepares
the Way

IT is to the seventeenth century that we must look for some contributions destined to have an important influence in preparing the way for the era of congregational hymn singing. One of the first to be observed is the work of George Wither, who in 1623 published *Hymns and Songs of the Church*. Wither was then thirty-five years of age. It is remarkable that until recent date none of his verses appeared in any of our hymn books, for his place in the formative period of English hymnody was an important one. George Wither had an interesting career. He was in the service of Charles I as a captain of the horse, but became a supporter of Cromwell, on whose behalf he raised a troop of horse, selling his estates for the purpose.

He was imprisoned by James I for a pithy satire, *Abuses Whipt and Stript*, and wrote some of his best poetry during his detention. It is strange that we should have been so long unaware of Wither's devotional writings, for it can be said with truth that he was the pioneer of the modern hymn. His *Hymns and Songs of the Church* won royal favour, and a patent was obtained for it to be included with every copy of the metrical Psalms. The Company of Stationers strongly opposed this concession, and the patent was eventually withdrawn in 1634. This book of George Wither's has been described as the earliest attempt at an English hymn book. It appears to have been eagerly bought by the younger people of the time, and its popularity was undoubtedly enhanced by the delightful

13

tunes set to a number of the hymns by Orlando Gibbons, the most noted composer of the period.

Some years later Wither published another collection of hymns, under the title of *Hallelujah, or Britain's Second Remembrancer*, and this work was addressed to the High Court of Parliament, with the statement that he had directed to their attention "the sweet perfume of pious phrases compounded according to the art of the spiritual apothecary". He was clearly a man of delightful humour. He attached a note to each hymn suggesting the occasion for which it was specially written. Thus, "To be sung when washing" and "When we cannot sleep" and another, "When slandered". Others were intended for particular persons, such as Members of Parliament, doctors, lovers, artists, merchants, and, perhaps most delightful of all, "For a Widow delivered from a troublesome yoke-fellow". How many themes his pen would find to-day! No wonder such caustic wit was not popular with the somewhat humourless James I. Pope spoke of Wither as "sleeping among the dull ancient days, where no critics damn". Whatever the reason, it is remarkable that a writer of such charm and felicity should have remained neglected by the compilers of our hymn books.

Wither wrote a hymn for the anniversary of marriage, so quaint and beautiful, yet so sound and practical in sentiment, that it deserves to rank with the best of our wedding hymns, and would prove an acceptable change from *The Voice that breathed o'er Eden* by the omission of the first verse, adding this verse on subsequent anniversaries.

Here are the verses:

> Lord, living here are we,
> As fast united yet,
> As when our hearts and hands by Thee
> Together first were knit!
> And in a thankful song
> Now sing we will Thy praise
> For that Thou dost as well prolong
> Our loving as our days.

Together we have now
Begun another year,
But how much time Thou wilt allow
Thou mak'st it not appear.
We therefore do implore
That live and love we may
Still so, as if but one day more
Together we should stay.

Let each of other's wealth
Preserve a faithful care,
And of each other's joy and health
As if one soul we were.
Such conscience let us make
Each other not to grieve,
As if we daily were to take
Our everlasting leave.

The frowardness that springs
From our corrupted kind,
Or from those troublous outward things
Which may distract the mind;
Permit Thou not, O Lord,
Our constant love to shake,
Or to disturb our true accord,
Or make our hearts to ache.

But let these frailties prove
Affection's exercise,
And that discretion teach our love
Which wins the noblest prize.
So time which wears away
And ruins all things else,
Shall fix our love on Thee for aye,
In whom perfection dwells.

15

The century that produced Wither marked the emergence of another remarkable group of men, the metaphysical poets, as we now call them. Most of them were members of the truly distinguished circle of friends who gathered around Izaak Walton. Of these, possibly, George Herbert, the gracious and saintly Public Orator of Cambridge, and later Rector of Bemerton, is the best known. In this fellowship we find Donne, the famous Dean of St. Paul's, Wotton, Crashaw, Ferrar, Ken, and other leading churchmen of the period. To these should be added Vaughan and Traherne. The extent to which our modern hymn books have been enriched by them will be seen in a later chapter, when the treasures gleaned from poetry are considered more fully. They were writing lines of unfading power and beauty, with little or no thought that they were providing hymns for a later age. The ban which continued to rest on the congregational singing of hymns discouraged any such enterprise as the deliberate writing of hymns for congregational use. But their work should be borne in mind not only as evidence of the skill and capacity which then existed in the realm of poetry, and which could, beyond question, have produced hymns of the first quality, but also because the literature and language of England have never been marked by a greater wealth of creative genius.

At this stage we must notice one of these poets, because he had a composition set to music, and sung in his own cathedral, in the reign of James II. At the time it was probably sung as an anthem, but it has now been included in two of our modern hymn books. This is John Donne's hymn *Wilt Thou forgive that sin where I begun*. It was written when Donne was Dean of St. Paul's, and during an illness which was the occasion of his volume of *Devotions*.

> Wilt Thou forgive that sin, where I begun,
>   Which was my sin though it were done before?
> Wilt Thou forgive that sin, through which I run,
>   And do run still, though still I do deplore?
> When Thou hast done, Thou hast not done,
>   For I have more.

Wilt Thou forgive that sin which I have won
  Others to sin, and made my sin their door?
Wilt Thou forgive that sin which I did shun
  A year or two, but wallowed in a score?
When Thou hast done, Thou hast not done,
                For I have more.

I have a sin of fear, that when I've spun
  My last thread, I shall perish on the shore;
But swear by Thyself, that at my death Thy Son
  Shall shine, as he shines now and heretofore:
And, having done that, Thou hast done:
                I fear no more.

Izaak Walton, in his *Life of Donne*, tells us that the author of this poem, after his recovery from the illness during which it was composed, "caused it to be set to a most grave and solemn tune, and to be sung often by the Choristers of St. Paul's in his own hearing; especially at the Evening Service". We may rightly assume that this act was something in the nature of an innovation, which would not be surprising when we remember Donne's original and creative mind.

During the Restoration period a number of works of private devotion were published, and their value lies in the fact that they helped to influence the form of subsequent English hymns, by the verses they contained. One was the work of Samuel Crossman, who became Dean of Bristol Cathedral. It contained a long poem in two parts on the Heavenly Jerusalem, and this, shortened and somewhat altered, has become the familiar hymn *Jerusalem on High*, which is now found in most of our hymn books. Another beautiful hymn included in the same book of devotions, but less familiar, was *My song is love unknown*, which now finds a place in several of the more recent hymn books. The merit of this is the impressive restraint and, therefore, true reverence, which marks the references to Our Lord's Passion. It was a theme which when dealt with by both Catholic and Evangelical writers tended frequently to assume forms marred by a cloying sweetness, or else by a morbid concentration on physical details bordering on the sadistic and repulsive.

The absence of these defects, and a natural beauty of treatment, make Crossman's hymn distinctive. As it is not so widely known as the previous hymn of the same author, it is reproduced.

> My song is love unknown,
> My Saviour's love to me;
> Love to the loveless shown,
> That they might lovely be.
>   O who am I,
>   That for my sake
>   My Lord should take
>   Frail flesh, and die?
>
> He came from His blest throne
> Salvation to bestow;
> But men made strange, and none
> The longed-for Christ would know;
>   But O! my Friend,
>   My Friend indeed,
>   Who at my need
>   His life did spend.
>
> Sometimes they strew His way,
> And His sweet praises sing;
> Resounding all the day
> Hosannas to their King;
>   Then "Crucify!"
>   Is all their breath,
>   And for His death
>   They thirst and cry.
>
> Why, what hath my Lord done?
> What makes this rage and spite?
> He made the lame to run,
> He gave the blind their sight.

Sweet injuries!
Yet they at these
Themselves displease,
And 'gainst Him rise.

They rise and needs will have
My dear Lord made away;
A murderer they save,
The Prince of life they slay.
Yet cheerful He
To suff'ring goes,
That He His foes
From thence might free.

In life, no house, no home
My Lord on earth might have;
In death, no friendly tomb,
But what a stranger gave.
What may I say?
Heaven was His home;
But mine the tomb
Wherein He lay.

Here might I stay and sing,
No story so divine;
Never was love, dear King!
Never was grief like Thine.
This is my Friend,
In Whose sweet praise
I all my days
Could gladly spend.

This hymn first appeared in the *Public School Hymn Book*, and it is surprising that verses of such depth and sensitive feeling should have remained so long neglected, and that well-known hymn books continue to overlook them.

Another name belonging to the middle of the seventeenth century is that of John Austin. Here, again, verses of unusual quality and beauty have only recently been included in a few of our hymn books.

John Austin, who died in 1669, belonged originally to the Church of England, but subsequently entered the Roman communion, and issued a devotional manual, including prayers and meditations for private and family use. It contained forty-three hymns, some from his own pen and others by Richard Crashaw. More than one adaptation of Austin's book was made for the use of English Churchmen, for it was a work distinguished by sincere devotion and spiritual insight. Three of the hymns have been published in one or two recent hymnals, and these are *Blest be Thy love, dear Lord; Hail, glorious spirits, heirs of light*; and *Hark, my soul, how everything*. The latter is in the true Franciscan tradition, in that it expresses the unity of creation, including man, in the worship of God. Here are the six verses which have been selected for popular use in congregational worship.

Hark, my soul, how everything
Strives to serve our bounteous King;
Each a double tribute pays,
Sings its part and then obeys.

Nature's chief and sweetest choir
Him with cheerful notes admire;
Chanting every day their lauds,
While the grove their song applauds.

Though their voices lower be,
Streams have too their melody;
Night and day they warbling run,
Never pause, but still sing on.

All the flowers that gild the spring
Hither their still music bring;
If heaven bless them, thankful, they
Smell more sweet and look more gay.

20

Wake! for shame, my sluggish heart,
Wake! and gladly sing thy part;
Learn of birds, and springs, and flowers,
How to use thy nobler powers.

Call whole nature to thy aid,
Since 'twas He whole nature made;
Join in one eternal song,
Who to one God all belong.

One sound method to employ in discerning the quality of a hymn is to abstract single lines, and ponder their significance. A hymn which appears at first sight almost childlike in its simplicity will, by this method, yield treasures of thought and vision beyond expectation, if it is truly a hymn of merit. Apply this method to the above lines, as well as to others already quoted, and the reward will prove generous. The hymn by John Austin expresses a mysticism, valid and profound, yet clothed in a form so exquisitely lucid and simple that a child can sing the lines with delight. Is there not an inescapable loveliness in the thought of the flowers, because heaven blesses them, being thankful, and because thankful, "they smell more sweet and look more gay"? There are thoughts here not to be passed over lightly or hastily.

The name of Richard Baxter is probably better known, and we must regard him as one of the pioneers of hymn making and hymn singing, anticipating the notable work of Isaac Watts, who was soon to appear.

Baxter was a prolific writer; a leading Puritan preacher, and one with a wide outlook and catholicity of mind far beyond the average religious thought of his day. A saint, mystic, and scholar, this truly remarkable man exercised an influence on the minds of men and women in all the Churches, and an influence that still endures. The vicissitudes of his life were unique in many ways. He was for a time chaplain in Cromwell's army; then at the Restoration chaplain to Charles II, who offered him the bishopric of Hereford, which he declined. On the passage of the Act of Uniformity in 1662 he resigned

21

his church at Kidderminster, and lived in retirement from 1663 to 1672. Following the Act of Indulgence in the latter year he took a leading part in Nonconformity. In 1685 the infamous Judge Jeffreys condemned him to prison, and his trial was the occasion of a well-known repartee that revealed his wit. To a sneer by the Judge, "Baxter, I see the rogue in thy face", the retort was made, "I did not know, my Lord, that my face was a mirror!" Baxter was imprisoned on a charge of sedition, the common and false accusation frequently made against Nonconformists at the time, but after eighteen months he was pardoned and released.

The grace and beauty of Baxter's character and personality shine through his words and works. It was of the latter that Dr. Johnson remarked, "Read them all, they are all good"; sound advice which can be followed with much profit. George Macdonald proclaimed his merit as a poet, and it is no exaggeration to regard him as one of the greatest men of the century in which he lived. He was a man who knew in his soul the unconquerable peace of God, yet he endured years of conflict and turmoil; driven from place to place; imprisoned for preaching at one period, and in royal favour at another. Offered the see of Hereford, he declined it; following his convictions consistently and fearlessly, yet keeping a grace and humility of spirit manifest in all he said and did, and dreaming of the ultimate unity of the Church of God in a time of religious intolerance and strife.

One of the best-known hymns he wrote has come to us in a revised form. This is the familiar, *Ye holy angels bright*. Another, contained in one of his volumes of poetry, is the beautiful hymn, *Lord it belongs not to my care*. This hymn as we have it now is part of a longer poem, called *The Covenant and Confidence of Faith*. It is quoted (although it may be well known to many readers) because it reflects so truly the spirit of Baxter, and, also, because it is a hymn which is a masterpiece of simplicity and rich thought with rare economy of expression. In form it anticipates the congregational hymns which were to attain their place later through the bold and fearless pioneer enterprise of Isaac Watts.

Lord, it belongs not to my care,
    Whether I die or live;
To love and serve Thee is my share
    And this Thy grace must give.

If life be long I will be glad,
    That I may long obey;
If short—yet why should I be sad
    To soar to endless day?

Christ leads me through no darker rooms
    Than He went through before;
He that unto God's kingdom comes,
    Must enter by this door.

Come, Lord, when grace has made me meet
    Thy blessed face to see;
For if Thy work on earth be sweet,
    What will Thy glory be!

Then I shall end my sad complaints,
    And weary, sinful days;
And join with the triumphant saints
    To sing Jehovah's praise.

My knowledge of that life is small,
    The eye of faith is dim;
But 'tis enough that Christ knows all,
    And I shall be with Him.

The last verse merits careful reflection. It remains, for all ages, the most complete expression of the soul's faith in relation to the life beyond. There seems nothing one can add or take from it. Can we wish to say more than it says?

One of the oldest hymns in the Christian Church is the *Veni Creator Spiritus*, which we have in translation as the

Whitsuntide hymn, beginning "Come, Holy Ghost our souls inspire". While the hymns derived from Greek and Latin sources will be considered in a subsequent chapter, this translation of the *Veni Creator Spiritus* should be mentioned here, for the beautiful translation we use is the work of John Cosin, who was Bishop of Durham after the Restoration. It had the unusual distinction of being included in the Ordinal of the English Prayer Book in 1662, and in this form and place may claim to be the earliest English hymn permitted to be sung in public. The translation made by Cosin first appeared in his *Collection of Private Devotions in the Practice of the Ancient Church*, published in 1627, when Cosin was rector of Brancepeth. It was intended to be said every morning at nine in memory of the descent of the Holy Spirit upon the Church. The original on which it is based was sung at Whitsuntide as far back as the tenth century, and at ordinations since the eleventh century.

It is to another seventeenth-century poet, John Dryden, that we owe a further rendering of the *Veni Creator Spiritus*, which now finds a place in most hymnals, in the form of the hymn beginning, "Creator Spirit, by whose aid".

Mention of Dryden suggests another writer to whom we are indebted for two of the best known hymns in the English language. These are the morning and evening hymns of Thomas Ken, who became Bishop of Bath and Wells in 1684. It is said that Dryden had Ken in mind when he wrote his lines on the *Good Parson*.

> Letting down the golden chain from high,
> He drew his audience upward to the sky.
> And oft with holy hymns he charmed the ears,
> A music more melodious than the spheres;
> For David left him, when he went to rest,
> His lyre; and after him, he sang the best.

Ken's morning hymn, *Awake, my soul, and with the sun*, and the one for evening, *Glory to Thee, my God, this night*, have become world famous. Probably many sing the doxology, which forms the last verse of both hymns, without even being aware of the author:

> Praise God, from whom all blessings flow;
> Praise Him, all creatures here below;
> Praise Him above, ye heavenly host;
> Praise Father, Son, and Holy Ghost.

The hymns were first published in the *Manual of Prayers*, for the scholars of Winchester College, who, in a preface, were exhorted to "sing the Morning and Evening hymns in your chamber devoutly".

Under James II, the good man was imprisoned for refusing to sign the Declaration of Indulgence, and in 1688 he resigned his see, rather than acknowledge the royal claims of William III. He died in 1711, and his friends buried him at Frome in the early morning. This had been his expressed desire, as he had wished to be laid "under the east window of the chancel, just at sunrising". It was done, and as the daylight brightened, those present sang Ken's own anthem of praise, *Awake, my soul, and with the sun.*

A famous literary figure of the same century, destined to have an enduring place in our hymnals, was Joseph Addison, although in the hymns from his pen we really move into the early-eighteenth century. Addison was born in 1672, and died in 1719. It was on August 9, 1712, that one of Addison's noted essays appeared in the *Spectator*, in the editing of which journal he secured his fame as a man of letters. The essay was on the theme of "Gratitude" and it was prefixed by the following words:

> I have already obliged the public with some pieces of divine poetry which have fallen into my hands; and as they have met with the reception which they deserve, I shall, from time to time, communicate any work of the same nature which has not appeared in print, and may be acceptable to my readers.

The essay then concluded with the verses beginning:

> When all Thy mercies, O my God,
> My rising soul surveys,
> Transported with the view, I'm lost
> In wonder, love and praise.

Some other fine hymns from the pen of Addison which owe their origin to *Spectator* essays are, *The spacious firmament on high*, verses pregnant with a mystic apprehension of the divine presence in nature; *The Lord my pasture shall prepare*, and a hymn for travellers, *How are Thy servants blest, O Lord!*, which concluded an essay on *The Sea*. All these appeared in the *Spectator* in the same year (1712), and are coming to be more rightly valued by modern congregations, although even yet not as widely known as their merit deserves.

John Wesley's tribute to Addison is worth remembering. "God raised up Mr. Addison, and his associates, to lash the prevailing vices, and ridiculous and profane customs of the country, and to show the excellence of Christianity and Christian institutions".

When considering the pioneers in the seventeenth century, who were quietly preparing the way for the rise of English hymnody, we must not omit reference to John Mason and Thomas Shepherd. The importance of both is that in a very real way they were forerunners of Isaac Watts in getting hymns not only written but *sung*. It is to the little village of Water Stratford in lovely Buckinghamshire that we owe the production of the first English hymns intentionally written for congregational singing. Here, on January 28, 1674, the good folk welcomed a new rector in the person of the Reverend John Mason, and to this little flock he faithfully ministered until he departed this life in 1694.

It was here he composed and published his *Songs of Praise*, and there is little doubt that these hymns were designed and intended for his own people to sing. They assumed a structure and metre which were to remain the norm for most subsequent

26

hymn writers for many years. They are marked by a simple devotion and unaffected style, and certainly reflect the influence of George Herbert.

Richard Baxter, whose work has already been mentioned, was a friend of Mason, and both, one may be sure, longed for the day when the oppressive prejudice against congregational hymn singing would be dispelled. Meanwhile, we may imagine the mild sensation caused in the little parish of Water Stratford when the rector introduced his bold innovation. It is safe to say that it was not approved by authority, nor adopted by the neighbouring clergy, who were, doubtless, much alarmed by the boldness of their colleague. His work had a great influence on Isaac Watts, who, writing of Mason at a later date, said that "his heart was always in heaven". It is of interest to members of the Anglican Church to reflect that although it was the Nonconformists who really established the practice of congregational hymn singing in England, yet it was a Church of England parson, John Mason, who prepared the way in his little parish, although it was destined to be a long while before his own branch of the Christain Church would follow his lead.

His collection of hymns passed through twenty editions, a fact which suggests that even at that period there were many who craved something more than was provided by the rigid limits of the authorised metrical psalters.

Of Mason's hymns which have found inclusion in modern hymnals, here is one that deserves to be more widely known:

> Thou wast, O God, and Thou wast blest,
>   Before the world began;
> Of Thine eternity possest
>   Before time's hour glass ran.
> Thou needest none Thy praise to sing,
>   As if Thy joy could fade;
> Couldst Thou have needed anything,
>   Thou couldst have nothing made.

Great and good God it pleased Thee
  Thy Godhead to declare;
And what Thy goodness did decree,
  Thy greatness did prepare;
Thou spak'st, and heaven and earth appeared
  And answered to Thy call;
As if their Maker's voice they heard,
  Which is the creature's all.

To whom, Lord, should I sing, but Thee,
  The maker of my tongue!
Lo, other lords would seize on me,
  But I to Thee belong.
As waters haste into their sea,
  And earth unto its earth,
So let my soul return to Thee,
  From whom it had its birth.

George Macdonald, a critic of merit, regarded this as the finest hymn in the language. Even if we do not go as far, we shall agree that it reveals a quality which stamps it at once with significance and promise, bearing in mind the period when it was written. Earlier in this chapter it was noted that the Baptist, Benjamin Keach, was making an effort to introduce hymns to his flock, but sad doggerel it was. There was something of an entirely different calibre in the work of John Mason. Another hymn to be found in this early collection, which comprised forty-one hymns, is *Now from the altar of our hearts*, which includes the verse of inspired beauty and simplicity:

Minutes and mercies multiplied
  Have made up all this day;
Minutes came quick, but mercies were
  More fleet and free than they.

Here, again, one can only wonder that the compilers of our hymn books persistently failed to include anything from Mason's collection, until Garrett Horder, to whom we owe enduring gratitude for adding many treasures to our English hymnody, reproduced several of Mason's hymns.

Mason appears to have been a man who at times experienced unusual visions and raptures. A few weeks before the end of his earthly life he had a vision of Jesus wearing a glorious crown, and with an aspect of wonderful majesty. Inspired by this, he preached a sermon on "The Midnight Cry", in which he proclaimed the approach of the second Advent. The opinion took root that this would occur at Water Stratford, and the little place became crowded with folk who brought in furniture and provisions, and scenes of extraordinary excitement followed. It was during this turmoil that the old rector passed away, but his last gentle words were, "I am full of the loving kindness of the Lord". The curious may find interest in this singular episode of his closing days, but his real interest for us, and his enduring reputation, will be in the contribution he made to the beginnings of English hymnody.

When John Mason passed away, Isaac Watts was a young man of twenty. He was already approaching his notable and creative work for English hymnody, for much of it was done in his early twenties. The spark ignited by Mason was to be fanned to a mighty flame by Isaac Watts.

3

"Goostly Psalmes" and "Godly Sports"

IT would, no doubt, startle a decorous modern congregation
if they were reminded before they began to sing the psalms
appointed for the day that they were about to indulge in
"godly sports"! Yet there reposes in the library of Queen's
College, Oxford, a book which would appear to justify the
description. It is a unique copy of *Goostly Psalmes and Spiritualle
Songs*, and is the work of Miles Coverdale, well known for his
translation of the Bible, and for the fact that he was Bishop of
Exeter in the middle of the sixteenth century. It is one of the
earliest examples in English of a version of metrical psalms,
and on its title page are these quaint lines:

> Be not ashamed, I warrande thee
>> Though thou be rude in songe and ryme,
> Thou shalt to youth some occasion be
>> In godly sports to passe theyr tyme.

So the designation has the authority of a famous bishop.
The intention was to provide for the youth of the period, and
also for those of riper years, an alternative to the secular folk-
songs of the age. This is made clear by some further words in
the preface:

Would God our carters and ploughmen had none other
thing to whistle upon save psalms . . . and if women . . .

spinning at the wheels had none other songs... they should be better occupied than with hey nony nony, hey troly loly.

This was a sign of the times. Not completely new in its intention, for even before the Reformation some earlier Catholic hymns found popularity through being set to profane melodies. One collection appears to have been printed in Venice in 1512, and a version of the Psalms in Flemish had the first line of a ballad at the head of each Psalm. John Wedderburn, one of the Scottish reformers, together with his two brothers, had gone to Germany in 1539. There they had been impressed by Luther's method of setting psalms and hymns to popular melodies. "Why should the devil have all the best tunes?" asked Luther. On his return to Scotland, John Wedderburn, with the aid of his brothers, set about a similar task, and performed it very thoroughly. The collection Wedderburn made was compiled very largely from German sources. It contained some carols, including the familiar *In Dulci Jubilo*, and verses of satire depicting the vices and weaknesses (as they alleged) of the Roman priesthood. The aim was to make the hymns and psalms popular with the common folk by the attraction of familiar tunes drawn from secular sources. The Salvation Army is not original in employing this method. It was a device that did an enormous amount to spread the sentiment and ideas of the Reformation, and one of many instances of the influence of music and song in furthering a movement. This is a fact the modern Church should not forget.

Had this Lutheran outlook and method been allowed full play it is certain that congregational hymn singing would speedily have become popular in England. Cranmer appears to have been in sympathy with this aim, and willing to promote it. Coverdale, in his collection, mentioned above, had included thirteen English translations of German hymns of the Reformation, one hymn to the Holy Spirit, and one more with the intriguing title, *Let go the whore of Babylon*; a title which seems to leave no doubt as to the sentiment!

What then, it will be asked, delayed for so long the congregational singing of hymns? Why, when they were written, were they restricted in use to primers of private devotion? For the answer we must look to the other great stream of Reformation thought which found its source in Geneva, and in which the influence of John Calvin became predominant. This was the centre which had the major influence on the thought and practice of religious life in England, due to the fact that many Protestant exiles from England, clerical and lay, had found asylum there, who, when they eventually returned to their native land, did much to spread the outlook and tradition they had imbibed at Geneva. This made the singing of the Psalms in metrical version the one form in which a congregation could express the emotions of worship and devotion. The restriction was justified by the appeal to the Bible as the one source of authority, by which, it was contended, only the singing of those hymns which the sacred book provided—namely, the Psalms—could be allowed.

Luther, as we have seen, took a more generous view of the use of hymns. While he promoted German metrical translations from the Psalms, he also encouraged the production of original hymns, and even allowed the use of Catholic material for this purpose, adapting it to Protestant thought where necessary. English authority, with the support of Henry VIII, while it conserved more of the Catholic tradition than was common with the Continental Reformed Churches, was yet dominated by the Calvinistic outlook in the sphere of hymnody. As a result the employment of hymns in congregational worship was strictly forbidden, and the production of an authorised metrical version of the Psalms was taken in hand, and became the collection known as the Old Version, or Sternhold and Hopkins, after the names of the compilers.

The preparation of metrical versions of the Psalms was much more complex than appears at first sight. The singular fact is that it was not solely a work prompted by the religious Reformers of the time. It was a task which seems to have captured the imagination and stirred the interest of many in high places, who patronised the arts. It is to the French Court

of the Valois that we have to look for the first translations of
the Psalter into the common tongue of a nation. One such
patroness of the arts was Marguerite, sister of Francis I, the
wife of the deposed King of Navarre, who was in sympathy
with the doctrines of the Reformation. One of the members
of her suite was the French poet, Clement Marot, and it was
he who began to translate the Psalms into French. The first
of these translations was included in a volume of poems in
1533, and he followed this with others, and these, set to popular
tunes of the time, became a vogue in Court circles. They were
adopted by courtiers, each of whom would have his special
psalm as he would have his particular arms, mottoes, or
liveries. The singer would be accompanied by a musician on
the viol or flute, and the psalms were received with delight
not as an act of worship, but rather as an artistic exercise.

They spread over the countryside, and did much to further
the Reformed doctrine and worship. So much so that the
religious authorities took alarm, and when, in 1542, Marot
published thirty of the psalms in a single volume, he was
compelled to seek refuge at Geneva. Here, in the following
year, he produced a new collection containing fifty psalms.
After his death, which occurred shortly after, the work of
translation was taken up by the famous Huguenot, Theodore
Beza, and in 1562 a complete edition appeared, which has
become known as the Genevan Psalter. Two musicians of
talent were available—namely, Louis Bourgeois, who was in
charge of the music at the Huguenot church in Geneva, under
Calvin, and Claude Goudimel, an equally accomplished man,
an ardent Protestant, and later a victim of St. Bartholomew's
Eve. These able composers set the translated psalms to airs
drawn from popular melodies of the time, and this psalter
became a store of song for the people. The psalms were heard
in castle and cottage. They were sung by workers in the fields
and the mills, they were the first lessons imparted to children,
and frequently became the last words heard on the lips of the
dying. Henri II sang Psalm 42, *Like as the hart,* as he hunted
in the forest of Fontainebleau, riding by the side of his mistress,
Diane de Poitiers, who, in turn, sang Psalm 130, *De profundis,*

and for whose portrait the King had chosen the first verse of his favourite psalm.

This "Genevan Psalter" became very widely used in translation, circulating not only in France and Switzerland, but in Germany, Holland, and Denmark.

In England a similar movement was in course of development. It was indicated, as we have seen, by the work of Miles Coverdale, but it was ten years after Coverdale's hymn book that Thomas Sternhold, Groom of the Robes to Henry VIII, began, in possible imitation of Marot, his version of the Psalms, nineteen of which were published in the year of his death, in 1549. There is a story preserved of how the young King Edward VI heard Sternhold singing psalms to an organ accompaniment and expressed a desire to hear more. When Sternhold published some of these psalms they were dedicated to the King in these words: "Albeit I cannot give your Majesty great loaves, or bring into the Lord's barn full handfulls, I am bold to present a few crumbs which I have picked from under my Lord's board".

After Sternhold's death a further edition was published which contained thirty-seven of the psalms, and the task which he had put in hand was continued by John Hopkins, who in 1551 added seven more versions to Sternhold's thirty-seven. Through the Marian persecutions the Reformers who escaped death were driven into exile, and most of them found refuge in Geneva, where the further development of the Psalter in English was carried forward, and in 1556 an enlarged English Psalter, with tunes, was published. This was placed in the centre of a *Forme of prayer and ministration of the Sacraments*, issued as a rival to the Book of Common Prayer, which had been discarded by the more extreme party of the Reformers. The number of psalms was now fifty-one, and to these was added a version of the Ten Commandments. These additions were made by William Whittingham, who had married Calvin's sister, and later became Dean of Durham. He was at the time pastor to the Genevan refugees.

The English Psalter continued to grow, and in 1561 two new books were issued, one at Geneva, and one in London.

The former was the parent of the Scottish Psalter, and was edited by William Kethe, whose name is of interest as the author of the now world-famous paraphrase of the 100th Psalm, *All people that on earth do dwell*, written expressly for the *Old Hundredth* tune to which it is now generally sung. The hymn is of great historic interest as the only fragment of this ancient psalter which has survived in popular use. It was contained in the English as well as the Genevan edition. In the English edition, Hopkins took up his work of adding further to Sternhold's collection, with a few additions from other sources. Gradually the Psalter was becoming a standard hymn-book, and in the following year, 1562, the first complete English Psalter was published, under the title of *The Whole Booke of Psalmes collected into Englysh metre, by T. Starnhold, I. Hopkins and others*. This was what is now known as the "Old Version" and it continued to be used for more than 235 years. About 350 editions were issued during this period, and it attained a domination which for long was without question. The musical quality of the collection was mediocre. Of the one hundred and fifty psalms only forty-seven had tunes of their own. The others had to fare as best they could with borrowed melodies. One may recall Fuller's pertinent opinion of the quality of the work, both as to its thought and music:

> Their piety was better than their poetry; they had drank more of Jordan than of Helicon. . . . Sometimes they make the Maker of the tongue speak little better than barbarism, and have in many verses such poor rhyme that two hammers on a smith's anvil would make better music.
> (*Church History of Britain*, iv, p. 73. Oxford ed., 1845.)

But although this version was to hold a position of authority for over two centuries, many others engaged in the task of arranging the Psalms in English, either as whole collections or in part. In the Court circles of Elizabeth it became a fashionable pursuit, and one outlet for the river of poetic feeling and expression then running at full tide. The Queen herself indulged in this work of paraphrasing, even though we are told she referred to the metrical psalms rather slight-ingly as "Geneva jigs", but she gave their use in congrega-tional worship official approval in the Royal Injunction:

> For the comforting of such as delight in music, it may be permitted that in the beginning or end of Common Prayer either at Morning or Evening, there may be sung an hymn or such like song to the praise of Almighty God in the best melody and music that may be devised, having respect that the sense of the hymn may be understood and perceived.

This Injunction became immediately the admitted authority for an anthem by the choir, and the metrical psalm by the people.

Sir Walter Raleigh, Edmund Spenser, and others joined in the popular task of paraphrasing, and Sir Philip Sidney attempted a complete psalter, an enterprise which, after he lost his life at Arnhem, was carried on by his sister, Mary, Countess of Pembroke. Meanwhile, the popularity of the metrical psalms provoked scenes rivalling those which had taken place on the Continent. As soon as they began to sing the psalms in one little church in London, other churches, not only in London, but in towns far distant, eagerly followed the same practice. It was said that after service at St. Paul's Cathedral six thousand persons would assemble outside singing together and praising God. One observer of the times declared that the effusions of Sternhold were "roared aloud" like orgies ("Godly sports", indeed!) in almost every street, as well as church, throughout the kingdom. The Papists looked on with disapproval, but even the children laughed at them as they passed in the streets. There was something of frenzy and excitement in such excesses, but it suggests the extraordinary popularity of the "Old Version" as it came to be called.

It was clear by this time that so far as congregational singing was concerned England (and even more, Scotland) was following the Calvinistic, rather than the Lutheran tradition. This will help to explain why England was two

centuries behind Germany in the singing of hymns, where hymns
had taken a prominent place in Lutheran thought and worship
from the beginning. A particular and rigid view of the
authority of the Bible kept the adherents of Calvin strictly
within the narrow limits allowed by the metrical versions.
Few readers to-day will be aware of the quaintness, and often
crudity of some of the lines in the "Old Version". It is difficult
to imagine what impulse of worship could be nourished, or
inspiration derived from such lines as the following, in the
Sternhold and Hopkins rendering of Psalm 58:

> The teeth, O Lord, which fast are set
> in their mouth round about:
> The lions teeth that are so great,
> do thou, O Lord, break out.
>
> Let them consume away and waste,
> as water runs forth-right,
> The shafts that they so shoot in haste,
> let them be broke in flight.
>
> As snails do waste within the shell
> and unto slime do run:
> As one before his time that fell,
> and never saw the sun.

This is one sample. Others, similar in character, could be
quoted. What is remarkable is that such a version could have
enjoyed predominance for so long. It is a reminder of the
conservative spirit that clings to religious worship, and in
modern days makes it so difficult to persuade congregations
to adopt and appreciate hymns of more worthy quality than
some of those to which they cling.

We may try to imagine how stark and barren worship must
have been in not a few churches, with nothing but the "Old
Version" to express whatever devotion may have been in the
hearts of the worshippers.

However, complacency is a remarkable quality, and one writer of the seventeenth century, Thomas Mace, confessed himself quite content with the few psalm tunes which were then in use. He claimed they were so excellently good that no art could mend or make better! But (and this we can well understand) the singing in many parish churches he found very unsatisfactory. "Tis sad", he wrote, "to hear what whining, toting, yelling or screeching there is in many country congregations".

This condition of things was made worse by the almost complete absence of organs, or any other musical instrument, due to the strong prejudice against these on the part of most congregations. The story is told of one countryman of the time who, hearing an organ played in church, danced and jigged all up the aisle, "having never heard anything like it except the bagpipes in an alehouse". Puritan sentiment objected to organs owing to the Romish and Laudian associations. It is not easy now to imagine what the services must have been like in many churches. Added to the frequently discordant singing of the metrical psalms, and the absence of any musical aid, there was the practice whereby the parish clerk read out the psalm line by line, the people repeating each line after him, until they could sing them from memory. This practice was officially provided for by an order of the Westminster Assembly in 1645, which stated:

Where many in the congregation cannot read, it is convenient that the minister, or some other fit person appointed by him and the other officers, do read the psalm, line by line, before the singing thereof.

Sometimes the clerk had not only to recite the psalm line by line, but also start the tune, and there is little doubt that it was not always easy to find a clerk who had the sensitive ear, or suitable voice for such a task. Occasionally he may have been like one old clerk in Staffordshire, who, after hymn singing had become a tolerated procedure, would proudly announce "the tew 'underd and tewty-tewth 'im". Certainly, all clerks were not as limited as this one; indeed, they were a worthy and praiseworthy race of men, who, in their day and generation, served God nobly and well. They were, in fact, one of the historic features of old England. But, at the best, the singing of the metrical psalms, both in matter and style, must have been a rather dreary affliction, with the folk repeating the lines after the clerk, and to a very dull tune. It is easy to understand the feeling that prompted Lord Rochester's epigram on a parish clerk singing the psalms.

> Sternhold and Hopkins had great Qualms,
> When they translated David's Psalms,
> To make the heart full glad:
> But had it been poor David's Fate
> To hear thee sing, and them Translate,
> By God, 'twould have made him mad.

The music of the Psalter underwent a progressive development, but it is not the theme of this chapter to trace this in detail. Further reference will be made to the subject.

It is important to bear in mind, that apart from the developing efforts to improve the musical setting of the Psalms, an increasing number of metrical translations came into existence, to compete with the supremacy of Sternhold and Hopkins. In the course of time scores of these versions came into print. An exhaustive list is given in Julian's *Dictionary*, for the information of the student who may wish to refer to them. It was not until the end of the seventeenth century that a successful rival to the "Old Version" appeared. This was a new translation, which came to be known as "Tate and Brady" or the "New Version", and was the work of two Irishmen, Nahum Tate and Nicholas Brady. It was published in 1696, at which time Tate was Poet Laureate, and it was given permissive authority by King William III in Council. This authority did not supplant the "Old Version" of Sternhold and Hopkins, but allowed the use of the new work as an alternative. At once the two versions became a cause of dispute, and heated controversy. In this debate the bishops did not fail to share.

One good prelate denounced the intruder for its "fine and modish character, flourished with wit and fancy", and also complained of the inconvenience of having two versions. John Wesley's father admitted the merits of the "New Version", but declined to use it in his church at Epworth, for the reason that the people "have a strange genius at understanding nonsense", a genius, it may be said, not confined to the parishioners of Epworth. The reception given to the version of Tate and Brady seems to have justified the opinion of Samuel Wesley. Many people viewed the "Old Version" as having little less than Divine approval, and there is a story of a maid in one house who refused to join in family prayers, giving to her employer the reason: "If you must know the plain truth, Sir; as long as you sung Jesus Christ's psalms, I sung along with ye, but now that you sing psalms of your own invention, ye may sing by yourselves".

While an attitude of mind so extreme as this may have been rare, there is no doubt, as events proved, that the Old Version held its ground for many years. Even Brady's own church cast out the new book as "an innovation not to be endured". Yet in some parishes it made headway, and was followed in the year 1700 by a *Supplement*, which provided additions in the form of alternative words, and a few hymns, including the now world-famous Christmas hymn, *While shepherds watched*. Two other hymns from the New Version have survived in popular use, namely, *As pants the hart*, the hymn, as now used, being a selection from the more numerous verses of the original. It will be seen that it is a metrical form of Psalm 42. Another version of Psalm 34, which in the collection of Tate and Brady has eighteen verses, appears in most hymnals in shorter form as *Through all the changing scenes of life*. Three others, less known, which remain in *Hymns Ancient and Modern*, are *Thou, Lord, by strictest search hast known*, also, *O God of hosts*, and, *Have mercy, Lord, on me*.

It is now possible to understand clearly why so few hymns were written in English before the eighteenth century. John Ellerton, one of our leading English hymnologists, computed that of the many thousands of English hymns now in existence, leaving out of count translations, not above one hundred at most are of an earlier date than 1700. This is not surprising when we bear in mind the tremendous hold which the Psalters, and particularly the Old Version, had on the religious public in England, and even more in Scotland. Many attempted versions of the Psalms, but very few took in hand the writing of hymns, and then only for purposes of private devotion. We have marked one or two conspicuous exceptions, covering the somewhat unhappy effusions of the Baptist pastor, Benjamin Keach, and the much more felicitous, and indeed, significant verses of John Mason. But it can be understood what a bold venture it was to challenge the rule of psalmody, and to attempt the introduction of congregational hymn singing.

4

The Victory of Isaac Watts

WITH this background in mind we can appreciate better the courage and enterprise of young Isaac Watts. The adjective is important, because to those unfamiliar with the story of this remarkable man the reference to *Dr.* Isaac Watts usually suggests an elderly and grave divine, writing stately hymns which, we assume, came at once into general favour. The facts are quite otherwise.

Isaac Watts was an Independent (or Congregationalist, as we should now call him) and it is worth reflecting that it was from the Puritan wing of the Church, that had so tenaciously opposed the singing of hymns, and had fastened the dominion of the Psalter most firmly on the English people, that there emerged the great pioneer of English congregational hymn singing. Watts was the real founder of English hymnody. He did for the English what Ambrose did for the Latins; what Clement Marot gave to the French, and, in regard to hymn singing, what Luther did for Germany.

It is fairly certain that when Watts began his work, congregational hymn singing was restricted to a few isolated churches. William Barton, a Puritan cleric, who conformed to the Anglican settlement after the Restoration, published a small collection of hymns as early as 1659, and this was expanded by further additions. It met with no response from the Anglican Church, but was probably used in a number of Independent churches, and was one of the early influences which helped to prepare the way for Isaac Watts, as also did the small collection by John Mason, previously noted, to whom Watts paid generous tribute. But the work of Isaac Watts marked the beginning of a new era.

Watts found congregational singing restricted almost entirely to the metrical psalms and to the Old Version of Sternhold and Hopkins. This practice was firmly entrenched, and supported by a venerable tradition, reaching back over centuries in the life of the Christian Church, and with a rich inheritance from its Hebrew ancestry. Before the Reformation, the Psalms were recited weekly in every monastery and convent in Europe, and by every priest and deacon as part of his daily duty. In the Calvinistic wing of the Reformed Church, whose influence became most dominant in England, the Psalter was held firmly to be the only form of congregational singing sanctioned by Holy Scripture.

One result of this, and one to be kept clearly in mind if the aim of Isaac Watts is to be understood, was that the thought of Christian congregations became over-weighted with Old Testament material. There is a wealth of grand and sublime spiritual thought in the Psalms, as well as a profound range of emotion and experience which ensure for them a unique place in the religious poetry of the world. At the same time, we must allow, sound judgment and critical discrimination should be exercised in their use. The Psalter is, in fact, a collection of religious poems representing the developing religious consciousness of the Jewish nation. They vary greatly in theme, outlook, sentiment, and quality of expression. If we compiled an anthology of English religious poetry, ranging from the time of King Alfred to John Masefield, we should find, and rightly expect to find, a varied, often widely differing, and even contradictory, expression of religious belief. The same truth should be borne in mind when reading the Psalms. Some of the earlier poems, for example, clearly belong to a period when there was no belief in individual survival after death, while later work, following the time of the Exile, reveals the growing belief in a life beyond, grounded in the glorious conviction that nothing can separate the devout soul from the ever-living God. There is something incongruous to-day in listening to a congregation singing the former, and, shortly after, affirming belief in the resurrection. It is only the power of long usage that blunts our sense of this incongruity. Furthermore, it is equally distressing to a sensitive and intelligent worshipper to sing such a verse as

> That thy foot may be dipped in the blood of thine enemies: and that the tongue of thy dogs may be red through the same.

or:

> The tabernacles of the Edomites, and the Ismaelites: the Moabites and Ilagarens:
> Gebal, and Ammon and Amalek: the Philistines, with them that dwell at Tyre.
> Assur also is joined with them, and have holpen the children of Lot.
> But do thou to them as unto the Madianites: unto Sisera, and unto Jabin at the brook of Kison;
> Who perished at Endor: and became as the dung of the earth.
> Make them and their princes like Oreb and Zeb: yea, make all their princes like as Zeba and Salmana.

Yet if it chances to be the thirteenth or sixteenth day of the month, verses of this nature are still appointed for Christian worship, and the 83rd Psalm, containing the above verses, is followed the same evening with the exquisite beauty and devotion of the poem which begins, *O how amiable are thy dwellings.* It is remarkable that no serious effort is made to provide a revised Psalter which a Christian congregation can use, satisfying to both intelligence and devotion. It is desirable on every ground that verses such as those quoted, and others to which space cannot be given, should be eliminated, and then the large deposit of magnificent poetry, adorned by exalted sublimity of outlook, would shine the more clearly. There is everything to gain by omitting verses which are simply expressions of hate and passion, or obscure allusions to events, places or customs which convey no jot of meaning to a Christian

44

congregation at the present day. It is true that in the revised English Prayer Book of 1928 some of these undesirable verses are bracketed for omission *if desired*, but even this timid option is rarely exercised.

This plea for revision is not a digression for it bears directly upon the work and witness of Isaac Watts. He was not only a hymn writer of conspicuous genius, and the effective pioneer of congregational hymn singing. He was much more, for he was a critic and reformer, who saw clearly the need for a Christian edition of the Psalter.

This conviction, and his endeavour to initiate such a reform, give the clue to many of his hymns. He challenged boldly the prevailing attitude to the Psalter, and stressed the fact, mentioned above, that not a few of the psalms are markedly unsuitable for Christian worship. Thus, in an *Essay* which appears in the 1707 edition of his *Hymns*, he wrote (concerning the Psalms):

Some of them are almost opposite to the spirit of the Gospel: Many of them foreign to the State of the New Testament, and widely different from the present circumstances of Christians .... Thus by keeping too close to David in the House of God, the Veil of Moses is thrown over our hearts.

Sound criticism, and a sensible point of view could hardly be put better than in the words with which Watts continued his judgment.

Some Sentences of the *Psalmist* that are expressive of the temper of our own hearts, and the Circumstances of our Lives, may compose our Spirits to Seriousness, and allure us to a sweet retirement within ourselves; but we meet with a following line which so peculiarly belongs but to one Action or Hour of the Life of *David* or of *Asaph*, that breaks off our Song in the midst; our Consciences are affrighted, lest we should speak a falsehood unto God: Thus the Powers of our Souls are shock'd on a sudden, and our Spirits ruffled before we have time to reflect, that this may be sung only as a History of ancient Saints: And perhaps in some instances that *Salvo* is hardly sufficient neither. Besides, it almost always spoils the Devotion by breaking the Uniform Thread of it. For while our Lips and our Hearts run on sweetly together, applying the Words to our own Case, there is something of Divine Delight in it: But at once we are forced to turn off the Application abruptly, and our lips speak nothing but the heart of *David*: Thus our own Hearts are as it were forbid the Pursuit of the Song, and then the Harmony and the Worship grow dull of meer necessity.

These salutary words were written nearly 250 years ago. They are as pertinent and applicable to-day as when they were written. It remains true that "while our Lips and our Hearts run sweetly together . . . there is something of Divine Delight in it". This is a sound criterion to apply to our hymns. They provide the test by which a hymn can be ranked as good and worthy—namely, that it does not include sentiments or ideas which naturally provoke question or criticism, and so deflect sincere, spontaneous worship. It will be seen how the greatest hymns of Isaac Watts pass this test.

In order to appreciate the work he did, we must know a little concerning the man himself. Isaac Watts was born on July 17, 1674. The important event of the year of his birth was the repeal of the Declaration of Indulgence, which had granted a measure of toleration to Nonconformists. Important, because it renewed the persecution of his father, a Southampton schoolmaster, and deacon of the Independent church in that town. Both the minister and the deacon were imprisoned, and Mrs. Watts often sat on the stone near the prison gate, with the infant Isaac in her arms. When Isaac was nine years of age, his father was again imprisoned for his Nonconformist convictions, this time for six months, and on his release was forced to live away from home, quietly in London for two years, to avoid further arrest. But in 1688 relief came, in some degree, to Nonconformists, when William of Orange ascended the throne. Isaac was now showing promise of the fine scholarship which was to adorn his career, and friends in Southampton offered to provide a course for him at Oxford or Cambridge if he would subscribe to the Church of England, for both universities were then closed to Nonconformists. This he declined to do, and entered an academy at Stoke Newington, then a charming village adjacent to London, and with which district Watts was to be closely associated all his life. In 1694, when he was twenty, he returned home to Southampton, where he remained for the following two years. They were not fruitless years, for it was as a young man of twenty that 'Dr.' Isaac Watts (as he later became) wrote his first hymns. One may well ask, how did he get a foothold in view of the prevalent attitude to congregational hymn singing? For an answer it must be held as probable that the Southampton congregation was a little in advance of most, and that possibly Barton's small collection of hymns was in use, though, doubtless, the metrical psalms held first place. Isaac Watts was both scholar and poet, and it was natural that the material provided for singing in the Southampton chapel left him dissatisfied. His father challenged him to provide something better, and in response he wrote his first hymn, of which the opening verse is

> Behold the glories of the Lamb
> Before His Father's throne;
> Prepare new honours for His name,
> And songs before unknown.

There was certainly much significance in the last line! The Southampton congregation sang the hymn, and wanted more. The work of reform had begun. From that date forward it became an ever widening stream. Isaac Watts returned to Stoke Newington as a tutor to the children of a local family. This episode helps to explain the origin of his quaint *Divine and Moral Songs*. Some of its contents have become familiar as household words for many who have forgotten the author of the sayings they quote. It is the source of the verses beginning

How doth the little busy bee
    Improve each shining hour,
And gather honey all the day
    From every opening flower.

How many know that it is in the same verses we find the
oft-quoted words

For Satan finds some mischief still
For idle hands to do.

But Watts could not write hymns for children. It is interesting to observe how few of our leading hymn writers have
contributed hymns of any real merit for young people. It is
the great distinction of Watts that in much of his work he
transcended the gloomy Calvinism of his time, and it is certain
that many of his hymns indicate a humane and liberal theology,
in contrast to the harsh tenets of Geneva. Yet for some reason
not easy to explain, when writing for children it was the harsh
Calvinistic strand that seemed to predominate in his thought.
This mars many of his poems written expressly for the young.
It is not easy to justify such verses as the following:

There is a dreadful hell,
    And everlasting pains:
There sinners must with devils dwell
    In darkness, fire and chains.

Can such a wretch as I
    Escape this cursed end?
And may I hope, whene'er I die,
    I shall to heaven ascend?

The same note intrudes and spoils the lovely theme of the
Cradle Hymn, opening as it does with the tender verse

Hush, my dear! Lie still and slumber!
    Holy angels guard thy bed!
Heavenly blessings, without number
    Gently falling on thy head.

48

II ISAAC WATTS, eighteenth century pioneer of English hymnody, and
author of our great national hymn, *Our God, our help in ages past.*

From an engraving by J. Cochran after W. G

III   CHARLES WESLEY, poet of the eighteenth century Evangelical Revival
and author of nearly seven thousand hymns.

Yet this poem contains the verse

> 'Twas to save thee, child, from dying,
>   Save my dear from burning flame,
> Bitter groans and endless crying,
>   That thy blest Redeemer came.

A verse from another of the *Divine Songs* reads

> There is an hour when I must die
>   Nor do I know how soon 'twill come:
> A thousand children, young as I,
>   Are call'd by death to hear their doom.

> Just as a tree cut down, that fell
>   To north or southward, there it lies,
> So man departs to heaven or hell,
>   Fix'd in the state wherein he dies.

These verses are a reminder of the appalling religious ideas conveyed to children of the early-eighteenth century. They serve to explain why no satisfactory hymns for young people can be found in the compositions of the period, and indicate the distorted version of the religion of Jesus which it was the concern of the time to present to youthful minds.

Yet this defect and limitation which Isaac Watts shared in common with the religious teachers of his age, helps to throw into bold relief the true genius and unique insight of the man. The striking fact to remember is not that his thought expressed in some measure the harsh and limited outlook of the Calvinism which then dominated so much of the religious thought of England. The greatness of Watts is evident in the degree in which he transcended the prevalent view, and helped to cleanse it of its unworthy and repellent aspects, while retaining and giving clearer definition to its valuable and enduring features. If he failed to do this in the verses he attempted for children, he certainly achieved it in the great hymns he wrote, now found in all our hymnals, and which are certain to keep a permanent place in Christian worship.

Watts took hold of the outstanding feature of value in the thought of Calvinism—namely, the sovereignty of God, and invested it with an invigorating faith and joy, which were sadly lacking in much of the orthodoxy of the period. In no hymn is this more conspicuous than in one of the best known and best loved, now the treasure of all the Churches, and, indeed of the whole nation. *Our God, our help in ages past,* may be regarded as the greatest hymn in the language. This first appeared under the heading of "Man frail and God eternal" in the collection of metrical psalms which Watts published in 1719. It will be noted that the first line begins as quoted above, and not *O God, our help in ages past,* as given in several of the standard hymnals. The change was made by John Wesley in his *Collection of Psalms and Hymns* in 1737. It is not easy to understand why Wesley made the change. This exclamatory and vocative opening loses the significance implicit in the original *Our,* with its suggestion of a common fellowship in God. It is good to see that the original form was used by Garrett Horder in *Worship Song,* and also appears in the *Revised Baptist Church Hymnal* and the *Congregational Hymnary.* The hymn contained nine stanzas. Dr. Julian held that the three which are omitted are unequal to the remainder, but this is a verdict which may be open to question. In these days of arrogant nationalism, and frequent disregard of the temporal nature of human institutions, the additional three verses seem very pertinent:

> Thy word commands our flesh to dust,
>   'Return, ye sons of men;'
> All nations rose from earth at first,
>   And turn to earth again.

> The busy tribes of flesh and blood,
>   With all their cares and fears,
> Are carried downward by the flood,
>   And lost in following years.

> Like flow'ry fields the nations stand,
>   Pleas'd with the morning light:
> The flow'rs beneath the mower's hand
>   Lie with'ring ere 'tis night.

These verses, in common with the whole of this noble hymn, express the majestic conception of the prophet in the fortieth chapter of Isaiah:

The voice said, Cry. And he said, What shall I cry?
All flesh is grass, and all the goodliness thereof is as the flower of the field:
The grass withereth, the flower fadeth, but the word of our God shall stand for ever.

The same thought is voiced in the 90th Psalm, which Watts paraphrased in this famous hymn. The reader who will compare the two will be able to appreciate better the inspiration of this metrical version.

The hymn was written about 1714, shortly before the death of Queen Anne, when there was widespread national anxiety about the succession. The human mind, in the presence of social stresses and national troubles, finds assurance and steadying direction in the majestic vision and virile faith of this great hymn. It is easy to understand the degree to which it has become entwined in our thought through the vicissitudes of our recent history.

One other very important aspect of this hymn should be borne in mind. It is a perfect example of a hymn which can be a common treasure of all the Christian Churches. Its spacious vision and depth of sentiment transcend lesser doctrinal differences. Yet there is implicit a firm dogmatic faith in God, which can be shared by all. Those who demand that hymns should be the means of expressing dogmatic convictions make the mistake, not infrequently, of desiring a hymn to convey some particular theological dogma of which divergent views may exist; as, for example, some particular doctrinal view of the Atonement. Those who object to this use of the hymn do so for two good reasons. First, because a hymn written deliberately with the intention of conveying a definite theological tenet is likely to be a poor hymn. The purpose of a hymn book is not simply to be a manual of theology put into rhyme and metre. In the second place, objection to making hymns subordinate to dogmas, is that in so doing they cease to express "the unity of the Spirit in the bond of peace". The test of a truly great hymn is that it springs from the fundamental, enduring convictions which are at the root of our common spiritual experience, and speaks a universal dialect. More examples of this can be observed in the chapters which follow. Here it is sufficient to point to this superb hymn *Our God, our help in ages past*, as an example of the truth.

The hymn also serves to demonstrate another feature in the outlook of Isaac Watts, expressing, it may be said, the best and most enduring feature of Calvinism, namely, its sense of the universal, cosmic significance of the Gospel. This was, however, marred and spoiled by the harsh and repellent doctrine of Predestination with which it was mixed. In Watts a new note became manifest. He recaptured the joy and spaciousness of the original Gospel. Notice how this is the clue to another of his famous hymns, which ranks in popular esteem with the one quoted above. *When I survey the wondrous Cross.* Mark the last verse:

> *Were the whole realm of nature mine,*
> That were a present far too small;
> Love so amazing, so divine
> Demands my soul, my life, my all!

The whole realm of nature. There is the cosmic view. Nothing paltry or trivial can linger within the sweep and range of this outlook. Again, observe the accent on joy, in another of Isaac Watts great hymns:

> Come let us join our cheerful songs
> With angels round the throne;
> Ten thousand thousand are their tongues,
> But all their joys are one.

How this must have broken like a ray of sunlight into the gloom of the prevailing Calvinism. In this hymn, also, we sound again the cosmic note:

Let all that dwell above the sky,
　　And air, and earth and seas,
Conspire to lift Thy glories high,
　　And speak Thine endless praise.

The whole creation join in one
　　To bless the sacred name
Of Him that sits upon the throne,
　　And to adore the Lamb.

The whole creation join in one. If one sings this sincerely the soul must be lifted out of all that is merely sectarian and petty. We begin to glimpse something of what this young scholar and poet was doing for the religious thought of his day and generation. After over two hundred years our own catholicity of spirit is not such a *fait accompli* that we can afford to undervalue this accent.

A hymn in which the inspiring doctrine of the Communion of Saints finds noble expression is the following:

Give me the wings of faith to rise
　　Within the veil, and see
The saints above, how great their joys,
　　How bright their glories be.

I ask them whence their victory came;
　　They, with united breath,
Ascribe their conquest to the Lamb,
　　Their triumph to His death.

They marked the footsteps that He trod,
　　His zeal inspired their breast;
And, following their incarnate God,
　　Possess the promised rest.

Our glorious Leader claims our praise
　　For His own pattern given;
While the long cloud of witnesses
　　Show the same path to heaven.

53

Again, as an example of the delightful manner in which his spirit soared above the gloomy Puritan Calvinism of his time in its outlook on the Future Life, another of his well-known hymns may be recalled. As we have seen, when writing for children Watts lapsed into the grim perspective of his time when contemplating the world beyond this one. But now let us picture the young poet walking around his native Southampton and gazing across the meadows of Netley, and seeing their green, and beyond the blue waters of the Solent. It is said this vista inspired the words

> There is a land of pure delight
>   Where saints immortal reign;
> Infinite day excludes the night,
>   And pleasures banish pain.

> Sweet fields beyond the swelling flood
>   Stand dressed in living green;
> So to the Jews old Canaan stood,
>   While Jordan rolled between.

How human and gently understanding is the next verse:

> But timorous mortals start and shrink
>   To cross this narrow sea,
> And linger shivering on the brink,
>   And fear to launch away.

And how simple and strong the faith inspiring the two closing stanzas:

> O could we make our doubts remove,
>   Those gloomy doubts that rise;
> And see the Canaan that we love,
>   With unbeclouded eyes.

Could we but climb where Moses stood,
    And view the landscape o'er,
Not Jordan's streams, nor death's cold flood
    Should fright us from the shore.

Nearly all the hymns written by Isaac Watts, which are now so familiar, were composed when he was a young man. After his work as tutor, he became pastor of the Mark Lane Independents, or Congregationalists. With the passing of Queen Anne there came increasing toleration and freedom for the Dissenters, and Watts was soon a leader of Nonconformist thought and worship. He became the friend of Sir Thomas Abney, who was Lord Mayor of London in 1700, and he and Lady Abney gave Watts encouragement and support, and he lived under their hospitable roof for the remainder of his life, until he passed away in 1748. His health was always feeble, and had been impaired by the strenuous studies and manifold mental activities of his early manhood. Yet, undaunted by his frail physique, Watts continued his remarkable work as pastor, preacher, and writer. The care bestowed upon him by the Abneys made much of this possible, and after the death of Sir Thomas Abney his widow and daughters continued to care for Watts until the end of his life at the age of seventy-four. Watts' personal income, it is said, never exceeded one hundred pounds a year, and a third of this was spent in charity. He lived to see his textbook on Logic adopted by Oxford University, from which place of learning his nonconformity had excluded him, and the University of Edinburgh conferred the degree of Doctor of Divinity upon him in 1728. His mortal remains were buried in Bunhill Fields, where lies John Bunyan's body, almost within sight of the famous chapel of the next great hymn writers—the Wesleys.

At this distance of time it is possible to judge more soundly the true merit and significance of Isaac Watts. It is easy to point out his defects and limitations. His effusions for children tend now to provoke a smile of amusement. Many of his hymns were inferior in quality and short lived in use. It should be remembered that he wrote hundreds of hymns, due partly to the practice of writing one for use at the end of a sermon, to enforce the theme. Frequently, the results were poor, and many of these hymns are forgotten or only recalled for antiquarian interest. But it is true to affirm that he wrote some of the greatest English hymns, and possibly in *Our God, our help in ages past*, the greatest hymn in our tongue. Jowett, the Master of Balliol, once asked a group of Oxford dons to name the English hymns they esteemed the best. Each returned one hymn only: *Our God, our help in ages past*, which each regarded as fulfilling the conditions of a perfect hymn. It should be remembered also that Watts wrote a number of excellent hymns which are not so well known as those mentioned. One is grateful to find that *Songs of Praise* has recovered the truly beautiful hymn *Christ hath a garden walled around*. It deserves to be far more widely known.

Christ hath a garden walled around,
A paradise of fruitful ground,
Chosen by love and fenced by grace
From out the world's wide wilderness.

Like trees of spice his servants stand,
There planted by his mighty hand;
By Eden's gracious streams, that flow
To feed their beauty where they grow.

Awake, O wind of heaven, and bear
Their sweetest perfume through the air:
Stir up, O south, the boughs that bloom,
Till the beloved Master come:

That he may come, and linger yet
Among the trees that he hath set;
That he may evermore be seen
To walk amid the springing green.

Although there was much prejudice to be overcome, and many years were to elapse before congregational hymn singing became general in all the English Churches, the new era was well established before the end of Watts' earthly life in 1748. It is certain that the response in some of the Independent Churches was swift and cordial. It may be assumed that many of these congregations eagerly welcomed the new hymns by Isaac Watts, and the completely different type of metrical psalm which he provided. Evidence of this is that in 1720 another hymn writer, the Reverend Simon Browne, published *Hymns and Spiritual Songs in Three Books,* designed as a supplement to the work of Isaac Watts, which, it is clear from this, was already becoming widely popular. Browne was for a time a near neighbour of Isaac Watts, being pastor of an Independent church in Old Jewry. He wrote over two hundred and fifty hymns. They were of small merit, and the only one to survive in our modern hymnals is the hymn, *Come, gracious Spirit, heavenly dove.* But his work bears witness to the firm progress which the hymns of Isaac Watts were making in the Independent Churches. These Churches were, however, to exhibit another form of conservatism. Just as they had previously excluded everything but the older versions of the metrical psalms, so now they would admit no hymns except the hymns of Isaac Watts. None the less, the new era was born. Isaac Watts was a portent. Not only were hymns being written, but they were being written for *Congregational* singing. The foundation was firmly laid for one of the most remarkable achievements in English religious history.

The genius of Watts was attested by the fact that he clearly formulated principles of style which have left a lasting impression on all subsequent hymnody.

His hymns are clear and simple in expression, marked by dignity and melody. They reveal strong emotion under firm control, and at their best they deal with themes of universal spiritual experience, ensuring for a substantial percentage of them a permanent place in all English and American hymnals.

A statistical analysis of any group of hymn books in general use to-day will bear witness to this fact. Watts continues to hold a leading place among the hymn-writers of the English tradition on both sides of the Atlantic. It vindicates the judgment of an American writer, Frederic Palmer, that Watts "was the first Englishman who set the gospel to music, and in his special field of song he has never been surpassed".

While much of his thought was naturally clothed in the thought forms familiar to his age, in important matters his vision went far beyond the range of his period. This was marked in his desire for a revised psalter, and after two centuries this remains an important need. It is one direction in which we may well travel along the road indicated by the Christian vision of this sensitive and far-seeing pioneer.

[*Note*. Space forbids fuller analysis and criticism of the hymns of Isaac Watts, but the reader is urged to pursue the subject in *The Hymns of Wesley and Watts*, by Bernard L. Manning (Epworth Press). Mr. Manning's book is the reprint of a series of papers, and they give a penetrating and most suggestive appreciation of the hymns of Watts. It is a pity that Mr. Manning allowed his unbounded (and fully justified) enthusiasm for both Wesley and Watts, to lead him into uncritical gibes and quips at some very excellent modern hymns and tunes, but allowing for this defect, his treatment of Watts is masterly, and is of the greatest value for the general reader.

Bernard Lord Manning was a Fellow of Jesus College, Cambridge, and a young Congregational scholar of outstanding ability. His untimely death has been a great loss.]

5

"For the Use of the People
called Methodists"

IT has been pointed out by more than one critic, that when Isaac Watts began writing hymns, there existed already a substantial number which would have enabled the publication of a good collection without any addition being made to them. The material thus available has already been indicated in the first chapter. But it must be remembered that these verses were for the most part contained in manuals of private devotion and not regarded as hymns, while others, now employed as hymns, were written originally as poems. The use of the latter marks a much later stage in the development of English hymnody.

Demand creates supply, and so it is from the time of Isaac Watts, marking the true beginning of congregational hymn singing, that we trace a steady and increasing body of hymn writers. One name which must be remembered, forming a link between the pioneer work of Watts and the rich harvest of the Methodist Revival, is that of Philip Doddridge, who was born in 1702, and died shortly after Watts, in 1751. The son of a London oil merchant, he had ancestors who had suffered for their religious convictions. His paternal grandfather had been one of the ministers ejected under the Commonwealth, while his maternal grandfather had been a Lutheran pastor who had fled from Bohemia "with his little store of money bound up in his girdle, and Luther's Bible for all his heritage". Like Watts, Philip Doddridge declined the offer of admission to the University, preferring to remain a Dissenter. He became pastor of the Congregational church at Northampton, and principal of the Theological Academy there. He wrote 364 hymns, which during his life appeared only in manuscript. A selection was published after his death, in a volume called *Hymns founded on Various Texts*, edited by the Reverend Job Orton, who had been one of Doddridge's students at the Northampton Academy. Some of the hymns are well known, and most of these are included in modern hymnals. The best known is, *Hark! the glad sound the Saviour comes*, which so discerning a critic as Garrett Horder acclaimed as "one of the noblest hymns ever written, alike as to style and substance". Another hymn, *Ye servants of the Lord*, is frequently included in ordination services, while one of the most familiar and beautiful Communion hymns is, *My God, and is Thy table spread*, and another of the best known is *O God of Bethel by whose hand*. Philip Doddridge was an intimate friend of Isaac Watts, and the importance of his hymns lies in the fact that while they retain the form common to the hymns of the Independents, they anticipate in spirit and expression the forthcoming Methodist hymns, and are a bridge connecting the two types of hymnody.

The coming of the Wesleys opened the most remarkable epoch in the history of English hymns. The achievement of Charles Wesley in this field remains unique and without a rival. His output alone was astounding. He was the author of not less than seven thousand hymns. If many of these are now unknown, or forgotten, nevertheless those which find inclusion in our hymnals are in number without parallel. They have become the common inheritance of all the Christian Churches. It is interesting to note the quantity contained in various leading hymnals excepting the *Methodist Hymn Book*, which, as is natural, includes the greatest number. *Hymns Ancient and Modern* has thirty-two, *The English Hymnal* twenty, *Songs of Praise* twenty-one, *Worship Song* fifteen, with an equally generous proportion in the hymnals of other Churches, including twenty in the Unitarian hymnal, *Hymns of Worship!* Song was the life blood of the amazing Methodist movement, which will ever remain one of the most astonishing events in

English history. Without the hymns of Charles Wesley it seems impossible to imagine the movement. It was proof of the English response to hymns, and makes it the more astonishing that religious organizations in this country could have neglected an influence so potent and effective.

The figures given above are impressive from the standpoint that they are the hymns of one writer, and if we take all the standard books now in use in the Churches no other hymn writer can claim so generous a number. It may be said, of course, that these figures relating to Charles Wesley's hymns represent a very small percentage in relation to the enormous output of 7,000, even if we bear in mind the large number, nearly 250, included in the *Methodist Hymn Book*. This is true, and it is a reminder of the high mortality rate in hymns. Hymns which have survived through centuries, and remain in *common* use (as opposed to merely sectarian or party use) do so because, whatever weakness or flaws may be in them, in the light of modern eyes they enshrine qualities which appeal to a universal spiritual experience, expressed with some measure of poetic genius. There are probably many more hymns by Charles Wesley which would well merit revival, in addition to those already to be found in the *Methodist Hymn Book*, but others would be found to "date" and would be of interest only as they reflect the doctrinal controversies of the time. This emphasizes the fact already stressed, that hymns which are truly great, while they quite naturally echo the mighty themes of the Christian faith, are not simply rhymed dogmatic pronouncements, or theological tracts in verse. If they are no more than this they may have a temporary vogue for purposes of sectarian propaganda, but they will not endure in the affection of generations, as will those hymns which express the abiding realities of the soul's experience.

All the same, in every really Christian hymn, which by its nature is more than vaguely religious poetry, there will be a spine of dogmatic conviction. But it will be conviction of a fact, rather than a particular interpretation of it. To make this clear, the fact of the death of our Lord as an atonement is, beyond question, a common Christian conviction. This is the foundation of the famous hymn by Isaac Watts, *When I survey the wondrous cross.* It is implicit in every line. But it does not involve one particular *theory* of the Atonement, of which there are a number in the history of Christian doctrine. In the same way the hymns celebrating the Holy Communion, which pass into common use, must not bear the burden of a special doctrinal interpretation, such as the Roman dogma of transubstantiation.

This may seem a digression, but it is important and relevant in an effort to judge rightly the hymns of Charles Wesley. The advocate of dogmatic hymnology may, and often does, invoke him in support of the plea for definitely *doctrinal* hymns. Yet the hymns of this writer which have endured as the common treasure of all the Churches, are the hymns which imply broadly the basic convictions of Christian thought. That even these hymns were not without polemical significance at the time they were written, is beyond dispute. If, indeed, their tremendous attraction and overwhelming power is to be understood rightly, they must be seen within the context of the religious disputes of the time. The major dispute, and it is the clue to the Methodist movement, was the conflict with Calvinism. This has an importance which cannot be exaggerated. It has been noted that the entrenched strength of the Old Psalters in public worship was an expression of the power of Calvinism over English religious life and thought. This was true of both the Anglican and Dissenting Churches. It was the Calvinistic stream of Reformation thought and life that had moulded the religious mind and practice of England, except for the tenacity with which the Anglican Church held to the episcopacy. The influence of Luther, and the German type of Reformation thought, had touched but slightly the religion of England. It was the distinctive work of John and Charles Wesley to make this latter influence dominant, with the refinement and enrichment contributed by their own Anglican tradition and inheritance.

This is an aspect of the Methodist movement often forgotten or overlooked; an aspect that changed the religious thought of the English people. It was a mighty, seemingly almost incredible achievement. When the two brothers began their work, Calvinistic theology dominated the minds of the religious teachers of England, but at its close what may be called the great Evangelical movement emerged, both in the Anglican and the Dissenting Churches. The Calvinism remaining was a purified and transformed version; a change foreshadowed by Isaac Watts, which was realized and carried through by the two Wesleys. It was nothing less than a second Reformation, or a Reformation within the Reformation. In this task hymns played a tremendous part, even as they had in the work of Luther himself. It would be a counsel of perfection to ask congregations to sing *historically*, but if they did they would enter into the significance of Charles Wesley's hymns in a new way. They would understand that in the mind of the writer there was always present the thought and wonder of the free, unmerited, universal Love of God, reaching out and embracing all His creatures, without distinction of nation, class or race. It can be seen how fond Charles Wesley was of the words *free* and *freely*, and because these do not appear in italics they are sung without recognizing the impact they were meant to produce—and must have produced—on the Calvinistic thought then prevailing in England.

It may be well to recall the nature of this thought. Charles Wesley once quoted from Calvin a characteristic, and to us now, a revolting, statement concerning the reprobate: "God speaketh to them that they may be the deafer: He gives light to them that they may be the blinder; He offers instruction to them that they may be the more ignorant; and uses the remedy that they may *not* be healed". Dr. Henry Bett, a leading authority on the hymns of Methodism, mentions this, and adds the detail that in Bristol, during Charles Wesley's exposition of a controverted passage of Scripture, one of his hearers "called for damnation upon his own soul if Christ died for all, and if God was willing that all men should be saved". Yet, as opposed to Calvinism, this was the universal Gospel which the Wesleys expounded, and which the hymns were designed to proclaim. They repudiated completely the perversion of the idea of election which, as John Wesley said,

taught that "one in twenty (suppose) of mankind are elected;
nineteen in twenty are reprobated. The elect shall be saved,
do what they will; the reprobate shall be damned, do what
they can". In place of this the founders of Methodism proclaimed that the love of God was boundless. "Your God is
worse than my devil", said John Wesley, to one Calvinistic
protagonist "for whereas my devil tempts one to sin, your God
compels one to do so". It was a well aimed shaft. It was against
this type of doctrine that many of the hymns were directed.
Mark some of the verses:

> Father, whose everlasting love
>   Thy only Son for sinners gave,
> Whose grace to *all* did *freely* move,
>   And sent Him down *a world to save*

> Help us Thy mercy to extol,
>   Immense, unfathom'd, unconfined;
> To praise the Lamb who died *for all*,
>   *The general Saviour of mankind.*

Observe carefully the thoughts here in italics. Mark the
title, *the general Saviour of mankind.*

See it again in a verse of one of the hymns of Christian
fellowship,

> We meet the grace to take
>   Which Thou hast *freely* given;
> We meet on earth for Thy dear sake,
>   That we may meet in heaven.

Notice how the word here underlined comes again in the
verse of one of the best known and loved of Methodist hymns,
Jesu, Lover of my soul:

> Thou of life the fountain art,
>   *Freely* let me take of Thee,
> Spring Thou up within my heart,
>   Rise to all eternity.

IV REGINALD HEBER, Bishop of Calcutta, whose famous hymns helped
to win over the Catholic wing of the Anglican Church to hymn singing.

VI JOHN HENRY NEWMAN, whose great hymn *Lead, kindly Light* is world famous.

V JOHN KEBLE, compiler of *The Christian Year*, an English devotional classic.

Then, as another example, out of a host that could be cited, recall these two most characteristic verses:

O unexampled love!
   O all-redeeming grace!
How swiftly didst Thou move
   To save a fallen race:
What shall I do to make it known
What Thou *for all mankind* hast done?

O for a trumpet voice,
   On all the world to call!
To bid their hearts rejoice
   In Him who died for all;
For all my Lord was crucified,
For all, for all my Saviour died.

For all ... *For all*: Charles Wesley cannot repeat the words too often. They express the dynamic *motif* of the Methodist Revival. They help to explain the new touch of hope, the personal appeal and sympathy, which reached out to masses of neglected, forgotten, and outcast souls in the England of the eighteenth century. It warmed and stimulated philanthropic enterprises of all kinds; care for the poor, the untaught, the sick, the prisoners, and the unfortunate. It helped to explain why the new Evangelical movement inspired the agitation for the abolition of the slave trade. The same impulse took Charles Wesley into the foul prison of Newgate, with a new message of the Love of God for the neglected creatures there. The latter part of his life was devoted to this service, and again it lights up the emphasis made in the hymns mentioned. In the *Journal* written by Charles Wesley, we have this entry under date July 10, 1738:

I went ... to Newgate; and preached to the ten male-factors under sentence of death. ... a sudden spirit of faith came upon me, and I promised them all pardon in the name of Jesus Christ, if they would repent and

E   65

believe the Gospel. Nay . . . I could not help telling them, "I had no doubt but God would give me every soul of them".

A faith which, the *Journal* goes on to tell us, was completely fulfilled.

It was a further instance of the faith expressed in his great conversion hymn:

> Outcasts of men, to you I call,
> The invitation is to all.

These examples will suffice to demonstrate the challenge which this interpretation of the Gospel made to the dominant Calvinism of the period. It was a practical application of the truth expressed by Luther in his great doctrine of Justification by Faith. How thoroughly it achieved victory may be judged from the fact that those Churches which inherit the Calvinistic tradition in England, to-day sing and treasure the great hymns of Charles Wesley in common with their Methodist friends. It is now forgotten that some of these hymns were polemic in their origin. But this is only because they deal with the immensities of faith and experience, and not with secondary or lesser themes. If, in the religious climate of to-day, the harsh gloom of early Calvinism is unthinkable, it should not be forgotten that it was the Methodist Revival, and particularly its hymns, which made this change possible.

It is also to the hymns of Charles Wesley that we look for examples of another outstanding feature of the Evangelical movement, and an abiding feature of hymns which are now so designated. This feature is the note of intimate, personal experience. Just as at the other end of the scale, Isaac Watts, as was mentioned, related the historic Gospel to the wide sweep of the cosmic purpose of God, so in the hymns of Charles Wesley we have this historic Gospel related to the individual. In modern thought there has been a fashion to discount what is termed the individualism of the Evangelicals, and to encourage the sense of the community in its place. It is a shallow criticism, and one of which we are likely to hear less in an era when the individual is being reduced to little more than a registered number! The Evangelical valuation of the individual is one of the most precious and indispensable truths of the Gospel of Jesus Christ, and has received immortal illustration in the wonderful parables in the fifteenth chapter of St. Luke. This note rings out with clarion clearness in hymn after hymn that Charles Wesley wrote:

> See there my Lord upon the tree!
> I hear, I feel, He died *for me*.

This is from the same hymn which emphasizes, *For all, for all.* . . . See how perfectly Charles Wesley has related self and community, the one and the many. Again:

> 'Tis mercy all, immense and free;
> For, O my God, it found out *me*!

Possibly in no stanza is this thought more beautifully expressed than in one which combines a note of deep humility; he is writing of the grace of God:

> Throughout the world its breadth is known,
>   Wide as infinity;
> So wide *it never passed by one*,
>   Or it had passed by me.

These are the authentic notes of Evangelical experience. Linked with the wide vision of all mankind, embraced within the orbit of the Divine grace, it can be said that in Charles Wesley the two wings of Christian outlook and experience, what we now designate the Evangelical and Catholic, unite. It is a reminder that a true Catholicism must ever be Evangelical, and a soundly Evangelical standpoint, Catholic. The two are not contradictory, but complementary, and this is a sure reason why the hymns of Charles Wesley are treasures now common to both types of Church.

It would be wrong to suggest that all the hymns are of equal merit. It could not be expected in view of their immense number. Charles Wesley had remarkable gifts and qualities as a lyric poet. In this fact, combined with his own vivid spiritual experience, mystical understanding, and zeal as an evangelist, we have the clues to his supreme powers as a writer of hymns of enduring worth. But no poet can claim uniform quality for all his work. No such claim could be made for Shakespeare, Keats, Browning, Tennyson, or any of the great poets of our language. Many hymns were inspired by purely passing and even local events; Charles despised nothing that offered suggestion to his lively imagination. But this meant that much verse was ephemeral and transitory. Dr. Bett rightly reminds us that Charles Wesley wrote many verses dealing with the political events of his time, and the affairs of the nations. "These are generally uninspired and sometimes they are singularly wrong-headed". We can afford to forget these for the wealth of treasure that is left.

Of the Methodist hymns that have become the common possession of all the Churches to-day, *Jesu, lover of my soul* would, on vote, undoubtedly, secure first place. Critics have made various objections to it, and some strange results have accrued from efforts to produce a revised form. John Wesley omitted it altogether from the *Methodist Collection*, of 1780, but time has given it the seal of approval. Henry Ward Beecher said, "I would rather have written that hymn than to have the fame of all the kings that ever sat upon the earth". There is one story associated with this hymn that merits repetition, if only because it suggests the healing power of the common treasures of worship, in a world broken by faction and strife:

A party of Northern tourists were on the deck of an excursion steamer, on the Potomac, one summer evening in 1881. One of the party, who had a remarkable voice, began to sing hymns to the others. When he had sung two verses of *Jesu, lover of my soul*, a stranger made his way from the outskirts of the crowd: "Beg your pardon, sir,

68

but were you actively engaged in the late war?" Yes, I fought under General Grant", replied the singer. "Well", the first speaker continued, "I did my fighting on the other side, and I think I was very near you one bright night eighteen years ago this month. It was much such a night as this. If I am not mistaken, you were on guard duty. We of the South had sharp business on hand. I crept near your post of duty my weapon in my hand; the shadows hid me. Your beat led you into the clear light. As you paced back and forth you were singing that same hymn. I raised my gun and aimed at your heart—and I had been selected for the work because I was a sure shot. Then out upon the night floated the words:

> Cover my defenceless head
> With the shadow of Thy wing.

Your prayer was answered. I couldn't fire after that. And there was no attack made upon your camp that night. I felt sure when I heard you singing this evening that you were the man whose life I was spared from taking". The singer grasped the hand of the Southerner and said: "I remember the night very well, and the feeling of depression with which I went forth to my duty. I knew my post was one of great danger. I paced my lonely beat, thinking of home and friends, and all that life holds dear. Then the thought of God's care came to me with peculiar force, and I sang the prayer of my heart and ceased to feel alone. How the prayer was answered I never knew until this evening".

A hymn which remains number 1 in *The Methodist Hymn Book* is the familiar one *O for a thousand tongues to sing*. It is fitting that it should be given this premier position, for it was written by Charles Wesley to commemorate his own conversion, composed on the first anniversary of his profound spiritual change, May 21, 1739. It is probable that the hymn was the expansion of a thought lodged in his mind by a remark by Peter Bohler, one of the Moravian leaders, who, when Charles spoke to him a year previously about confessing Christ, replied, "Had I a thousand tongues, I would praise Him with them all".

Another of the hymns which has held a firm place in the increasing affection of all the Churches is *Love divine, all loves excelling*. It is certainly one of the most beautiful of Charles Wesley's hymns, and if we recall the theological 'climate' of the period in which it was written, depressed by the sombre gloom of the grim Calvinist conception of God, then the gracious tenderness and warm glow of this lovely hymn become all the more apparent.

Possibly nothing that Charles Wesley wrote exceeds the last verse in aspiration and devotion:

> Finish then Thy new creation
>   Pure and spotless let us be;
> Let us see Thy great salvation,
>   Perfectly restored in Thee:
> Changed from glory into glory,
>   Till in heaven we take our place,
> Till we cast our crowns before Thee,
>   Lost in wonder, love and praise.

Others that are now treasured wherever Christian hymns are sung are the fine Easter hymn, *Christ the Lord is risen to-day* (strangely weakened in the amended form given in *Songs of Praise*), a hymn vibrant and throbbing with the poetry and passion revealed by the writer at his best; *Soldiers of Christ, arise*, another hymn of distinctive strength and power, originally in thirty-two verses, containing one, now omitted, of striking thought and phrasing:

> But, above all, lay hold
>   Of faith's victorious shield
> Armed with that adamant and gold
>   Be sure to win the field.

While another firm favourite, and a hymn of outstanding merit, is *Rejoice, the Lord is King*, marked by inspired strength and simplicity. This is one of the three Wesley hymns for which Handel composed the tunes, and, in this instance, the tune "Gopsal" brings out to the full the thought and sentiment of the hymn, an example of the happy and desirable congruity between *thought* and *sound*, of which more will be said in a later chapter, and of which Handel was a master.

O Love Divine, how sweet Thou art is another example of the combination of poetic ability, and devotional fervour, which is the peculiar genius of Charles Wesley's hymns. What could be finer that the thought and structure of the second verse?

> Stronger His love than death or hell;
> Its riches are unsearchable;
>   The first-born sons of light
> Desire in vain its depths to see,
> They cannot reach the mystery.
>   The length, and breadth, and height.

One of the greatest of the Methodist hymns, held by some to be the greatest, is *Come, O thou Traveller unknown*. It is really a passionate devotional poem, so intimate and mystical, and, therefore, so intensely personal, that it may be doubted if in congregational use the significance of its thought can be fully appreciated. In the original there are fourteen verses, usually reduced to four in most hymnals. *The Methodist Hymn Book* gives twelve of the original verses, followed by the abbreviated version. Some of the verses omitted from the latter bring out the spirit of this matchless hymn with such power and beauty that they should be recalled:

> My prayer hath power with God, the grace
>   Unspeakable I now receive;
> Through faith I see Thee face to face
>   I see Thee face to face, and live!
> In vain I have not wept and strove;
> Thy nature and Thy name is Love.

I know Thee, Saviour, who Thou art,
　　Jesus, the feeble sinner's Friend;
Nor wilt Thou with the night depart,
　　But stay and love me to the end;
Thy mercies never shall remove;
Thy nature and Thy name is Love.

While in the verse which is now given as the last verse of the shortened version, Charles Wesley reveals his true greatness as mystic and poet:

'Tis Love! 'tis Love! Thou diedst for me!
　　I hear Thy whisper in my heart;
The morning breaks, the shadows flee,
　　Pure, universal love Thou art;
To me, to all, Thy mercies move;
Thy nature and Thy name is Love.

When we think of hymns such as these, we can understand how the dark shadows of a grim Calvinism were giving place to the light and warmth of this Christian renaissance. We can see, too, more clearly the amazing combination of gifts and qualities in the writer of these hymns; poet, mystic, scholar, evangelist, and simple-hearted Christian. He has left a legacy to English religious thought and worship which will never be lost.

The quality of these hymns, together with the impact of them upon the religious consciousness of the time, seems to justify the claims made in the preface by John Wesley to the *Collection* of 1779:

... No such Hymn Book as this has yet been published in the English language. In what other publication of the kind have you so distinct and full account of scriptural Christianity? ....
1. In these hymns there is no doggerel; no botches; nothing put in to patch up the rhyme; no feeble expletives.
2. Here is nothing turgid or bombast, on the one hand,

72

or low and creeping on the other. 3. Here are no *cant* expressions; no words without meaning . . . 4. Here are . . . both the purity, the strength, and the elegance of the English language; and, at the same time, the utmost simplicity and plainness, suited to every capacity. Lastly, I desire men of taste to judge (these are the only competent judges) whether there be not in some of the following hymns the true Spirit of Poetry, such as cannot be acquired by art and labour, but must be the gift of nature. By labour a man may become a tolerable imitator of Spenser, Shakespeare, or Milton; and may heap together pretty compound epithets . . . but unless he be *born* a poet, he will never attain the genuine spirit of Poetry.

But . . . . That which is of infinitely more moment than the Spirit of Poetry, is the spirit of piety. And I trust all persons of real judgment will find *this* breathing through the whole Collection. It is in this view chiefly, that I would recommend it to every truly pious reader, as a means of raising or quickening the spirit of devotion; of confirming his faith; of enlivening his hope; and of kindling and increasing his love to God and man. When Poetry thus keeps its place as the handmaid of Piety, it shall attain, not a poor perishable wreath, but a crown that fadeth not away.

Reference must be made to one other body of hymns composed by Charles Wesley. Those dealing with the Sacrament of Holy Communion. These are important not only as further examples of merit and quality, but because they serve to confirm the importance which the Wesleys attached to this Sacrament, and centre of Christian worship. Both brothers were staunch Anglican Churchmen, and Charles remained in fellowship with the parent body until the end, while we know it was the desire of John that the members of the Methodist Societies should remain in this fellowship. It may well be that the first practical step in official Reunion in England will unite these two branches of the Church Universal, and to this end it will help to recall the great hymns devoted by Charles

Wesley to the observance of the Lord's Supper. The brief *Author of life divine*, may be held to rank as one of the best. It is in perfect accord with the true Anglican doctrine of the Eucharist:

> Author of life divine,
>   Who hast a table spread,
> Furnished with mystic wine
>   And everlasting bread,
> Preserve the life Thyself hast given,
> And feed and train us up for heaven.
>
> Our needy souls sustain
>   With fresh supplies of love,
> Till all Thy life we gain,
>   And all Thy fullness prove,
> And, strengthened by Thy perfect Grace,
>   Behold, without a veil Thy face.

The most orthodox Anglican theologian could take no exception to the following:

> Come, Holy Ghost, Thine influence shed,
>   And realise the sign;
> Thy life infuse into the bread,
>   Thy power into the wine.
>
> Effectual let the tokens prove
>   And made, by heavenly art,
> Fit channels to convey Thy love
>   To every faithful heart.

To these we must add the well-known hymn, *Victim divine, Thy grace we claim*, as well as *Jesus, we thus obey*.

John Wesley's own contribution to hymnody was mainly in the work of translation, to which task we are indebted for some of the excellent German hymns in the Lutheran tradition. These will be dealt with further when considering the hymns we have gleaned from other than English sources.

John Wesley's work in editing and sifting the amazing collection of his brother's hymns must not be overlooked. If he did not possess such a full measure of the poetic gift as Charles (though his own endowment was of no mean order) yet his critical judgment, and skill in literary discernment, were probably greater. It may be assumed that in his final selection he eliminated a considerable amount of the more ephemeral, and less valuable work of Charles, with resultant gain in the amount of pure gold contained in the ultimate *Collection*.

6

A Group of Evangelicals

WITH the advent of Isaac Watts and the Wesleys, the future of hymn-singing in English religious worship was assured. The process of development was slow, but moved through well marked stages. The Independents were the first to favour hymns in public worship as a general practice, due mainly to the inspiration given, and contribution made by Watts. Even here the approval given to the innovation was not at once general. But there is no doubt that within the boundaries of the Independent Churches, the singing of hymns became well established during the life of Watts. But for a considerable time the hymns used were confined to those written by him, even as with the Methodist 'Societies', which were coming into existence in the middle of the eighteenth century, the hymns used were restricted to those written or translated by the Wesley brothers. It was later that worshippers in both bodies began to see how much there was in common in the thought of Watts and that of both John and Charles Wesley, so that the hymns of all three were enjoyed as treasures to be shared.

With the growing, if still limited, popularity of hymns in Dissenting circles, it was natural that an increasing number of hymn writers appeared. It may be assumed that not a few followers of Charles Wesley felt impelled to add their own contributions to the growing volume. But few of their efforts have survived, and it is small wonder that they were overshadowed by the genius of their leader. One or two, however, are remembered by the hymns they wrote, a few of which still find place in our hymnals. Of these, "that majestic ode" as it has been called, *The God of Abraham praise*, reminds us of Thomas Olivers, one of the itinerant preachers of John Wesley, although he owed the experience which led to his conversion to the preaching of Whitefield, at Bristol. He became one of the most noted of the first group of Methodist travelling preachers, and laboured at first in Cornwall, and later in other parts of England and in Ireland. Had he kept a journal, as his famous leader did, there is no doubt it would have been stored with many similar adventures. It is said he travelled fully a hundred thousand miles, and frequently encountered much opposition and persecution. He was an unlettered man, who had been a blacksmith's apprentice, but a man of rich spiritual experience, and evangelical zeal, and a typical example of the early Methodist lay preacher. It is said that about 1770 Olivers chanced to hear the *Yigdal*, or doxology of the thirteen articles of the Hebrew faith, sung at the Great Synagogue, Duke's Place, London. Soon after this he wrote the verses of his now well-known hymn, which he claimed as a Christian version of the Hebrew *Yigdal*, and he obtained from the Jewish chorister, Leoni (Meyer Lyon), the melody to fit the words, the familiar tune "Leoni" to which the hymn is usually sung. It has also been provided with a fine alternative tune, "Covenant" by Stainer.

The hymn, in most of the books now in use, is somewhat amended, and abbreviated, although eight verses are given in *The English Hymnal*, seven in *Songs of Praise*, and ten in *Hymns Ancient and Modern* where it appears as a processional hymn, while twelve verses appear in *The Methodist Hymn Book*. One verse, usually omitted in the shorter version, enshrines the spirit of Methodism so aptly that it calls for quotation:

> Though nature's strength decay,
> And earth and hell withstand,
> To Canaan's bounds I urge my way
> At His command.

The watery deep I pass,
With Jesus in my view;
And through the howling wilderness
My way pursue.

Richard Pattison, a devoted Methodist missionary in the West Indies, said that he often quoted to himself the last four lines of the verse above, when passing through storms on the ocean, or crossing from one island to another in small vessels, and felt his faith in God wonderfully strengthened.

The hymn was written at the house of a friend, another leading Methodist lay preacher of the time, John Bakewell, who resided at Greenwich, where he had founded a nonconformist academy. He was active for a great number of years in the Methodist movement, a fact mentioned on his tombstone, which is near to the one in memory of John Wesley, in City Road Chapel, London. From this we learn that Bakewell lived to be ninety-eight; that his Christian life covered eighty of these years, and that he had been a lay preacher for seventy of them. One may doubt if this record has ever been excelled. It is believed that Bakewell wrote several hymns, but the only one which we can attach to his name with certainty is *Hail, thou once despiséd Jesus*! Something needs to be said about this hymn, for it is omitted, strange to say, from the three most widely used Anglican hymn books. It seems to be regarded as the property of a somewhat exclusive evangelical section of the Church, but fortunately is contained in the leading Free Church hymnals, at present in use. This is an example of the limitation imposed upon a hymn by an obvious expression of doctrine. It seems to many to involve a particular view of the Atonement, more especially in the second verse:

Paschal Lamb by God appointed,
All our sins on Thee were laid;
By almighty love anointed,
Thou hast full atonement made:

> All Thy people are forgiven
>   Through the virtue of Thy blood;
> Opened is the gate of heaven;
>   Peace is made 'twixt man and God.

This may be doctrinal, but it is sound doctrine, and we may be sure Charles Wesley would have approved. It is singular that it should be an offence to compilers who have been content to give space to far inferior compositions, and much more debatable statements of belief. One feels that such slightly intolerant omission is the more to be regretted when the noble, catholic spirit of this great hearted man is remembered. When he was very old he wrote the following beautiful prayer, which may well be on our lips and in our hearts at the dawn of the World Council of Churches:

> May God of His infinite goodness grant that we, and all serious Christians of every denomination, may labour for a perfect union of love, and to have our hearts knit together with the bond of peace, that, following after those essential truths in which we all agree, we may all have the same spiritual experience, and hereafter attain one and the same kingdom of glory.

Another name associated with the beginnings of Methodism was John Cennick, the author of the original verses on which is based the familiar Advent hymn *Lo! He comes with clouds descending*. This hymn calls for several comments. In the first place, in the form in which it is now known it had a mixed origin. Cennick, who, early in life, had been converted through the preaching of the Wesleys and Whitefield, was for a time a Methodist preacher, but later parted from the Methodist movement owing to doctrinal differences, and attached himself to the Moravians. He was only thirty-seven when he died in 1755, but by this time he had written a number of hymns, and the Graces, which it was once the vogue to sing at congregational tea parties: *Be present at our table, Lord*, and *We thank Thee, Lord, for this our food*. He wrote an evening hymn, marked

79

by gentleness and devotion, *Ere I sleep, for every favour*, found in some current hymnals, as well as one, better known, *Children of the heavenly King*; a good hymn, simple and sincere in sentiment.

Lo! He comes with clouds descending, the familiar hymn with which Cennick's name is linked, is a very much altered version of the verses as he first wrote them. It is not essential to give the verses in full, but two will suffice to show their quality:

> Lo! He cometh, countless trumpets,
>   Blow before His bloody sign!
> 'Midst ten thousand saints and angels
>   See the Crucified shine.
>   Allelujah!
> Welcome, welcome bleeding Lamb!
>
> All who love Him view His glory,
>   Shining in His bruised Face:
> His dear Person on the rainbow,
>   Now His people's heads shall raise:
>   Happy mourners!
> Now on clouds He comes! He comes!

These verses, with the others which formed the original hymn, came to the notice of Charles Wesley. It is not surprising that his poetic sensibility shrank from their crudity. He altered them into the form which, with some further changes, is now familiar to us. In fairness to Cennick, it may be allowed that he was capable of writing some good verse, but this is certainly an example of vastly inferior work. In the light of it we can understand John Wesley's disinclination to encourage any of his helpers, except his brother, to write hymns. "Were we to encourage little poets, we should soon be overrun", he once remarked. John Wesley knew well that to write a good hymn is a difficult task, and his judgment has been abundantly confirmed by the vast output of a later period. The revision made by Charles Wesley in this instance failed to produce a good hymn. This opinion may shock those who have come to venerate it through long usage, and through affection for the tune "Helmsley", to which it is usually sung. It is an obvious example of the way *doctrine* should *not* be employed in writing a hymn. No belief has given rise to such fantastic ideas, or wild imaginings, as the belief associated with what is called the Second Advent. The imagery used in the hymn is born of the strange Messianic outlook which marked the post-exilic beliefs represented in the writings contained in what we know as the Book of Daniel, and in other religious books of the same period, not included within the canon of our Scriptures. How far the subtle Oriental mind may have used such imagery simply as metaphors and symbols of deeper spiritual thought is another matter. What is clear is that the very literal Western mind has extracted from these writings crude and revolting ideas which have found expression in some medieval art, and, as here, in later hymnody. This is not a manual of theology, so that it is not possible to pursue the nature and significance of this belief. It is an important belief, and one which calls for careful re-interpretation, but that the former crude notions should still find congregational utterance is an occasion for regret.

It suggests one other practical reflection. Would it not be correct to say that the popularity of *Lo! He comes with clouds descending* is due to the tune "Helmsley", enriched now by a Vaughan Williams descant? Would it retain its popularity if continued to be sung to "St. Thomas", the tune with which, at one time, it was usually linked? One even suspects that *Songs of Praise*, in many other instances strangely fastidious, included this hymn because of the tune. It seems an instance of straining out the gnat, and swallowing the camel! However, if space is given to this criticism it is because of the desirability of keeping sincerity in mind when offering our worship to God, and a hymn is an important, and most widely prevalent, act of worship. If objection is made to the inclusion of a good hymn because it is suspected of a too positive doctrine of the Atonement, on what grounds can exemption be granted to a hymn conveying an even more doubtful interpretation of the second coming of Christ?

Another member of the Methodist preaching band, Edward Perronet, wrote a hymn which has become .one of the most famous and widely cherished. This is *All hail the power of Jesu's Name*. It first appeared without a signature in the *Gospel Magazine* in 1780, and it was not known for a while who was the author. Edward Perronet was the son of the Vicar of Shoreham, Kent, the Reverend Vincent Perronet. John Wesley was an intimate friend of the Perronets, and often stayed with the Vicar at Shoreham, and preached in the parish. Edward appears to have been a gentleman of lively wit, and a pungent critic. It was of the Anglican Church he said, "I was born and brought up, and am likely to die in the tottering communion of the Church of England, but I despise her nonsense". A somewhat premature view of an institution that is far from tottering! Again, in 1757 he published a poem called *The Mitre* a forcible and satirical piece of work which did not spare celebrities in Church or State. It much annoyed John Wesley, who called for its instant suppression, which was done, although Edward continued to circulate it privately. All the same he was for some years a loyal and hard-working helper of the Wesleys. At Bolton, during mob violence which greeted the preachers, he was thrown down and rolled in mud and mire, and there is clear evidence that John Wesley thought very highly of him. Subsequently he parted company with his leader, owing to a difference of opinion concerning the administration of the Sacraments, and attached himself to an independent body with Calvinistic views, known as the Countess of Huntingdon's Connexion, after the name of its distinguished founder. Later, however, he became the minister of a Congregational church in Canterbury. He died at the age of sixty-six, and his earthly body was buried in the cloisters of Canterbury Cathedral.

All hail the power of Jesu's Name is one of the most popular English hymns, and is an example, of which there are many, of a writer being known by one hymn which retains its place in the affection of all Christian congregations.

Outside the Methodist circle there were some hymns written at this period which have held an enduring position. They were produced by other sections of what we call the Evangelical Movement, one being the Moravian Brethren. This Christian sect, which had its origin in Bohemia, spread to America and England, through the refugees who came for religious freedom. In 1735 a party sailed for America in company with John and Charles Wesley. Reference will be made in another chapter to the contribution made to English hymnody by the translations from the German which John Wesley made. This community exerted a profound influence on the Wesleys, and it will be remembered that it was at one of their meetings in Aldersgate Street, London, that John Wesley experienced his conversion. Apart from the German hymns, which have come to us from this source through John Wesley, there are a few other well-known hymns written by members of this community. Many have not survived. They were often emotionally extravagant, and crudely expressed, and met with John Wesley's strong disapproval. The name of John Cennick has already been noticed in his association with the Wesleys, before he linked himself with the Moravian community, and one, which must be dealt with more fully, is James Montgomery. He is of considerable importance in the record of English hymnody, for not only was he a hymn writer of real merit, but may also be regarded as the first critic, or hymnologist. He was the son of a Moravian minister, and became a journalist and editor of the *Sheffield Reporter* in 1796. He is mentioned at this stage, because he represents the more disciplined and refined type of hymn contributed by a Moravian. In point of time it will be seen he is slightly later than the names so far given in this chapter. It is by his hymns that Montgomery is remembered, for various poems he wrote (and he appears to have had considerable poetic ability) are now mostly forgotten. He was a man of fearless political views, which were not always acceptable to the Government of the day, and twice he was fined and imprisoned for his liberal pronouncements in the paper which he edited. It is to these imprisonments that we are indebted for some of his best hymns. It appears he could "sing the Lord's song in a strange land!" He certainly knew much of "the changes and chances of this mortal life", for eventually the Government gave him a literary pension of two hundred a year! For nearly half a century he enriched the hymnody of the Church, and must certainly merit a place with England's leading hymn writers.

The sound and durable quality of Montgomery's hymns may be due in some measure to the fact that he was not a facile writer. He confessed that he composed his verses very slowly, and only by fits and starts. Moreover, he was a man of quiet, restrained temperament, shy and retiring. It may have been this diffidence of nature that prevented him from becoming a member of the Moravian Church until he was over forty. It is remarkable that he should have been in the Moravian communion, for the restraint and sobriety of his verse contrast with the lavish outpourings of earlier Moravian hymns. That most discerning hymnologist, Garrett Horder, said of Montgomery's hymns that "for variety, clearness, strength, suitability of form to subject they have rarely, if ever, been excelled". Moreover, Montgomery's hymns are interesting as an indication of the rapid strides made in English hymnody, following the great pioneer work of Watts and the Wesleys. Their quality is confirmed by the large percentage that have endured, and found inclusion in all modern hymnals. There are thirteen in *Hymns Ancient and Modern*; eight in *Songs of Praise*; ten in *The English Hymnal*; fifteen in *Worship Song*, and thirteen in *The Methodist Hymn Book*. It will be seen at once what a large number these represent in relation to the total, a higher percentage than applies to Watts or Wesley.

The best way for the interested reader to assess the merit of these (and other) hymns, is to look them up in one of the standard hymn books named. One or two examples are quoted in illustration of the qualities indicated, which will help to explain the enduring hold Montgomery has secured in the esteem of all the Churches; the proof and test of the writer who is bigger than all sects and parties. One further interesting illustration of this is that thirteen of Montgomery's hymns find inclusion in the hymn book of the English Unitarian Church, *Hymns of Worship*, so that this quiet Moravian now occupies a position in English hymnody shared by very few.

True to the Moravian tradition, Montgomery was enthusiastic in the cause of missionary work overseas. One of his best and most popular hymns was inspired by this interest. *Hail to the Lord's Anointed*, remains, and rightly, one of our greatest missionary hymns, with its firm, confident ending:

> O'er every foe victorious,
> He on His throne shall rest,
> From age to age more glorious,
> All blessing and all-blest;
> The tide of time shall never
> His covenant remove;
> His name shall stand for ever;
> That name to us is Love.

Another example is a hymn little known in Anglican circles, due to its regular omission from the chief hymn books of this Church. This is the hymn of God's victory, *Hark! the song of Jubilee*, a hymn which any congregation will find an excellent antidote to the flagging faith and nerveless despairs of these difficult days.

> Hark! the song of Jubilee,
> Loud as mighty thunder's roar,
> Or the fulness of the sea,
> When it breaks upon the shore;
> Hallelujah! for the Lord
> God omnipotent shall reign:
> Hallelujah! let the word
> Echo round the earth and main.
>
> Hallelujah! hark! the sound,
> From the centre to the skies,
> Wakes above, beneath, around,
> All creation's harmonies;
> See Jehovah's banner furled,
> Sheathed His sword: He speaks—'tis done;
> And the kingdoms of this world
> Are the kingdoms of His Son.

He shall reign from pole to pole,
With illimitable sway;
He shall reign, when like a scroll
Yonder heavens have passed away;
Then the end; beneath His rod
Man's last enemy shall fall;
Hallelujah! Christ in God,
God in Christ, is all in all.

Another fine missionary hymn is *O Spirit of the living God.*
One of the tenderest hymns on the Passion is the little fragment,
When on Sinai's top I see, with the exquisite tenderness of the
third verse:

When on Calvary I rest,
God in flesh made manifest,
Shines in my Redeemer's face,
Full of beauty, truth and grace.

While it seemed an act of wonderful faith, in anticipation
of the Assembly of World Churches, that prompted Montgomery to write *Millions within Thy courts have met.*

Soon as the light of morning broke
O'er island, continent or deep,
Thy far-spread family awoke,
Sabbath all round the world to keep.

One other familiar hymn of Montgomery's which must be
mentioned, and some will deem it his greatest, is *For ever with
the Lord.* It may not be an exaggeration to say it is a hymn
which is a model of what any hymn dealing with death should
be—sincere, restrained, an expression of living faith, not
dimmed or entangled by a clutter of elaborate imagery or
points of theological dispute. Contrast it, for example, with
the hymn already criticised, *Lo! He comes with clouds descending.*
We can understand why this hymn of Montgomery's has
found universal favour. It reaches to the core of a simple,
sincere feeling in contemplation of the Future Life. In no

field of religious thought is the need for simple and clear restatement more urgent than in relation to this subject. In illustration of this must be mentioned a hymn of a later date than Montgomery's, but one which is still widely sung. In fact, it has become so entrenched in a certain type of religious sentiment that any criticism of it may sound well-nigh sacrilegious. This is the familiar hymn by S. Baring-Gould, *On the Resurrection morning*. There is no mistaking its viewpoint.

> On the Resurrection morning
> Soul and body meet again;
> No more sorrow, no more weeping,
> No more pain.

> For a while the wearied body
> Lies with feet toward the morn;
> Till the last and brightest Easter
> Day be born.

> On that happy Easter morning
> All the graves their dead restore;
> Father, sister, child, and mother
> Meet once more.

It is a matter of wonder that the compilers of *The English Hymnal* could have included this in a collection marked by a considerable degree of discrimination. No hymn could better indicate the difficulty confronting the reformer in hymnology. It has gathered around itself certain associations, at least to an older generation of worshippers. It has been employed almost exclusively at moments when emotions are unusually sensitive and receptive owing to sorrow and bereavement; and when the critical faculties tend to be stilled. It contains lines which are rhythmic and well expressed, and it has been linked with a tune adding to the appeal. None the less, one must say frankly, it is an example of a hymn which projects a particular conception of the existence of human personality after death which is not likely to carry conviction to thoughtful minds to-day. It is easy to understand the confusion caused by this hymn, followed by an exposition by the preacher of the text, "To day shalt thou be with me in paradise", or with an enlightened and inspiring exposition of our Lord's beautiful promise, "And if I go and prepare a place for you, I will come again, and receive you unto myself; that where I am, there ye may be also" (St. John XIV. 3). The resurrection faith is the Church's most precious asset, and it is not one to be obscured or confused by the persistence of pre-Christian ideas, even when these are enshrined in a rhythmic and tuneful hymn.

Observe the wise restraint and simplicity of faith, in Montgomery's fine hymn, *For ever with the Lord*, and the familiar concluding verse.

> So when my latest breath
> Shall rend the veil in twain,
> By death I shall escape from death,
> And life eternal gain.
> Knowing as I am known,
> How shall I love that word,
> And oft repeat before the Throne,
> 'For ever with the Lord!'

It is to James Montgomery we owe the inspiring hymn of worship, *Stand up and bless the Lord*, with a verse that perfectly expresses the spirit of worship at its truest and best:

> Oh, for the living flame
> From his own altar brought,
> To touch our lips, our mind inspire,
> And wing to heav'n our thought.

The verdict of time has more than justified Montgomery's own modest belief that some of his hymns would survive. When asked by a friend in Whitby, "Which of your poems will live?" he replied, "None, sir; nothing, except, perhaps, a few of my hymns".

It is necessary to go back a little in time to make reference to another famous hymn, *Rock of ages*. The author was Augustus Toplady, who was Vicar of Broadhembury, Devon, and who died at the early age of thirty-eight in 1778. Toplady was an almost fanatical Calvinist, and this brought him into violent dispute with John Wesley, who, however, declined to enter into controversy on the ground that "he did not fight with chimney-sweeps". There is no need to disinter the dry bones of these ancient disputes, but it is interesting to recall the origin of the hymn, which first appeared at the end of a controversial and singular article by Toplady, in the *Gospel Magazine*, of which he was the editor. The article appeared in March 1776, and was called "A remarkable calculation Introduced here for the sake of the Spiritual Improvements subjoined. Questions and answers relating to the National Debt." He then dealt with the said Debt, which he claimed was so large that it could never be discharged. It is interesting to reflect what he would have thought of our present liability! He then applied the analogy to the vast total of human sins, calculating these in relation to each day, hour, minute and second, and then estimating what this calculation signified for the various decades of human life.

Our dreadful account stands as follows: At ten years old each of us is chargeable with 315 millions and 360,000 sins. At twenty with 630 millions and 720,000. At thirty with 946 millions and 80,000 . . . At eighty, with 2,522 millions and 880,000.

It was the thought suggested by this fantastic piece of arithmetical theology that inspired the verse:

> Not the labours of my hands
> Can fulfil Thy law's demands;
> Could my zeal no respite know,
> Could my tears for ever flow,
> All for sin could not atone;
> Thou must save, and Thou alone.

The hymn, and the curious calculation mentioned, were prompted by what Toplady held to be error in the Wesleys' teaching on entire sanctification in this life. It must be said that there is no basis in fact for the attractive legend that the hymn was inspired by the shelter provided by a rock in the delightful Mendip country of Somerset. Garrett Horder suggested that *Rock of ages* is the most popular hymn in the English tongue. It cannot be held, in this instance, that this is due to the tune, for more than one tune is now attached to it, and no particular melody has been linked with it in popular affection. The reason goes deeper. The hymn has made an extraordinary appeal to all kinds of people. It seems clearly an example of the truth that, by a happy inspiration, a hymn expressing a particular form of doctrine may give to the doctrine such a universal and abiding type of utterance that it will dwell in the affection of worshippers who may not be in sympathy with the original outlook which framed the hymn. Thus, *Rock of ages* was a great favourite with the High Churchman, Gladstone, whose theological sympathies were far removed from those which animated Toplady. It was sung in Westminster Abbey at Gladstone's funeral, and so discerning a critic as A. C. Benson, who was present, said "To have written words which should come home to people in moments of high, deep and passionate emotion; consecrating, consoling, uplifting . . . there can hardly be anything worth better doing than that".

Yet the popularity of this hymn was not immediate. It did not enjoy this distinction until over fifty years after the author's death. After this it achieved a firm place in the esteem of worshippers in all parts of the world. There can be no question as to its power of appeal, and the simple strength with which it utters the feeling of complete dependence on the grace and mercy of God; a feeling which is the essence of the Christian experience. It is strange that Dr. Dearmer, while admitting to the full the greatness of this hymn, should yet say, "It may be questioned whether we ought to sing the hymn to-day; but it remains a notable monument of the religion which gripped our fathers". This comment echoes, no doubt, the temporary weakening in the profound sense of sin which has marked the more liberal theological thought of the past half-century, but this conviction of sin and acknowledgment of Divine Grace is inseparable from the Christian faith. The shallow optimism that would ignore these truths is alien from the realistic view of life which belongs to Christianity. The facts of Sin and Grace are not transient modes of theological thought; they are abiding, inescapable verities. It is certain that *Rock of ages* has kept its hold because it does boldly and vividly recognise and express these facts. However much its true nature may be disguised, man does not outgrow his sense of the need of deliverance. This lies at the root of his modern confusion and restlessness.

A few years after Toplady, in 1779, there appeared one of the most important early collections of hymns in the Evangelical movement. It was a collection known as *Olney Hymns*. This was the joint work of two remarkable men: John Newton and William Cowper. The former was the Vicar of Olney, Bucks, from the name of which place the hymn book received its title. William Cowper was the friend of Newton, and lay-reader at Olney. It was a remarkable friendship, for it would be difficult to find two men whose temperaments and careers present such a complete contrast. The life-story of John Newton is epitomized in the inscription to be found in the church of St. Mary Woolnoth in the City of London; an inscription which he wrote himself:

> JOHN NEWTON, Clerk,
> Once an infidel and libertine;
> A servant of slaves in Africa:
> Was by the rich mercy of our Lord and Saviour
> Jesus Christ,
> Preserved, restored, pardoned,
> And appointed to preach the Faith
> He had long laboured to destroy.
> Near sixteen years at Olney in Bucks,
> And twenty-seven years in this Church.

The reader of this epitaph will infer that Newton's early experiences were remarkable. His father was for many years the master of a ship, and later entered the service of the Hudson Bay Company. His mother died before he was seven.

He had only two years at school, and at the age of eleven John
went to sea with his father. Then followed some adventurous
years. He was flogged as a deserter from the Navy, and for
over a year was servant to a slave-dealer in Africa. His
spiritual awakening began with a chance reading of the
Imitatio Christi of Thomas à Kempis during a voyage in 1747,
when a terrible storm overtook the ship. Newton was at the
pumps from three in the morning until noon. Called in about
an hour he could only muster strength to steer. It seemed
impossible that the ship could survive the ordeal. Newton
continued at the wheel through the terrible storm, and it was
not until six the following evening that the vessel emerged in
safety. He marked the experience as the date of the decisive
change in his life, although his adventures were by no means
at an end. It did not prevent him continuing in the slave
traffic, and purchasing many slaves whom he sold in the
West Indies. But he continued to undergo a spiritual development and deepening, and eventually left both slave trade and
sea, and was ordained to the ministry of the Church of England
in 1764, when nearly forty years of age. Then followed his
sixteen years' ministry at Olney, and twenty-seven years at
St. Mary Woolnoth.

The *Olney Hymns* were mostly written for the little village
community whom Newton first served. He contributed 280
to the collection. Many are now forgotten, but a few achieved
enduring fame. Of these possibly the best known is *How sweet
the name of Jesus sounds*, included in all the leading hymn books,
while almost equally popular is *Glorious things of thee are spoken*
(linked as it is with several fine tunes). One of Newton's hymns,
less known perhaps, but reflecting his earlier experiences, is
Begone unbelief; my Saviour is near, with the last line of the first
verse prompted by the tempest at sea, which had marked the
beginning of his spiritual change:

> Begone unbelief; my Saviour is near,
>   And for my relief will surely appear;
> By prayer let me wrestle, and He will perform;
>   With Christ in the vessel, I smile at the storm.

Observe, too, the quiet, uplifting faith of the third verse:

> His love in time past forbids me to think
> He'll leave me at last in trouble to sink:
> Each sweet Ebenezer I have in review
> Confirms His good pleasure to help me quite through.

A verse, however, no doubt weakened for modern ears, deficient in familiarity with the Bible, by the reference to "Ebenezer"!

William Cowper contributed only sixty-eight hymns to the Olney collection, but he is of special interest for the reason that he was one of the first English poets of distinction to write hymns for public worship. In modern books we find included as hymns many verses written by English poets, from the time of Elizabeth to the present day, but it should be understood that this is because modern compilers have selected devotional treasures from the poets, not because the verses were written for use as hymns. In Cowper, we have a poet of conspicuous merit, who deliberately wrote hymns for the use of the Olney congregation. Here, again, the personality of the writer is of importance for a full appreciation of the hymns. The story of Cowper's life is probably familiar to many, but its main details may be recalled for those who do not know them. Born in 1731, son of the Rector of Berkhampstead, he lost his mother when he was only six years of age, a misfortune which left a lasting effect on him. On leaving Westminster he read for the Bar, but never practised. He suffered from severe attacks of depression, and a haunting fear that he would lose his reason. He was in love with his cousin, Theodora, but their contemplated marriage was opposed by her family, who suspected Cowper's mental disability. They parted, and never met again, although both remained single to the end. Later, through the suggestion of John Newton, Cowper went to live at Olney, and assisted in Newton's church. Soon after going there Cowper was afflicted with another attack of insanity, caused by the death of a much-beloved brother. Further attacks occurred from time to time. It seems clear that it was the poet's overwhelming sense of a Divine care and providence preserving him, that prompted the greatest of his hymns, and one that is certain to endure:

> God moves in a mysterious way
> His wonders to perform:
> He plants His footsteps in the sea,
> And rides upon the storm.

> Blind unbelief is sure to err,
> And scan His work in vain;
> God is His own Interpreter,
> And He will make it plain.

Hymns equally well known are *O for a closer walk with God*, and *Hark, my soul, it is the Lord*, both expressive of Evangelical conviction and experience, clothed in the tenderness and grace characteristic of the poet. Although it had a wide vogue in certain Evangelical circles, possibly the least satisfactory of Cowper's hymns is *There is a fountain filled with blood*. One cannot avoid the feeling that it is a rather florid and extravagant outburst on the theme of the blood of sacrifice. This defect is the more obvious when the verses are compared with such a hymn as *When I survey the wondrous cross*. The grace and felicity of expression always found in Cowper is expressed again in the delightful hymn, written for the opening of a church room, *Jesus, where'er thy people meet*, with the inspired simplicity of the second verse:

> For Thou, within no walls confined,
> Inhabitest the humble mind;
> Such ever bring Thee where they come,
> And going, take Thee to their home.

The same qualities are expressed in the hymn of real mystical beauty *Far from the world, O Lord, I flee*. Garrett Horder, whose valuation was seldom wrong, regarded Cowper's hymn *Ere God had built the mountains*, as probably the grandest hymn the poet wrote. Many who know the hymn will agree with this judgment, but it is the more remarkable that it finds so little recognition in any of our current hymn books, except the one in general use in the Methodist Church. In view of Garrett Horder's opinion it is strange that he omitted it from the fine collection included in *Worship Song*. As it may be unknown to many readers who do not possess *The Methodist Hymn Book*, it is given in full:

> Ere God had built the mountains,
>   Or raised the fruitful hills;
> Before He filled the fountains
>   That feed the running rills;
> In me, from everlasting
>   The wonderful I AM
> Found pleasures never wasting,
>   And Wisdom is my name.

> When, like a tent to dwell in,
>   He spread the skies abroad,
> And swathed about the swelling
>   Of ocean's mighty flood,
> He wrought by weight and measure,
>   And I was with Him then;
> Myself the Father's pleasure,
>   And mine, the sons of men.

> Thus Wisdom's words discover
>   Thy glory and Thy grace,
> Thou everlasting lover
>   Of our unworthy race:
> Thy gracious eye surveyed us
>   Ere stars were seen above;
> In wisdom Thou hast made us,
>   And died for us in love.

And couldst Thou be delighted
  With creatures such as we,
Who, when we saw Thee slighted
  And nailed Thee to a tree?
Unfathomable wonder,
  And mystery divine;
The voice that speaks in thunder
  Says: Sinner, I am thine.

A final assessment of the *Olney Hymns* may be best expressed in words which are again Garrett Horder's:

From the little volume of *Olney Hymns* the Church has drawn a far larger number of hymns, and these greatly prized, than from many more voluminous collections. Its somewhat narrow theology is softened by the reality and tenderness of the religious experience of the authors, of both of whom it may be said, 'They learnt in suffering what they taught in song'.

The last statement is important, for it provides the clue to the right understanding of what are sometimes designated "Evangelical" hymns, that have survived the test of time. They have one thing in common. They are the utterance of an intimate, personal experience of God; of His love, mercy, providence, and redemption. They were not written in cold blood, but born of the spirit's passion. Only in like mood can they be truly understood, and it is the glory of the eighteenth century that it gave us so many of these hymns.

7

A Christmas Present for Dolly

ON Christmas morning 1749, little Dolly Byrom came
down to breakfast, eagerly anticipating, as children
rightly and properly do, the gifts which would be awaiting
her on this important day of the year. Some days before her
father had asked her what she would like for a Christmas
present, and the little maid, knowing Daddy's fondness for
writing verse had said, "Please write me a poem" but, no
doubt, hoping for other good things as well. Now, as she sat
down to breakfast on this happy Christmas morning, she saw
a slip of paper on her plate, which is still preserved in Manchester. It contained a poem Daddy had written for her, and
was headed "Christmas Day. For Dolly". These were the
opening lines she read:

> Christians, awake, salute the happy morn,
> Whereon the Saviour of the world was born;
> Rise to adore the mystery of love,
> Which hosts of angels chanted from above;
> With them the joyful tidings first begun
> Of God Incarnate and the Virgin's Son.

Dolly's father, Dr. John Byrom, did not dream that the
verses jotted down in this way for his little daughter would
in after years become one of the most treasured Christmas
hymns, and be heard each Christmas morning in thousands
of churches throughout the land. When the season was over
the piece of paper containing the verses was cast on one side,

but chanced later to fall into the hands of John Wainwright, organist of Manchester Parish Church, who set the words to the tune now familiar to everyone. The tune was named "Stockport" after his native place, but became known as "Yorkshire" under which title it appears in our hymn books.

Wainwright then got his choir boys together to practise the hymn, and the following year on Christmas Eve he took them quietly over to Kersal Cell, the quaint, half-timbered house in the vale of the Irwell, on the outskirts of Manchester, where Dr. Byrom lived. He marshalled the choir around the door, where they sang the hymn, to the surprise and delight of the author who listened within.

Byrom was a most interesting personality, and a man of varied achievements, wide sympathies and friendships. These friendships included the two Wesleys, and there is an entry in his journal, under date February 7, 1739: "Walked with John Wesley, and another young fellow from Mr. Bray's to Islington". He was a lover of the mystics, and a close friend of William Law, and we can picture him taking coffee with the Wesleys, and all three ardently discussing Jacob Boehme, Madam Guyon, Fenelon, and William Law. But he was cast in a different temperamental mould from the Methodist leaders; in many ways a genial, kindly man of the world, yet mystical and devout. He was a Cambridge scholar, with a keen relish for science. Some of his poems are an index to his sunny and genial mind, which loved to find expression in light verse. Here is one example; an extract from his *Colin and Phoebe*:

> When walking with Phoebe what sights have I seen.
> How fair was the flower, how fresh was the green,
> What a lovely appearance the trees and the shade,
> The cornfields and hedges and everything made!
>
> But now she has left me they all are in tears,
> Not one of them half so delightful appears,
> 'Twas nought but the magic I find of her eyes,
> Which made all these beautiful prospects arise.

One suspects that Byrom would have found real kinship with the parson poet, Herrick. Another little poem he wrote is worth recall for the gentle tonic it offers to our strained and anxious spirits in these middle days of the twentieth century. It was called *Careless Content*, which Southey declared was perfectly in the manner of the Elizabethans:

> I am content, I do not care,
> Wag as it will the world for me;
> When fuss and fret was all my fare,
> It got no ground, as I could see:
> So when away my caring went,
> I counted cost, I was content.
>
> With more of thanks and less of thought,
> I strive to make my matters meet;
> To seek what ancient sages sought,
> Physic and food in sour and sweet,
> To take what passes in good part,
> And keep the hiccups from the heart.
>
> With good and gentle-humoured hearts
> I choose to chat where'er I come,
> What'er the subject be that starts;
> But if I get among the glum,
> I hold my tongue to tell the truth,
> And keep my breath to cool my broth.

Not a bad philosophy of life. Most of us will do well in these strange times to "Keep the hiccups from the heart". Should any assume that this quiet, genial optimism arose from a shallow nature, it may be more true to say that it was the serenity born of a deep inner vision, the gift of the mystic, that the heart of life is good. The serious expression of this tranquil faith inspired another of the very few hymns Byrom wrote, in which, it will be noticed, the last line of each verse becomes the first line of the next. It is one of the many debts we owe to Garrett Horder that this beautiful little hymn, a

mystical gem, long neglected, was restored to us, and is now
included in several modern hymnals:

> My spirit longs for Thee
> Within my troubled breast,
> Though I unworthy be
> Of so divine a guest:
>
> Of so divine a guest
> Unworthy though I be,
> Yet has my heart no rest
> Unless it come from Thee.
>
> Unless it come from Thee,
> In vain I look around:
> In all that I can see
> No rest is to be found:
>
> No rest is to be found,
> But in Thy blessed love:
> O let my wish be crowned,
> And send it from above.

It should also be recalled that Byrom rendered indirect
service to hymnody in another unusual way. He invented a
system of shorthand, and he taught his system to the Wesleys,
who used it in making many of the entries in their famous
Journals, and the greater part of Charles Wesley's hymns were
jotted down in the same script. Thus, so far as the method
employed in writing it was concerned, Byrom may well have
had some share in another famous Christmas hymn, *Hark! the
herald angels sing*; a hymn that Dr. Julian held was one of the
four at the head of all in the English language. As this chapter
is concerned with Christmas hymns, a group much loved by
English folk everywhere, this hymn has been reserved for
notice here, rather than with other hymns by Charles Wesley
previously mentioned. It has undergone some alteration in
the form which is now so well known. As Charles Wesley
wrote it, the first verse ran:

> Hark, how all the welkin rings!
> 'Glory to the King of Kings,
> Peace on earth and mercy mild,
> God and sinners reconciled.'

> Joyful, all ye nations rise,
> Join the triumph of the skies;
> Universal nature say
> Christ the Lord is born to-day.

While in the original the last verse is one of deep significance and beauty:

> Now display Thy saving power,
> Ruined nature now restore,
> Now in mystic union join
> Thine to ours, and ours to Thine.

Few hymns have suffered more alteration and revision. It seems to have been too universal in its outlook for the Calvinist, Whitefield, who altered it in his collection of 1753, and it was given the now familiar first line. Further alterations were made by other compilers, and to-day variations will be noticed in the versions in our standard hymnals. The full original will be found as number 88 in *Songs of Praise*, and 23 in *The English Hymnal* and attests the poetic genius of its author. The 1904 edition of *Hymns Ancient and Modern* dared to restore the original first line, but the word "welkin" made the welkin ring with protests against such a departure from the revised form. The two later books mentioned above, while keeping to the revised version, also (very wisely) published the original as it was written by Charles Wesley.

An English Christmas hymn, earlier than either of the above, is the universal favourite *While Shepherds watched their flocks by night*. This was compiled by Nahum Tate, one of the joint authors of the New Version of the metrical psalms, mentioned in a previous chapter. It was contained in a supplement to this psalter which set out sixteen hymns, for various festivals and services. Of these only one has survived in use, and this is the famous Christmas hymn.

Our popular Christmas hymns have been derived from many sources, and, like Charles Wesley's hymn, have undergone various and extensive revisions. This is true of another universal favourite, *O Come, all ye faithful*. The precise origin of this great hymn is unknown, but it is generally thought to be from a French source of the late-seventeenth or early-eighteenth century. Yet the English sources in which it first appeared are earlier than the French, and it was in use in Roman Catholic circles in England in the second half of the eighteenth century. There have been something like forty different renderings of the hymn, a striking proof of its popularity, and in its earlier Latin form of *Adeste fideles* it was found in a collection of MS. music at Stonyhurst, dated 1751. The translation in use in our standard English hymnals is based on one made by the Reverend Frederick Oakeley in 1841, when he was incumbent of the church which is now All Saints, Margaret Street, London, and which had become a centre of the Tractarian movement in the Church of England. Subsequently Oakeley joined the Church of Rome (in the same year as Newman) and later became a canon of the Roman Catholic district of Westminster.

In the French version *Adeste fideles* is longer than the English version which has become familiar. The extra verses have been reproduced in *The English Hymnal*, where, in addition to the popular version, the longer one is given as a processional hymn. As these extra verses will be unknown to many readers, they are here quoted:

> See how the Shepherds,
> Summoned to his cradle,
> Leaving their flocks, draw nigh with lowly fear;
> We too will thither
> Bend our joyful footsteps.

> Lo! star-led chieftains,
> Magi, Christ adoring,
> Offer him incense, gold and myrrh;
> We to the Christ Child
> Bring our hearts' oblations.

Child, for us sinners
Poor and in the manger,
Fain we embrace thee, with awe and love;
Who would not love thee,
Loving us so dearly?

O come, let us adore him,
O come, let us adore him,
O come, let us adore him, Christ the Lord.

A Christmas hymn which has rapidly gained favour is one by E. H. Sears: *It came upon the midnight clear*. Like so many hymns that have enriched modern English hymnody, it is a gift from America, and is distinguished by real poetic strength and power. Sears was in the American Unitarian ministry, and was also active in religious journalism. It is surprising that this hymn is absent from one of the leading hymnals of the Anglican Church. Its lines seem charged with special appeal to the victims of a war-torn world:

Yet, with the woes of sin and strife,
The world has suffered long;
Beneath the angel-strain have rolled
Two thousand years of wrong;
And man, at war with man, hears not
The love-song which they bring:
O hush the noise, ye men of strife,
And hear the angels sing!

A glance at the more recent English hymnals will indicate the increasing number of Christmas hymns which are coming into popular favour. It will be seen that they are drawn from many sources, and they are, in fact, an excellent example of the varied origin of the large collection now contained in our standard hymn books. The poets have made their offering. A gem of beauty is Christina Rossetti's hymn, *In the bleak midwinter*, with two of the tenderest verses to be found in any Christmas song:

Enough for him whom cherubim
  Worship night and day,
A breastful of milk,
  And a mangerful of hay;
Enough for him, whom angels
  Fall down before,
The ox and ass and camel
  Which adore.

What can I give him,
  Poor as I am?
If I were a shepherd
  I would bring a lamb;
If I were a wise man
  I would do my part;
Yet what can I give him—
  Give my heart.

From the pen of Christina Rossetti, also, is another lovely fragment, now happily included in more recent hymnals, *Love came down at Christmas*:

Love came down at Christmas,
  Love all lovely, Love Divine;
Love was born at Christmas,
  Star and angels gave the sign.

Another modern poet, Laurence Housman, is author of a Christmas hymn, introduced in one or two recent books, which deserves to be more widely known and used:

The Maker of the sun and moon,
  The Maker of our earth,
Lo! late in time, a fairer boon,
  Himself is brought to birth!

How blest was all creation then,
  When God so gave increase;
And Christ, to heal the hearts of men,
  Brought righteousness and peace.

No star in all the heights of heaven
But burned to see Him go;
Yet unto earth alone was given
His human form to know.

His human form, by man denied,
Took death for human sin:
His endless love, through faith descried,
Still lives the world to win.

O perfect love, outpassing sight,
O Light beyond our ken,
Come down through all the world to-night,
And heal the hearts of men.

English hymnody has been much enriched by treasures brought through translation, as will be mentioned again in another chapter. This, also, has been the medium by means of which we have found some delightful Christmas hymns. J. M. Neale, one of the most diligent explorers in the field of Latin and Greek hymnody, has provided a translation of a Christmas hymn of the Eastern Orthodox Church in *A Great and mighty wonder*, by the seventh-century St. Germanus.

A Great and mighty wonder,
A full and blessed cure!
The Rose has come to blossom
Which shall for aye endure.

Catherine Winkworth, another able translator, has helped to open up a rich store of hymns from German sources. To her we owe the translation of Martin Luther's fine Christmas hymn, *Give heed my heart*, which one is pleased to see included in *The Methodist Hymn Book*, and which merits far greater recognition:

Give heed, my heart, lift up thine eyes:
Who is it in yon manger lies?
Who is this child so young and fair?
The blessed Christ Child lieth there.

Ah, Lord, who hast created all,
How hast Thou made Thee weak and small,
That Thou must choose Thy infant bed
Where ass and ox but lately fed?

Were earth a thousand times as fair,
Beset with gold and jewels rare,
She yet were far too poor to be
A narrow cradle, Lord, for Thee.

Ah, dearest Jesus, holy child,
Make Thee a bed, soft, undefiled,
Within my heart, that it may be
A quiet chamber kept for Thee.

My heart for very joy doth leap,
My lips no more their silence keep;
I too must sing with joyful tongue
That sweetest ancient cradle-song.

Glory to God in highest heaven,
Who unto men His Son hath given;
While angels sing with pious mirth
A glad new year to all the earth.

No season in the calendar of the Church has been so prolific as the Christmas festival in promoting song and verse. The Catholicism of the Middle Ages was fertile in the production of carolry, though much of it, of course, would not come normally within the category of hymns. But the imagination of poet and artist have found endless inspiration in the Nativity story, and it is a reminder that Christian truth is never fully interpreted without this imagination. It cannot be adequately expressed by the propositions of philosophers, or the definitions of theologians, necessary as these are within their own limited province. The Reformation movement in Germany was no less fertile in making use of popular carols. One secret of their popularity was that they were in the common tongue of the people. Moreover, they were frequently linked with some simple dramatisation of the Christmas story. St. Francis of

Assisi and his followers were quick to see the poetic and pictorial elements in the Nativity stories, particularly as described in St. Luke's record. St. Francis obtained the permission of the Pope to render a stage version of the sacred story in the Franciscan churches. One such performance was given in the little church in the village of Grecia, near Assisi. St. Francis prepared a stable, borrowing from a friendly farmer an ox, an ass, and a bundle of hay. When the simple play was given the villagers flocked to see it, and listened to the Franciscan brothers singing their carols to the Christ Child. Legend tells us that St. Francis remained in the church all night, his heart full of great joy, and in vision he saw the little Child stretch out his arms towards him in blessing.

The simple Christmas plays spread to other lands. In Germany in the fourteenth century, the priests impersonated Joseph and Mary, inviting each other to take turns at rocking the cradle. It was often the custom to set up the manger in a farmhouse, when the rocking of the cradle would be done by the children. It would need a separate volume to follow in detail the interesting practices which were prompted by these ever popular dramatisations of the Nativity stories. They indicate how an increasing fund of carols was inspired, some of which have found their way into our hymnody. It is a welcome fact that we have discovered a large number of these quaint and beautiful carols, and although it is certain that the old Christmas hymns will retain their place in our sentiment and affection, yet our Christmas music will be all the richer for the delightful poetry of these medieval verses. Many of them, naturally, are verses addressed in praise of Mary, but even the most zealous Protestant will not cavil at such a lovely and gracious allusion as the one from the Middle Ages, in the following lines:

> I sing of a maiden
> That is makeless,[1]
> King of all kinges
> To her son she ches.[2]

[1] Without a mate.
[2] Chose.

He came so stille
　There His moder was,
As dew in Aprille
　That falleth on the grass.
He came all so stille
　To His moderes bower,
As dew in Aprille
　That falleth on the flower.
He came all so stille
　There His moder lay,
As dew in Aprille
　That falleth on the spray.
Moder and maiden
　Was never none but she;
Well may such a lady
　Goddes moder be.

8

The Church of England joins in

FOLLOWING the development of English hymnody to the close of the eighteenth century, it will be observed that various hymn writers, and hymnals, emerged in what is called the Evangelical wing of the Church, both Anglican and Nonconformist. Yet although by this time a large body of hymns of abiding value had been written by Anglican Churchmen (for both the Wesleys, and the authors of the *Olney Hymns* come in this category) no official approval had yet been given by Authority in the Church of England, and in most parish churches the metrical psalms still held unchallenged supremacy. But the time was drawing near for the Anglican Church to join in the growing movement for the use of hymns in public worship. To-day it seems difficult to imagine that less than a century and a half ago, to hear a hymn sung in an English parish church would have been a rare and isolated experience. It may be, as was noticed earlier, that John Mason's hymns were sung at Water Stratford, but this is not certain. Nor is it clear that the *Olney Hymns* were at first employed in congregational worship. It may well have been that they were for a while restricted to private devotional use. The Anglican reception was cautious and timid. One of the first steps towards change was permission to use the metrical psalms in such a way as to mark the Church's times and seasons as they came round, while in a few parishes hymns were tolerated provided they did not form a feature of the liturgical service. Then it was allowed that they should form an item in the ordinary service if kept within strict moderation, and confined to the leading festivals. But such hymns were usually restricted to the very few included in the *Supplement* to the New Version. The conservative spirit, which seems one of the most conspicuous traits in all religious systems, is nowhere more in evidence than in the development of hymnody. It helps to explain why people who regularly attend church are still amazingly slow to employ and enjoy the great wealth of good hymns now at their disposal. This reflection will help us to be more charitable to the reluctance of our ancestors to allow in their public worship the use of the hymns steadily growing in volume. It was a reluctance by no means confined to the Church of England. It has already been noticed how fiercely the Baptists were opposed to the introduction of hymn singing, and that it was not until the advent of Isaac Watts that, in Dissenting circles, this prejudice began to disappear. Nor was this hostility to hymns restricted to England. When John Wesley went to America as a young man, he had a charge brought against him at Savannah in 1737, the statement presented to the Grand Jury being that he had made alteration in the metrical psalms, and also that he had introduced into the church and service at the Altar compositions of psalms and hymns "not inspected or authorized by any proper judicature". If we can learn anything from history (which frequently seems doubtful) such folly in the past should prompt us to be more discerning and responsive in the present.

An event of great importance in persuading the Church of England to join in the practice of hymn singing, occured in Sheffield in 1819. Thomas Cotterill, who was then the Vicar of St. Paul's in that city, published the eighth edition of his *Selection of Psalms and Hymns for public and private use, adapted to the services of the Church of England*. In this work he had the help of the Moravian, James Montgomery, whose important contribution to English hymnody has already been described. Montgomery printed Cotterill's book, and enriched it with fifty of his own hymns. It was at his suggestion, also, that Cotterill included the Christmas hymn, *Christians awake*, in the version with which we are familiar. When the book

110

was put into use a part of the congregation of St. Paul's objected, and an action was brought against the Vicar in the York Consistory Court. The Archbishop wisely undertook to mediate, and the Moravian editor again assisted the Church of England vicar in the production of a book which the Archbishop, Vernon Harcourt, not only criticised and revised, but to which he added hymns of his own, and produced the work at his own expense. The incident may be said to mark the victory of hymnody in the Anglican Church. Montgomery said that he and Cotterill had "clipped, interlined and remodelled hymns of all sorts" and it was to this collection that Montgomery contributed some of his best hymns which have secured lasting fame.

The impetus given by the Archbishop's lead had a marked effect. Hymnals began to appear in quantity. Metrical psalms did not disappear, but they were now mingled with hymns growing in popularity, and the day was over when the Old and New Versions held monopoly in the services of the Anglican Church.

Yet another effort had been made a little earlier than the date marked by the recognition of Cotterill's work, and an effort with an added significance in that it was made by one whom we should now designate as a High Churchman. It will have been plain so far that the Evangelicals, both inside and outside of the Anglican Church, were the pioneers of English hymnody, but in Reginald Heber there appeared a new influence in the hymnody of the Anglican communion. So far, in the wealth of hymns written, no real effort had been made to link them with the festivals and seasons marking the Church's year. Even in the *Olney Hymns* there was no special provision of hymns to mark the great festivals. In the month of October, 1811, there appeared the first four of a series of hymns intended to remedy this defect, the first instalment of a small but remarkable contribution to English hymnody, based avowedly on the lines of the Book of Common Prayer. They were published in a magazine called *The Christian Observer*, edited at that time by Zachary Macaulay, the father of Lord Macaulay. The hymns bore the initials "D.R." being the

111

final letters of the name of one whose gracious life and Christian culture will never be forgotten in the history of the Anglican Church—Reginald Heber.

It has been said that Heber represented the highest Christian culture in England at the beginning of the nineteenth century. He had a short life of remarkable influence and achievement, for Heber only lived to be forty-three. He was one of the most distinguished men at Oxford in his day, with a genius for friendship. He became Rector of Hodnet, a country living to which he gave his best. It was here he began hymn writing, and the project of a worthy hymn book for the Church he loved was always in his mind. A man of wide literary achievements, he edited the works, and wrote a life of Jeremy Taylor. Heber was made Bampton Lecturer in 1815, and Preacher of Lincoln's Inn in 1822, and at the early age of thirty-nine became Bishop of Calcutta. It was a sphere of work vast enough to intimidate the bravest spirit. At the time there was no other Bishop of the English Church in the Eastern hemisphere. All India, with Ceylon, and even Australia was supposed to be in the Bishop's charge! It is small wonder that his physical powers were overtaxed, and that he passed away after a few years of ceaseless toil in his vast charge, where he had made hosts of friends by whom he was loved and trusted.

In the year following his death there was published all that was complete of the *Hymns adapted to the weekly Church Service of the Year*. The collection was a portent for the future of English hymnody, for in it Heber had drawn from wide and varied sources, including many of the poets of his own, and earlier times. It was also notable for another reason, for he had the help of a valuable and gifted coadjutor—Henry Hart Milman, another famous and gifted Anglican Churchman; a leading ecclesiastical historian; Dean of St. Paul's, and author of the famous hymn *Ride on, ride on in Majesty!*

The collection included fifty-seven hymns by Heber himself; twelve by Milman, and twenty-nine by other writers. Heber enjoys a distinction possibly unique amongst those who have written a number of hymns—namely, that all his hymns remain in use, even if a few of them are little known. Some of the

VII Reproduction of the original MS of the familiar carol by John Byrom, *Christians, awake.*

IX WILLIAM COWPER, English eighteenth century poet and author of the well-known hymn *God moves in a mysterious way.*

VIII BISHOP KEN, seventeenth century divine who wrote two of our most familiar morning and evening hymns.

hymns are the most familiar in all our standard hymnals. One of the best known is *Holy, Holy, Holy, Lord God Almighty*, a truly glorious hymn for Trinity Sunday. Equally well known is the missionary hymn *From Greenland's icy mountains*. The story of its writing is of interest. On Whitsunday, 1819, the late Dr. Shipley, who was Heber's father-in-law, and Dean of St. Asaph, preached a sermon in Wrexham church in aid of the Society for the Propagation of the Gospel. The day was also fixed for the commencement of the Sunday Evening Lectures to be established in that church, and Heber had agreed to deliver the first lecture. During the previous day the Dean asked Heber to write something which might be sung at the missionary service the following morning, and it was in response to this request that the hymn was there and then written, with no expectation, we may be sure, that it would become a universal favourite. It had not taken more than twenty minutes to complete the verses. The hymns of Heber are so familiar that they are known by multitudes who know nothing of the author's name. One of the most popular is *The Son of God goes forth to war*, and others include *Lord of mercy and of might*; *Hosanna to the living Lord!* and the beautiful vesper, only one verse as written by Heber:

> God that madest earth and heaven,
>   Darkness and light;
> Who the day for toil hast given,
>   For rest the night;
> May thine angel-guards defend us,
> Slumber sweet Thy mercy send us,
> Holy dreams and hopes attend us,
>   This livelong night.

Two hymns which are less known reveal clearly the poetic power of Heber, indicated in all his hymns. One is the delightful hymn, *When spring unlocks the flowers to paint the laughing soil*, and one, so little known, and yet so typical of the author, that it demands quotation:

I praised the earth in beauty seen,
With garlands gay of various green;
I praised the sea, whose ample field
Shone glorious as a silver shield;
And earth and ocean seemed to say,
'Our beauties are but for a day'.

I praised the sun, whose chariot rolled
On wheels of amber and of gold;
I praised the moon, whose softer eye
Gleamed sweetly through the summer sky;
And moon and sun in answer said,
'Our days of light are numbered'.

O God, O good beyond compare,
If thus thy meaner works are fair,
If thus Thy beauties gild the span
Of ruined earth and sinful man,
How glorious must the mansion be
Where Thy redeemed shall dwell with Thee!

The value of Heber's work in hymnody for the Anglican
Church may be summed up as a step forward in the poetic
quality of hymns, and in their relation to a liturgical plan.
It can be said truly that he laid the foundations of definitely
Anglican hymnody, and that later developments were an
expansion of the lines of progress Heber had envisaged. The
further invaluable contribution he made was that he left a
legacy which stimulated both the creation and use of hymns
by the more Catholic wing of the Established Church. Hitherto
this section had held aloof. They doubted if hymns, mainly
favoured and encouraged by the Evangelical, and, as they
thought, often more rebellious element in the Church, were
quite consistent with proper regard for the liturgy and with
loyal churchmanship. But now a churchman as loyal, and as
catholic minded as Heber, had given a lead, and had actually
written a number of hymns marked by deep devotion and

literary beauty. The door was ajar for what had previously been viewed as a dangerous innovation. It so happened that another movement which almost immediately took place within the Anglican Church, pushed the door wide open. This was the famous Tractarian movement, linked with the names of Newman, Keble, and their companions.

In the same year in which Heber's hymns were first published (1827) John Keble published *The Christian Year*. It was not a hymnal, but a series of devout reflections and meditations on the fasts and feasts of the Church calendar; a poetic interpretation of the year as set forth in the Book of Common Prayer. It helped to capture the Catholic element, already touched by Heber's influence, for the author clearly belonged to this section of the Anglican tradition. It was, indeed, the opinion of Pusey, one of the foremost figures in the Tractarian movement, that *The Christian Year* was the real source of the Catholic revival in the Church of England. The concern of the movement was to recover those features of value in the ancient practice and tradition of the Church which, it was felt, had been lost or disregarded at the Reformation. This necessitated an examination of ancient liturgical material, and the discovery, as a result, that hymns were no mere modern innovation, but actually a valuable ingredient in the life and worship of the ancient Church. One outcome of this was the recovery through translation into English of a considerable body of Greek and Latin hymnody, much of which has found an abiding place in our present hymnals. This will be considered briefly a little later. The value of *The Christian Year* was that it encouraged a disposition to favour and welcome a type of hymn inspired by Catholic devotion, as well as Evangelical fervour, and prepared the way for the production of some of the most beautiful verses in English hymnody. Keble's collection of religious verse, published first anonymously in 1827, had a tremendous vogue, reaching a forty-third edition, with 108,000 copies sold in twenty-five years, and with continued further increase. Hursley church, of which Keeble was rector, was built from the profits. It had a profound effect resulting in nearly a hundred poems and centos being used as hymns in various hymnals. Another characteristic, and the echo of the true Franciscan note in religious devotion, was the joy in the mystical element in Nature. The verses are rich in the quiet beauty of the English countryside, and there is a close kinship with the great English poet, Wordsworth, in this respect. There is tenderness and gentleness of thought and spirit, native to Catholic piety at its best, which the more militant Protestant would do well to understand and embrace. The hymns derived from *The Christian Year* suffer somewhat in our versions by being separated from the context of other verses which frequently give to those we use an even more vivid and beautiful significance. This is seen in the very familiar evening hymn, *Sun of my soul*. The opening verses of the poem from which the hymn is taken picture the weary traveller pushing on after the sun has set, and before the first verse of the hymn, as it is generally known and used, occur the two following stanzas:

> 'Tis gone, that bright and orbed blaze,
> Fast fading from our wistful gaze;
> Yon mantling cloud has hid from sight
> The last faint pulse of quivering light.

> In darkness and in weariness
> The traveller on his way must press,
> No gleam to watch on tree or tower,
> Whiling away the lonesome hour.

Now with this wistful picture in our mind we can feel more deeply the devotional appeal of the opening verses of the hymn:

> Sun of my soul! Thou Saviour dear,
> It is not night if Thou be near;
> O may no earth born cloud arise
> To hide Thee from Thy servant's eyes.

When round Thy wondrous works below
My searching rapturous glance I throw,
Tracing out Widsom, Power and Love,
In earth or sky, in stream or grove.

When with dear friends sweet talk I hold,
And all the flowers of life unfold;
Let not my heart within me burn,
Except in all I Thee discern.

Another treasure from Keble's collection of verse which has become a loved and popular hymn is *There is a book who runs may read*. In this hymn, more than most, the mystical interpretation of Nature is prominent. It illustrates, too, with what poetic beauty Keble could invest the seasons and festivals of the Church. The hymn is derived from verses written for Septuagesima Sunday, when the Lessons for the day include the first two chapters of Genesis, and the poem was inspired by the Pauline thought in Romans I., 20, "The invisible things of Him from the creation of the world are clearly seen, being understood by the things that are made". Bearing this in mind we can see how finely Keble expresses the thought:

There is a book who runs may read,
    Which heavenly truth imparts;
And all the lore its scholars need,
    Pure eyes and Christian hearts.

The works of God, above, below,
    Within us and around,
Are pages in that book, to show
    How God Himself is found

Then the important truth expressed in these lines:

Two worlds are ours: 'tis only sin
    Forbids us to descry
The mystic heaven and earth within,
    Plain as the sea and sky

With the simple, sincere prayer of the last verse:

> Thou, Who hast given me eyes to see
> And love this sight so fair,
> Give me a heart to find out Thee,
> And read Thee everywhere.

A hymn of this character has another conspicuous value. It is a clear example of a truth more than once emphasized in these chapters—namely, that a hymn, to possess an enduring quality, must not be mainly concerned with rhymed expressions of doctrinal disputes and dogmas. The hymns that live are those which reach the universal and eternal realities in the soul, and give the vivid sense of the presence of God, without which no hymn can be truly great; the wonder and delight of our communion with God; our dependence as creatures upon Him, and the deepening sense of a realm of eternal and abiding beauty. These are the ingredients in the hymns that will endure when the noise and heat of theological contentions have been forgotten. Again, this does not mean that there is not profound dogmatic conviction behind a good hymn, but that with clearer vision the hymn will wing its way to a region where the words and symbols of men, so often confused, so frequently divisive, will merge into a unity of experience and understanding which is a foretaste of the heavenly.

Another familiar hymn of Keble's is the morning song of praise and prayer, "O timely happy, timely wise", but as the hymn often occurs with the omission of the verse of which these words are the first line, it is, perhaps, better known by the verse which begins, *New every morning is the love*. Yet the previous verse is a most suitable opening.

> O timely happy, timely wise,
> Hearts that with rising morn arise,
> Eyes that the beam celestial view
> Which evermore makes all things new.

Another hymn of Keble's which cannot be overlooked is the hymn to the Holy Spirit, *When God of old came down from heaven*, and the well-known marriage hymn *The voice that breathed o'er Eden*—a hymn, it must be allowed, not one of Keble's best.

A name at once suggested by the mention of Keble is that of John Henry Newman, with whom for a time he was so closely linked in promoting the Catholic Revival. *Lead kindly Light* remains, and is likely to remain, one of the most popular hymns in the whole of our English hymnody. More than once interesting analysis has been indulged in to discover the reason for this popularity. Newman himself does not seem to have thought very highly of the verses. He once affirmed, "They are not a hymn, nor are they suitable for singing and it is that which at once surprises and gratifies me, and makes me thankful, that, in spite of their having no claim to be a hymn, they have made their way into so many collections". Again, he once attributed its popularity to the tune by Dr. Dykes. But even if we allow to the full for the influence of tunes (and they can have a great influence) yet it is fairly certain that a hymn which makes an appeal so general and so abiding as *Lead kindly Light*, possesses some quality beyond the ordinary. There seems an echo of all true spiritual experience, which is aware of itself, in the verse:

> So long Thy power hath blest me, sure it still
>   Will lead me on
> O'er moor and fen, o'er crag and torrent, till
>   The night is gone;
> And with the morn those angel faces smile
> Which I have loved long since, and lost awhile.

Even the last two lines of this verse have been food for speculation. What did Newman mean by them? When the question was put to Newman fifty years after the lines were written, he replied that he simply did not know, and could not be expected to remember after half a century what he really meant when the words were penned.

It may well be that they symbolize in a way, almost unconscious for modern, sophisticated man, a wistful sense that, in an age over-weighted with materialism and the tyranny of the senses, he has lost for a while some deeper awareness of angelic truth and of celestial presences that shall one day be restored. It may be that the tender lines of the hymn awaken a genuine nostalgia in twentieth-century folk for a true home of the soul from which they feel, and rightly feel, that they are often exiles. What is certain is that *Lead kindly Light* remains one of the great treasures of our Christian hymnody.

The hymn was written by Newman when a young man. He was on an orange-boat, returning from Sicily, where he had been very ill. He was much concerned at the time about his future career, and felt there was important work he must do in England. The ship lay becalmed for a whole week in the Straits of Bonifacio, and during this period, and the whole course of the passage, Newman tells us he was writing verses, including those which have now become the famous hymn.

Newman was not a prolific hymn writer, but more of his verse which has found place as a popular hymn, is from his notable work, *The Dream of Gerontius*. This is the hymn, *Praise to the holiest in the height*. Those who know the work will recall that it describes the journey of a soul to Paradise, and, as entry is made into the presence of the Emmanuel, the "Fifth Choir of Angelicals" sing this noble hymn. The hymn belongs to a much later period in Newman's life, when he was in fellowship with the Roman Catholic Church. It may not be as popular as *Lead kindly Light*, but there can be no doubt it is a much greater hymn. It is, again, an eloquent instance of the fact that a hymn can have a firm "spine" of dogmatic theology, and yet express the truth in a way so spacious, and with such an emphasis on eternal verities, that it commends itself to all. This is certainly true of the Roman Catholic hymn, *Praise to the holiest in the height*, which is included in the most Protestant of hymnals.

It is reported that Newman thought so little of the poem, in which the hymn occurs, that he threw it in the waste-paper basket. It was fortunately redeemed by a friend, and later it was published by the editor of a religious journal. Newman was a man of such fastidious and exacting standards of excellence, which he applied ruthlessly to himself, that one doubts if he ever felt satisfied with any of his literary achievements, fine and distinctive as they were.

Newman's fame as a hymn writer rests almost entirely on the two hymns mentioned. There is another included in *The English Hymnal*, *Firmly I believe and truly*, a neat, doctrinal affirmation, which in no way compares with the two more popular hymns. Newman also made a few translations of verses from the Roman Breviary; a hymn for Terce, *Come, Holy Ghost, Who ever one*, and a Compline hymn, *Now that the daylight dies away*, but neither of these has obtained wide use in the English Church.

One of the most fruitful services rendered by the representatives of the Catholic Revival to English hymnody was found in the translation of ancient and medieval hymns, a work so important, together with similar enterprise by certain Evangelicals, that it must be dealt with in a separate chapter. Meanwhile, another name associated with Keble and Newman is that of Frederick William Faber, who provided numerous hymns, some of very real merit, and marked by a spirit of beauty and deep devotion. A few of these have become very popular, none more so than the famous hymn, *Hark! hark my soul*, while others have found larger space in recent Nonconformist hymnals, partly, we may believe, through the prominence given to Faber's hymns by Garrett Horder, first in *Congregational Hymns*, and later in *Worship Song*, one of the many debts all the Churches owe to Dr. Horder in the region of hymnody. *Worship Song* includes no less than seventeen of Faber's hymns compared with only ten in the much more Catholic book, *The English Hymnal*, while *The Methodist Hymn Book* admits only eight, and *Songs of Praise* no more than four. One grants that Faber was an uneven writer, and some critics accuse him of excessive sentimentality, although it is often difficult to define exactly what is meant by this charge. One critic referred to Faber's style as being at times "saccharine and caressing", having in mind, one may suppose, his fondness for the adjective 'sweet' as in the opening line of his well-known evening hymn:

Sweet Saviour, bless us ere we go;

and in the verse of another popular hymn which Faber wrote:

> Was there ever kindest shepherd
> Half so gentle, half so *sweet*.

But it is a word found frequently in the Catholic mystics, in whose minds, we may fairly assume, it was not so trivial an endearment as it sounds to some.

Dr. Horder, who has done so much to introduce Faber's hymns to a wider public, is our best guide as to this writer's merits, while being fully aware of some of the weak patches in his work. In Dr. Horder's view Faber is "truly one of the greatest hymnists of any age. The thought, the fervour, the poetic quality, which are all combined in his hymns, place him in that little circle which includes the chief singers of the Church".

Hark! hark my soul, is probably the best known of Faber's hymns, closely followed by the lovely evening hymn mentioned above, *Sweet Saviour, bless us ere we go. Souls of men! why will ye scatter* is now becoming better known. *O Paradise! O Paradise!* was better known a few years ago, when religious thought was rather less earthbound in its orbit than is common at present. But some of Faber's best hymns deserve to be much more widely known and used. The following belongs to this category, and is undoubtedly one of our truly great English hymns:

> O God! Thy power is wonderful,
>   Thy glory passing bright;
> Thy wisdom, with its deep on deep,
>   A rapture to the sight.

> Yet more than all, and ever more,
>   Should we Thy creatures bless,
> Most worshipful of attributes,
>   Thine awful holiness.

There's not a craving of the mind,
    Thou dost not meet and still;
There's not a wish the heart can have
    Which Thou dost not fulfil.

Thy justice is the gladdest thing
    Creation can behold;
Thy tenderness so meek, it wins
    The guilty to be bold.

All things that have been, all that are,
    All things that can be dreamed,
All possible creations, made,
    Kept faithful, or redeemed—

All these may draw upon Thy power,
    Thy mercy may command;
And still outflows Thy silent sea,
    Immutable and grand.

O little heart of mine! shall pain
    Or sorrow make thee moan,
When all this God is all for thee,
    A Father all thine own.

No hymn on the Passion of our Lord could be more full of
expressive tenderness and imagination than *O Come and mourn
with me awhile*, with the exquisite verses at the close,

A broken heart, a fount of tears,
Ask, and they will not be denied;
A broken heart love's cradle is;
Jesus, our Lord, is crucified.

O love of God! O sin of man!
In this dread act your strength is tried,
And victory remains with love;
For He, our Lord, is crucified.

Another hymn of unusual poetic beauty, and devotional insight, is *I worship Thee, sweet Will of God*, including a verse vibrant with power:

> Ride on, ride on triumphantly,
>   Thou glorious Will! ride on;
> Faith's pilgrim sons behind Thee take
>   The road that Thou hast gone.

A further brief hymn, rich in the devotional intimacy so characteristic of Faber, is the following.

> Thy home is with the humble, Lord,
>   The simplest are the best;
> Thy lodging is in child-like hearts
>   Thou makest there Thy rest.

> Dear Comforter! Eternal Love!
>   If Thou wilt stay with me,
> Of lowly thoughts and simple ways,
>   I'll build a house for Thee.

> Who made this beating heart of mine,
>   But Thou, my heavenly Guest?
> Let no one have it, then, but Thee,
>   And let it be Thy rest.

> Thy sweetness hath betrayed Thee, Lord!
>   Great Spirit! is it Thou?
> Deeper and deeper in my heart,
>   I feel Thee resting now.

Another hymn, better known, but not as widely used as it should be, is *O God! whose thoughts are brightest light*, of which this is a typical verse:

> When we ourselves least kindly are,
>   We deem the world unkind;
> Dark hearts, in flowers where honey lies,
>   Only the poison find.

A hymn which also cannot escape mention is, *Oh, it is hard to work for God*; a hymn that expresses so beautifully and certainly the emotion of almost every thoughtful, sensitive Christian soul in the conflict with evil. It is included in several hymnals, but may still be little known to many:

> Oh, it is hard to work for God,
>   To rise and take His part
> Upon this battlefield of earth,
>   And not sometimes lose heart!
>
> He hides Himself so wondrously,
>   As though there were no God;
> He is least seen when all the powers
>   Of ill are most abroad.
>
> Ill masters good; good seems to change
>   To ill with greatest ease;
> And, worst of all, the good with good
>   Is at cross purposes.
>
> It is not so, but so it looks;
>   And we lose courage then;
> And doubts will come if God hath kept
>   His promises to men.
>
> Ah! God is other than we think!
>   His ways are far above,
> Far beyond reason's height, and reached
>   Only by childlike love.

Space is given to these examples of Faber's verse so that a better appreciation can be reached as to the quality of his hymns at their best, and this is the true standard by which any hymn writer should be judged. What is clear is that the hymns of Faber which are most widely known and popular are not his best work. It is one more example of the perverse fact that a writer's best hymns are not necessarily the most widely accepted. All the same it is surprising that a number of the more excellent of Faber's hymns should have been omitted altogether from recent hymnals.

Faber, like Newman, was at first in the ministry of the Anglican Church, but subsequently joined the Roman communion. He was a Yorkshireman by birth, and was educated at Shrewsbury, Harrow, and Balliol. He won the Newdigate prize in 1836 for a poem on *The Knights of St. John*, and other academic honours were bestowed upon him. He was a friend of Wordsworth, and gave early proof of his poetic ability. He was an impressive preacher, devout and mystical, and became Rector of Elton, in Huntingdonshire, in 1843, but in 1845 was received into the Church of Rome. Three years later he joined the Oratorians at Oscott under Newman, and the following year removed to the London branch of the community, with its centre at the now well-known Brompton Oratory, where he continued until his death in 1863.

A hymn which has found a secure place in most hymnals is *Crown Him with many crowns*, allied with the inspiring tune "Diademta". It is an example of the work of an Anglican layman in the Tractarian movement, who later joined the Roman Church. Little is known of Matthew Bridges, the author, but of the hymns he wrote this is the one that has survived in general use, and has become extremely popular, though in a form revised and abbreviated when compared with the original. Henry Collins was another Anglican clergyman, of a later date, who also entered the Roman Church, becoming afterwards a Cistercian monk. Two of his hymns are preserved in current hymnals, *Jesu, meek and lowly*, verses of no particular merit, and a hymn of genuine power and beauty, *Jesu, my Lord, My God, my All*, a hymn that deserves to be widely known and used for an intimate quality of appeal which it has, expressed in this typical verse:

> Jesu, what didst Thou find in me,
> That Thou hast dealt so lovingly?
> How great the joy that Thou hast brought,
> So far exceeding hope or thought.

A hymn writer whose verses have achieved world fame is Henry Francis Lyte, author of *Abide with me*. There is no need

126

to quote this hymn, for it is certain that none is better known. It has attained a popularity which is astonishing. No hymn is more frequently or widely sung, both on occasions which are suitable and those which are not! It is the very popularity of the hymn which has disposed more sensitive and fastidious critics to discount its merit. But there is no warrant for any such disparagement. The hymn contains verses of real strength and power; the expression of a deep, personal experience and emotion. This is undoubtedly one secret of its wide appeal, for it touches something in the human spirit which, however much overlaid by the trivialities of the world, is latent and from time to time responsive. Whatever the reason, *Abide with me* has secured a place in popular esteem which is not likely to be shaken.

Lyte has an historical importance in the record of hymnody in the Church of England. He is a further example of the influences which were becoming active in the early nineteenth century within the Anglican communion, helping to facilitate the change by which the Church of England joined in the growing movement for the use of hymns in public worship. As we trace the work of a few of the representative Anglican hymn writers of the period, it is possible to see how the door was opening ever wider to the reception of an increasing volume of hymnody. Many of our great and enduring hymns were now being written by Anglicans, not merely as verses to be used in private devotion, but as hymns to be employed in public worship. To this important era of creation and change belongs the work of Henry Francis Lyte.

After holding several curacies, Lyte was appointed in 1823, at the age of thirty, to the Rectory of Lower Brixham, in Devon. For twenty-five years he laboured with devotion, winning the friendship and affection of the fisher-folk and others in his parish, and composing the hymns several of which were to enjoy lasting fame.

Contrary to the prevalent idea, still put forward, that he wrote *Abide with me* on the last Sunday of his ministry in Brixham, from which place he was compelled to retire owing to a breakdown of health, the fact seems to be that the verses were written as early as 1820, before he went to Brixham, and when he was a young man of twenty-seven. The real inspiration of the hymn was a visit which he paid to an old friend, William Augustus Le Hunte, during this gentleman's last illness. The dying man kept repeating the phrase "Abide with me" and it so impressed Lyte that he made the words the basis of the famous hymn, and gave the verses to his friend's brother. The hymn was not published at the time and this is not surprising when the general attitude of the Church of England to hymns, at this period, is borne in mind. On the last day of his ministry at Brixham, nearly thirty years later, he gave a copy of the hymn to a relative, together with an air of his own composition. This was on September 4, 1847. Lyte passed away in Italy in the following November, and the hymn was first published, with some other writings of the author, in 1850.

In addition to *Abide with me* Lyte wrote further hymns which are also well known, and included in all our present standard hymnals. These are *Praise my soul, the King of Heaven* and *Pleasant are Thy courts above*. These were taken from a work which Lyte published in 1834, and if this date is borne in mind it will be seen that it was a significant contribution to the change then taking place in the Church of England with respect to the use of hymnody. This work was *The Spirit of the Psalms*, in which Lyte was employing the familiar method, used from the time of Watts, of making the Psalms the basis of a free paraphrase in the form of hymns. Another well known hymn which had its origin in the same collection is *God of mercy, God of grace*, together with some excellent versions of the Psalms.

Lyte, it should be mentioned, belonged to the Evangelical wing of the Church of England, so that it will be seen that influences from both Catholic and Evangelical schools of thought were combining to bring the Anglican body within the new vogue of congregational hymn singing. It was the prelude to an ever increasing flow of hymnody which came from all sections of the Church, both Anglican and Dissenting.

A layman, Sir Robert Grant, was contemporary in time with Lyte, and must be mentioned as the writer of a hymn which has become a general favourite. This is *O worship the King, all*

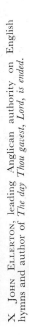

Douglas Scott

X John Ellerton, leading Anglican authority on English hymns and author of *The day Thou gavest, Lord, is ended.*

XI Percy Dearmer, creator of a new era in Anglican hymnals. Editor of *The English Hymnal* and *Songs of Praise.*

XII W. GARRETT HORDER, whose vital work for hymnody in the late
nineteenth century and after awakened new interest both in Great Britain
and America.

glorious above. Sir Robert was a Member of Parliament, and later Governor of Bombay. Of twelve hymns which he wrote, *O worship the King* is the only one which has found a place in the hymnals of all the Churches. It must suffice to mention two other names as belonging to the period when the use of hymns in the regular worship of the Anglican Church became approved and general. The first is Henry Alford, who was Dean of Canterbury from 1857 until his death in 1871, and, even if it is a digression, the inscription on his tomb is so apt and gracious that it must be quoted: *Deversorium viatoris proficientis Hierosolymam* (The inn of a pilgrim journeying to Jerusalem).

Alford was a Biblical scholar of distinction, and in 1834 became a Fellow of Trinity, Cambridge. He wrote a number of hymns and poems, and three of the former have become familiar in the hymnody of the Churches. One was written as a hymn for processional use for the festival of the Canterbury Diocesan Choral Union in 1871, *Forward be our watchword,* a lengthy hymn in the original of eight eight-lined verses, due, most likely, to the time it takes to perambulate slowly around the vast precincts of Canterbury's glorious cathedral. It was the last hymn the Dean wrote, and he did not live to hear it sung at the subsequent festival. At a much earlier date he had written what has now become one of the most familiar harvest hymns—*Come, ye thankful people, come.* It was first published in 1844, and has had a certain amount of revision and alteration in the form in which it is generally found. Slight differences in the text will be noticed if different hymn books are compared. The whole question of the alteration of hymns from the text originally used is one provoking discussion. It would seem there are instances where it has been done with advantage, but many others where it has been no improvement, but rather a departure from the meaning and intention of the writer. This is particularly so where the alteration has been prompted by the desire of a sect to accommodate the author's theological outlook to the doctrinal tenets of the denomination making the revision. The Unitarians have done this with Charles Wesley's great hymn, *Jesus, Lover of my soul,* and one feels it would have been better to omit the hymn from the denominational hymnal, rather than twist the theology of the author to suit the purpose.

This is not an irrelevant digression, but touches a subject of very real importance. Alford's lengthy processional hymn, *Forward be our watchword*, is, for example, much shortened in various hymnals, and although this seems unavoidable when used in an ordinary service of worship, in its original form it is more impressive. Thus, for example, it can be appreciated how verse six would light up with meaning when sung walking around the nave of Canterbury, or one of the other great cathedrals:

> Into God's high temple
> Onward as we press,
> Beauty spreads around us,
> Born of holiness;
> Arch, and vault and carving,
> Lights of varied tone,
> Soften'd words and holy,
> Prayer and praise alone:
> Every thought upraising
> To our city bright,
> Where the tribes assemble
> Round the throne of light.

One of the most inspiring hymns relating to the Future Life is *Ten thousand times ten thousand*, with its spacious range of imagination and its rising crescendo of thought. The Dean's Baptismal hymn, *In token that thou shalt not fear*, is one of the best in this category, and both hymns have the merit that while dealing with themes highly doctrinal and theological, they have such a range of outlook, with a firm grasp of essential truths, that they remain fresh and vital, where other hymns, dealing with the same subjects, 'date' in a marked manner.

The last name to which reference must be made here is that of the nephew of the poet, Wordsworth. Christopher Wordsworth, who became Bishop of Lincoln in 1869, contributed generously to the flow of hymnody which was then becoming a feature of the Anglican Church, with 117 hymns contained in *The Holy Year*, a book which altogether included 200 hymns, published in 1862. Later he added a few more hymns, and of the entire collection a number survive to the permanent enrichment of English hymnody, in hymns which are now well known. These include *O Lord of heaven, and earth, and sea,* an excellent offertory hymn, inspired, so one critic tells us, by the fact that in one of the parishes which came under his care, people attended the church mainly for what could be obtained in *material* benefits from the parochial charities. If this is true it is a weakness, it may be said, which is not confined to one parish. If this was the purpose of the hymn (which is doubtful) the author provided some loophole for the victims of cupidity, in the thought suggested by one verse:

> We lose what on ourselves we spend,
> We have as treasure without end
> *Whatever, Lord, to Thee we lend,*
> Who givest all.

The third line, here placed in italics, would seem to suggest a prudent motive for religious generosity, but it would not be fair to the writer of the hymn to press such a conclusion. All the same it is a line which is a flaw in an otherwise exceptionally fine hymn. But it may have served its purpose if, as is also alleged, as a result of making his congregation sing the hymn once a month, the offerings began to give sign of a substantial increase.

One of Wordsworth's best hymns is that dedicated to St. Paul's great chapter on love, (I. Cor. XIII). *Gracious Spirit, Holy Ghost.* Hymnals have a singular way of omitting different verses of this hymn, due, doubtless, to the peculiar predilections of various compilers. A frequent omission is the following verse:

> Faith, that mountains could remove,
> Tongues of earth or heaven above,
> Knowledge—all things—empty prove,
> Without heavenly love.

It is also to Bishop Christopher Wordsworth that we are indebted for the inspiring hymn *Hark, the sound of holy voices, chanting at the crystal sea,* a noble hymn, with a truly uplifting

sense of the victory of the soul through death. This hymn
serves to confirm the criticism made on an earlier page
respecting Baring-Gould's hymn, *On the Resurrection morning*.
Wordsworth's hymn suggests the immediate ascent and victory of the redeemed soul, and is, in every way, more satisfying.

The version of the hymn in *Songs of Praise* is another example
of the perverse alteration of hymns, without adequate reason,
for the original last two lines, as they were written, read:

> Pour upon us of Thy fulness,
> That we may for evermore
> God the Father, God the Son
> And God the Holy Ghost adore.

This has been altered to:

> God the Father, God the Spirit,
> One with Thee on high, adore.

To many it will seem that the triune formula of the original
is the more telling and emphatic.

O day of rest and gladness is another of Wordsworth's best
known hymns, and is frequently used in all the Churches in
Sunday morning worship.

Two hymns less known, but belonging to the best that
Wordsworth wrote are, *The Galilean fishers toil*, in which a
cluster of New Testament incidents are woven together in
appealing verses. One of the best is the last:

> The faithful few retire in fear,
> To their closed upper room;
> And suddenly, with joyful cheer
> They see their Master come.
> Lord come to us, unloose our bands,
> And bid our terrors cease;
> Lift over us Thy blessed hands,
> Speak, holy Jesus, peace.

The hymn for Ascensiontide, *See the Conqueror mounts in
triumph*, also offers some fine verses, with the suggestive and
inspiring thought of the following:

Thou hast raised our human nature
   In the clouds to God's right hand;
There we sit in heavenly places,
   There with Thee in glory stand;
Jesus reigns, adored by angels;
   Man with God is on the throne;
Mighty Lord, in Thine Ascension
We by faith behold our own.

But the chief significance of the hymns of Christopher Wordsworth lies in the witness they offer of the extent to which the Church of England was joining in the creation and use of hymnody by the middle of the nineteenth century. Not only were Anglican hymns being written, but they were being written expressly to fit in with the structure of the Book of Common Prayer, and to mark the celebration of appointed festivals and fasts. The foundation was being laid of the plan on which hymns are now distributed in the standard Anglican hymnals, and a pattern which, in a modified form, is followed by more recent Nonconformist collections. But in both the Established and Dissenting Churches the prejudice against observing days and seasons was for long strongly entrenched. It was, of course, a survival of Puritan influence, for the Puritans had held a strong objection to the observing of even such a day as Christmas. It was one of the results of the Oxford, or Tractarian, Movement, with its revival of Catholic elements within the Anglican tradition, that the marking of the main feasts and fasts was recovered. In the proposed revised Prayer Book of 1928 these have been greatly increased by the inclusion of lesser days. The interest here in this development is confined to its influence on hymnody. Sometimes the effect has been to stimulate the composition of a hymn of worth and beauty, but in many instances the result has not been so happy. Good hymns are seldom written to order, or produced in cold blood. Where they endure it is because they are in some way a passionate utterance of the soul, even if that passion is profoundly quiet and mystical in its form of expression. It must be confessed that a large amount of hymnody which began to emerge in response to the growing popularity of hymn singing in all the Churches was formal, stilted, mediocre and lifeless. A great quantity of it is forgotten, but with the dross there was a generous mixture of fine gold. It has endured, and there is now no season of the year in the Church that does not offer splendid hymns. Perhaps the least satisfactory are those concerned with Apostles and Evangelists, regarding some of whom we have little detail. Yet hymns have been written with the view that there must be a hymn for each of these days, and the fruits of this effort have not always been satisfactory, although one or two excellent hymns have resulted. What is important is to remember the response of the Anglican Church to the influences which were now at work to furnish her with a rich hymnody; influences emanating from both Evangelical and Catholic sources. By the middle of the nineteenth century the tide of development was flowing powerfully in the Established Church, and it is at this period that the original edition of the most popular and widely used Anglican hymnal was first published; *Hymns Ancient and Modern*. The opposition was past. The tyranny of the Psalter Versions, Old and New, was broken. A new era had begun. The Church of England had joined in, and her worship was being enriched increasingly by the ever growing volume of sacred song. If the Independents had Watts to their glory, and the Methodists could proudly lay claim to the immortal Wesleys, the Anglican Church had now a noble galaxy of names, Cowper, Newton, Keble, Newman, Faber, Heber, Milman, Alford, and Wordsworth, to mention only the most representative names of the time. It was an impressive assembly, and it was proof that if the Church of England had been slow in joining in, now that she had done so, she could offer a wealth of talent that would make her contribution a worthy one. Some bolder spirits, too, might even dare to mention that the inspired singer, perhaps greatest of all, Charles Wesley, had remained a devoted and loyal son of the Anglican Church to the end of his life. Be this as it may, there was no doubt about what had now happened—the Church of England had joined in.

9

Treasures of Translation:
German and others

IN one of John Wesley's sermons there is a reference which should not be overlooked by anyone interested in the development of English hymns. The words are as follows:

> It was between fifty and sixty years ago, that, by the gracious providence of God, my brother and I, in our voyage to America, became acquainted with the (so-called) Moravian Brethren. We quickly took knowledge what spirit they were of; six and twenty of them being in the same ship with us. We not only contracted much esteem, but a strong affection, for them . . . . *I translated many of their hymns, for the use of our own congregations.*

The words here placed in italics are important. They explain the origin of hymns which have become familiar, although their original source may have been forgotten by many who sing them. Moreover, we are reminded by this fact of the debt we owe to the work of translators who have enriched English hymnody by treasures from other sources. John Wesley in the above words refers to his own share in this task of translation.

If, in imagination, we can go back over the fifty to sixty years mentioned by John Wesley, we shall picture him as a young man spending hours on the ship during his memorable visit to America in the latter end of 1735 learning the German language. He was not doing this merely as a pastime, but, practical as he ever was, with a definite end in view. We know the reason from the statement above quoted. He was eager to give to English congregations the hymns which he was learning from the Moravians to whom he refers. Entries in his *Journal* during 1735 and 1736 contain numerous references to "German verse", "Translated German", "Made verses", and similar remarks. John Wesley was an accomplished linguist, with a remarkable facility for mastering a foreign tongue. In his knowledge of German, at the time, as in so much else, he was a pioneer. Few Englishmen then regarded German as a language worth learning. It was not until the end of the century in which John Wesley lived, that, through the influence of the literature of Goethe and Schiller, the German language became more widespread in this country.

English hymnody has been augmented greatly by the translation of hymns from other lands, and here, again, John Wesley was a pioneer, and his efforts are some of the best examples of translated verse that we possess. He was not content with German. While he was in Georgia he learned Spanish, in order to minister to some Spanish Jews who were in the colony, and he translated at least one Spanish hymn, the source of which is not known. It is a fine version of Psalm 63, and is a hymn of eight verses, of which the first is:

> O God, my God, my all Thou art:
> Ere shines the dawn of rising day,
> Thy sovereign light within my heart,
> Thy all-enlivening power display.

The translation is preserved to-day in *The Methodist Hymn Book*, in hymn 471. But John Wesley's great service to English hymnody was the number of German hymns, and these of the best, which he gave to us by his excellent translations, so accurate and skilful that they bring out the true spirit of the original. He was himself a mystic, as well as an amazingly practical man of affairs, and was profoundly influenced both by the German mystics and by the great English mystic,

136

William Law. Many of these German mystical hymns would
have become known to him through his contact with the
Moravians described above. Wesley's rational and critical
mind sifted the gold from the dross, and he firmly discarded
the more extravagant and emotionally cloying hymns which
not infrequently served the Moravian hymnody. The Lutheran
Reformation, unlike the Calvinistic, fostered and encouraged
hymn singing from the beginning, and the result was that an
enormous flood of hymns marked the German Protestant
movement. Zinzendorf wrote two thousand; Schmolke, over
eleven hundred; Heerman, four hundred; Bogatzky, Garve,
and Soloman Frank, some hundreds, while a host were written
by an army of enthusiasts whose zeal and piety exceeded their
poetic ability. One collection alone contained over three
thousand hymns. It is easy to understand what a mass of
mediocre and tawdry material would be found in such an
assembly, and it is the more striking that John Wesley, who
must have made acquaintance with a large amount of this
work, should have selected for translation the cream of German
religious verse. His translations were few in number, but it
proves their merit that they have survived. Among the
abiding treasures are the translations of the hymns of Paulus
Gerhardt. Gerhardt, who was born in 1607, has been called
"the typical poet of the Lutheran Church, as George Herbert
is of the English". He has also been designated "The Wesley
of the Fatherland", for there is in his hymns much of the quality
one discerns in the verses of Charles Wesley, though, of the
two, Gerhardt is quieter and more subdued in tone. He was the
author of over one hundred and twenty hymns, all of conspicuous merit, of which nearly forty are still in common use.
He lived through the Thirty Years' War, and it is this fact that
gives added significance to the deep, strong beauty of his
verses. He is for the time in which we live a splendid example
of the inner peace which abides in the soul firmly anchored to
the Peace of God. How much of interruption, disappointment,
and frustration there was in his life may be judged from the
fact that Gerhardt did not attain any settled position until he
had reached his middle forties. He was then a private tutor,

and a candidate for holy orders. At the close of 1551 he was ordained, and became minister of a country church at Mitten-walde. It was at this time he wrote his beautiful Christmas hymn, which should be known by everyone.

> All my heart this night rejoices,
>   As I hear, far and near,
>   Sweetest angel voices:
>   Christ is born! their choirs are singing,
>   Till the air, everywhere,
>   Now with joy is ringing

This hymn was translated by Catherine Winkworth, to whom further reference will be made. One of the most notable of Gerhardt's hymns translated by John Wesley is *Commit thou all thy griefs*. In English hymnals it is given now in various, and often abbreviated forms owing to the length of the original, which was fifteen stanzas of four lines each. It can be claimed without hesitation that it is one of the greatest hymns in any language. Owing to the difficulty of finding the complete version (*The Methodist Hymn Book* is one of the very few where it is given in full) it is reproduced here, for it is a hymn of such outstanding beauty and power, and such a worthy memorial of John Wesley's work as translator, that it should be known in its completion:

> Commit thou all thy griefs
>   And ways into His hands,
> To His sure truth and tender care,
>   Who heaven and earth commands.
>
> Who points the clouds their course,
>   Whom winds and seas obey,
> He shall direct thy wandering feet,
>   He shall prepare thy way.
>
> Thou on the Lord rely,
>   So safe shalt thou go on;
> Fix on His work thy steadfast eye,
>   So shall thy work be done.

No profit canst thou gain
By self-consuming care;
To him commend thy cause; His ear
Attends the softest prayer.

Thy everlasting truth,
Father, Thy ceaseless love,
Sees all Thy children's wants, and knows
What best for each will prove.

Thou everywhere hast sway,
And all things serve Thy might;
Thy every act pure blessing is,
Thy path unsullied light.

When Thou arisest, Lord,
What shall Thy work withstand?
Whate'er Thy children want, Thou giv'st;
And who shall stay Thy hand?

Give to the winds thy fears;
Hope, and be undismayed;
God hears thy sighs, and counts thy tears,
God shall lift up thy head.

Through waves, and clouds, and storms
He gently clears thy way:
Wait thou His time; so shall this night
Soon end in joyous day.

Still heavy is thy heart?
Still sink thy spirits down?
Cast off the weight, let fear depart,
Bid every care be gone.

What though thou rulest not?
Yet heaven, and earth, and hell
Proclaim: God sitteth on the throne,
And ruleth all things well!

Leave to His sovereign sway
To choose and to command;
So shalt thou wondering own His way,
How wise, how strong His hand.

Far, far above thy thought
His counsel shall appear,
When fully He the work hath wrought
That caused thy needless fear.

Thou seest our weakness, Lord;
Our hearts are known to Thee:
O lift Thou up the sinking hand,
Confirm the feeble knee!

Let us in life, in death,
Thy steadfast truth declare,
And publish with our latest breath
Thy love and guardian care.

One other reason for giving space to this magnificent hymn is that in addition to its place as an example of John Wesley's invaluable work in translation, it is a hymn for our own times. Gerhardt lived in disturbed and troubled days. Nearly two-thirds of his life were spent in the dark days of the Thirty Years' War, and his career was no smooth one. He touches this generation very closely in the atmosphere of violence in which so much of his life was set. Yet he writes with an inner conviction that had proved the reality of the immortal words of Christ, "Peace I leave with you, my peace I give unto you: not as the world giveth, give I unto you. Let not your heart be troubled, neither let it be afraid." (John XIV. 27). There is no hymn that can meet more perfectly the condition of our time. It is a masterpiece of simplicity, felicity of expression, and vibrant sincerity. It portrays all the features of what makes a great and enduring hymn that time cannot 'date'.

The hymn has been fortunate, too, in having wedded to it the firm, terse tune of "Doncaster" composed by John Wesley's

nephew, Samuel Wesley. Its decisive notes emphasise the quiet
confidence of the thought, and is another striking example of
the close link between sense and sound.

A lovely evening hymn of Gerhardt's, little known in England, is indicative of his sensitive poetic gift. It is a gem of
beauty.

> Now woods and wolds are sleeping,
> And darkness fast is creeping
> O'er byre, hearth and hall:
> But thou, my soul, ere slumber,
> For blessings passing number
> Exalt the Giver of them all.
>
> Though all around be darkling,
> Yet golden stars are sparkling
> From out yon azure spheres:
> So may I shine in lustre,
> As one of that fair cluster,
> When call'd to quit this vale of tears.
>
> O tarry Thou beside me;
> Jesu, my joyaunce, hide me
> Beneath Thy sheltering wing:
> And would the fiend infest me,
> Forbid him to molest me,
> But bid Thine Angels round me sing.
>
> Ye also, O my dearest,
> My friends and kindred nearest,
> God rest you safe from harm!
> His Angel-hosts attend ye,
> Their golden shields defend ye
> From nightly danger and alarm.

The translation of these delightful verses is the work of the
Reverend Dr. G. R. Woodward, who has thus made them
available for English readers.

Well known is the moving Passion hymn, *O sacred head once wounded,* appearing now in several variants, and derived by Gerhardt from a medieval Latin hymn, *Salve caput cruentatum,* and translated into English by Dr. J. W. Alexander. Another, translated by John Wesley, is the hymn of intimate devotion, *Jesu, Thy boundless love to me,* while to Catherine Winkworth is due the translation of the hymn, radiant with hope and faith, *Cometh sunshine after rain,* with the triumphal final verse:

> So the passing years employ,
> Greeting life and death with joy,
> Till at last you meet the grave
> With a heart still glad and brave,
>   Whom the Almighty doth defend,
>   Whom the Highest counts His friend,
>   Cannot perish in the end.

Devotion and philosophy epitomized in a perfect verse. Well may it be that the source of the power of Gerhardt's hymns lay in the man himself. Just as there is no great sermon without the soul of the preacher in it, so there is no truly great hymn without something of the soul of the writer given to it and through it. Gerhardt knew victory in struggle; peace in conflict; hope in darkness, and a triumphant love. Perhaps this is best expressed by the inscription on his portrait at Lubbe, describing him as *Theologus in cribro Satanae versatus* "a divine strained in the sieve of Satan".

One of the most remarkable of the German mystics, whose hymns provided John Wesley with material for translation, was Gerhard Tersteegen, born in 1697. He was a mystic of the purest type, holding that each individual soul may have direct communion with God, and so walk by an inner light apart from and independent of revelation, a mysticism closely allied to that of our own George Fox. His life was one of wonderful simplicity. It was intended that he should be ordained to the ministry, but he resolved to serve God in a lay capacity, and at the age of sixteen retired to a lonely cottage in the country.

There he supported himself by weaving silk ribbons, but his fame as spiritual adviser and counsellor spread far and wide, and so many sought his aid that more and more he had to give time to an informal ministry. When his work was done Tersteegen would spend hours of solitude in the woods, and sometimes whole nights would be passed in this way in prayer. Seasons of rare illumination and vision would be granted, and it is said that during one of these he drew blood from his veins, and penned with it words to his Saviour, offering his love and all his heart to "The sweet Friend of his soul".

Meanwhile, in the neighbouring town of Mulheim a group of like-minded men and women met each week for prayer. They were known as *Stillen in Lande*, "The Quiet in the Land". Tersteegen began to meet with them, and to speak words of guidance and comfort to his fellow worshippers. Later he compiled a hymnal for use at these meetings, and included within it a number of his own hymns. Subsequently he gave up weaving, and became the Warden or Head of a retreat known as the *Pilgerhutte*, or Pilgrims' Hut, where a small circle of seekers after the deeper life of the Spirit lived under his care and the inspiration of his teaching. One of the activities he developed was a dispensary, and sick folk came to him from far and near. No doubt Tersteegen possessed in a high degree the gift of healing. His influence and ministry were remarkable, and in the achievements of German mysticism he holds one of the highest places.

During the voyages to Georgia, John Wesley heard the Moravians who were on the ship singing Tersteegen's hymn *Thou hidden love of God*, and we can understand how it appealed to him, and with what eagerness he made the translation so that it should be available for English worshippers.

> Thou hidden love of God, whose height,
>   Whose depth unfathomed, no man knows,
> I see from far thy beauteous light,
>   Inly I sigh for thy repose;
> My heart is pained, nor can it be
> At rest, till it finds rest in Thee.

Like many German hymns, in the original it was very long, having ten stanzas. This feature of German hymnody is due to the practice of dividing a hymn into verses for use throughout a service. The result has been that English books in accommodating these hymns have had to keep in mind the different custom here. This has, however, caused abbreviations and revisions that have weakened the original power and beauty of the hymn. It would be a better method to print the entire hymn, and then divide the stanzas and employ it as two hymns in the service. It is certainly to be regretted that the beauty of verses like these should be impaired by the mutilation of the translated version.

Thou hidden love of God was judged by two eminent American critics, Emerson and Oliver Wendell Holmes, to be the greatest hymn in the English language. Different critics, as is noticed, assign this distinction to various hymns. What we can say for certain is that this hymn, like the great hymns of Gerhardt's described above, are treasures of translation by which English hymnody has been vastly enriched, and which form some of the most worthy features in our modern collections.

Another of Tersteegen's hymns, translated by John Wesley, which is well known and widely used, is *Lo, God is here! Let us adore.*

Tersteegen was a disciple of the German mystical leader, Johann Scheffler, known as Angelus Silesius, having adopted the name after a Spanish mystic of the sixteenth century, John of Angelus, adding Silesius because his birthplace, Breslau, was in Silesia. Scheffler was born in 1624, and became a doctor of medicine. Early in life he became interested in metaphysical and theological subjects, but found no congenial setting in the dogmatic Lutheranism of his time. He was deeply influenced by the teachings of the great mystics, Jacob Boehme, Tauler, and Ruysbroeck, and he entered the communion of the Roman Church in 1653. After a period as physician to the Emperor Ferdinand III, Scheffler took orders, and in 1671 entered the Jesuit monastery of St. Matthias in Breslau, then adopting the name of Angelus. Two of the hymns

144

which he wrote have found wide acceptance in English hymnals.
One is a translation by John Wesley; the hymn beginning,

> Thee will I love, my strength my tower,
> Thee will I love my joy, my crown;
> Thee will I love with all my power,
> In all Thy works, and Thee alone.
> Thee will I love, till the pure fire
> Fills my whole soul with strong desire.

This hymn is strangely absent from modern Anglican hymnals,
but is inserted in several of the Nonconformist collections. One
more generally known and used is the beautiful hymn beginning,

> O Love, Who formedst me to wear
> The image of Thy Godhead here;
> Who soughtest me with tender care
> Through all my wanderings wild and drear;
> O Love, I give myself to Thee,
> Thine ever, only Thine to be.

In 1644 there was composed what has proved to be both in
Germany and England one of the noblest and best known
hymns.

> Now thank we all our God,
> With heart, and hands and voices,
> Who wondrous things hath done,
> In whom His world rejoices;
> Who, from our mothers' arms,
> Hath blessed us on our way
> With countless gifts of love,
> And still is ours to-day.

This hymn may be called the *Te Deum* of Germany, used on
all great occasions of national thanksgiving, and in England
it now ranks with our own great English hymn, *Our God, our
help in ages past*, as a natural and spontaneous expression of
thanksgiving at all great moments when, as a people, our

hearts are lifted to God in praise. It will be recalled that Mendelssohn introduced these verses into his *Hymn of Praise*.

Martin Rinkart, the author of this magnificent hymn, was the son of a poor coppersmith. By dint of tireless industry, allied to his musical gifts, he went to the University of Leipzig, entered the Christian ministry, becoming precentor of the church at Eisleben, and at the age of thirty-one was made Archdeacon of his native town of Eilenburg, in Saxony. He went there at the outbreak of the Thirty Years' War, and laboured with his people all through those terrible years, enduring with them the miseries and hardships wrought by the conflict. The plague of 1637 visited Eilenburg with extraordinary severity, and eight thousand people died as a result. The pestilence was followed by a famine so extreme that groups of starving people were frequently clamouring at the door of Rinkart's house, although he had but the barest rations for himself and his family. After all this appalling suffering, the Swedes imposed upon the unhappy town a levy of thirty thousand florins, a demand which mainly through Rinkart's influence was reduced to two thousand. Even that was more than the stricken town could pay, and Rinkart was forced to mortgage his own income for several years ahead to provide the barest things necessary for his family.

When at last the good news came that peace had been made in Westphalia, it is easy to imagine the fervour and rapture with which Rinkart's great hymn was sung, and it is certain that no words can ever voice more perfectly the gratitude of the human heart.

Another glorious hymn of praise from a German source is one which although not yet so well known as the above is growing rapidly in favour, and deserves to rank with the greatest hymns of thanksgiving. This is Neander's:

Praise to the Lord, the Almighty, the King of Creation;
O my soul, praise Him, for He is thy health and salvation;
    All ye who hear,
    Now to His temple draw near,
Joining in glad adoration.

With an unforgettable second verse:

> [reigneth,
> Praise to the Lord, Who o'er all things so wondrously
> Shieldeth thee gently from harm, or when fainting
> Hast thou not seen   [sustaineth:
> How thy heart's wishes have been
> Granted in what He ordaineth?

The writer of this hymn was Joachim Neander (or Neumann), a man of remarkable talent and gifts. Not only was he a theological scholar, but was accomplished as well in letters, music, and poetry. In his short life of thirty years (for he died of consumption at the age of thirty) he composed sixty hymns, as well as the tunes for them. At the age of twenty-four he was appointed head master of the Reformed Grammar School at Dusseldorf, but the great zeal which he exhibited in this office seems to have been disapproved by the authorities, and he left the town. For some while he lived in a cave near Mettman on the Rhine, which is still named "Neander's Cave", after which he returned as preacher to St. Martin's, in his native city of Bremen; a ministry cut short by premature death. A tune of his composition is now familiar to English congregations, under the name of "Neander", and usually set to the hymn, *Come, ye faithful, raise the anthem*.

One tremendous lesson enforced by a study of the German hymns is that tragedy may blossom into song in the human soul, and a vale of tears become the source of divine music. As we have already observed some of the greatest German hymns date from the terrible Thirty Years' War. There is one other which must be included in this survey. It is probably not yet well known to English congregations, but it is a confident prediction that it will be, linked as it is to the majestic German tune "Wachet Auf". But before the hymn is read, recall the circumstances which prompted it.

In 1597, when a fearful pestilence raged in Westphalia, Philip Nicolai was pastor of the little town of Unna. In six months during the plague over 1,300 people died. Nicholai was burying on an average thirty a day, and during the brief

147

intervals in this exhausting and depressing labour, he was moved to read afresh St. Augustine's great work *The City of God*, and felt the profound contemplation of the eternal world which it inspired. The ravages of mortality were all around him. Evidence of life's precarious brevity met his gaze as he looked out of the parsonage window on the now too-familiar churchyard. The world of sense and time seemed to challenge (as it so often does) the postulates of faith in the eternal and abiding. With new force the moving thoughts of St. Augustine's classic touched the mind of Nicolai. He wrote at the time:

> There seemed to me nothing more sweet, delightful and agreeable than the contemplation of the noble, sublime doctrine of eternal life ... I gave to my manuscript the name and title of *Mirror of Joy*, and took this, thus composed, to leave behind me (if God should call me from the world) as the token of my peaceful, joyful Christian departure, or (if God should spare me in health) to comfort other sufferers.

So were the words of this glorious chorale composed. There have been several translations; an admirable one by Dr. F. C. Burkitt, contained in the *The English Hymnal*, and a very free rendering which is in *Songs of Praise*, but the earlier translation by Catherine Winkworth seems nearest to the original, and is reproduced here.

Wake, awake, for night is flying!
The watchmen on the heights are crying:
Awake, Jerusalem, at last!
Midnight hears the welcome voices,
And at the thrilling cry rejoices:
Come forth, ye virgins, night is past!
The Bridegroom comes; awake,
Your lamps with gladness take;
Hallelujah!
And for His marriage feast prepare,
For ye must go to meet Him there.

Zion hears the watchmen singing,
And all her heart with joy is springing;
  She wakes, she rises from her gloom;
  For her Lord comes down all glorious
The strong in grace, in truth victorious;
  Her Star is risen, her Light is come!
    Ah come, Thou blessed One,
    God's own beloved Son;
      Hallelujah
We follow till the halls we see
Where Thou hast bid us sup with Thee.

Now let all the heavens adore Thee,
And men and angels sing before Thee,
  With harp and cymbal's clearest tone;
  Of one pearl each shining portal,
Where we are with the choir immortal
  Of angels round Thy dazzling throne;
    Nor eye hath seen, nor ear
    Hath yet attained to hear
      What there is ours;
But we rejoice, and sing to Thee
Our hymn of joy eternally.

These few examples will be sufficient to indicate the German
hymns which have found their way into our English collections,
and because of the noble strength of their thought and the
majesty of their music many more are likely to become known
and treasured in the future. It would be impossible to leave
the subject of the translation of German hymns without
remembering the distinguished work of Catherine Winkworth,
whose name has been mentioned already. It is to John Wesley
we owe a few of the earliest translations, but it was through
the work of Catherine Winkworth that the English Churches
began to understand more clearly what treasures awaited them
in the store of German hymns. Miss Winkworth's book
Christian Singers of Germany, provided a rich feast of delight for
all who were ready to understand the value of the material

she translated. Her work has had a permanent influence on English hymnody, and, as the spectator is reminded when reading the inscription to her memory in Bristol Cathedral, she "opened a new source of light, consolation, and strength in many thousand homes".

Very little material from the French is to be found in English hymnals, but one hymn of merit and considerable interest is due to a translation made by William Cowper. His friend, the Reverend William Bull, suggested to the poet that he should translate the *Spiritual Songs* of Madame Jeanne Guyon, the French mystic, whose personality and career make one of the most interesting stories in the history of mysticism. She was born in 1648, and after receiving education in a convent, married at sixteen, her husband being Monsieur Guyon, more than twenty years her senior. Her married life seems to have been marked by extraordinary trials, including her own disfigurement by an attack of smallpox when she was only twenty-two. Then came domestic bereavements, including the loss of her husband within twelve years of their marriage, followed by deep spiritual experiences of a type making her worthy to be ranked with the great mystics of history. She won the devotion of the gifted Fenelon, and had much influence in the court of Madame de Maintenon. She came into conflict with the official Church of her time, and suffered imprisonment in the Bastille, and it was in prison that she wrote the verse:

> My cage confines me round;
> Abroad I cannot fly;
> But though my wing is closely bound,
> My heart's at liberty.
> My prison walls cannot control
> The flight, the freedom of the soul.

One hymn written by Madame Guyon, contained in Cowper's translation, of deep mystical thought and beauty, is entitled, *The soul that loves God finds Him everywhere*. It is puzzling to understand why nearly all our standard hymnals have failed to include verses of such value, and it is again a tribute to the unfailing discernment of Garrett Horder, that he reproduced this hymn in *Worship Song*. The verses proclaim their own worth:

> O Thou by long experience tried,
> Near whom no grief can long abide,
> My Lord! how full of sweet content
> My years of pilgrimage are spent.
>
> All scenes alike engaging prove
> To souls impressed with sacred love;
> Where'er they dwell, they dwell with Thee,
> In heaven, in earth, or on the sea.
>
> To me remains nor place nor time;
> My country is in every clime;
> I can be calm and free from care
> On any shore, since God is there.
>
> While place we seek or place we shun,
> The soul finds happiness in none;
> But with my God to guide my way,
> 'Tis equal joy to go or stay.
>
> Could I be cast where Thou art not,
> That were, indeed, a dreadful lot:
> But regions none remote I call,
> Secure of finding God in all.
>
> Then let me to His throne repair,
> And never be a stranger there:
> Then love divine shall be my guard,
> And peace and safety my reward.

Apart from the treasures garnered from German sources, very little addition has been made to our hymnody by translation from other European countries. It is certain that a large amount of fine material is available and invites the translator's skill and the interest of English congregations. This will be one of the ways in which English hymnody will develop further, and it is appropriate that it should do so along these lines in an era when the ecumenical movement is making rapid strides. It is a most fertile method of enabling people to realise the common dialect of the human spirit, deeper than all the wide variations of time and place.

A most delightful Danish hymn has found its way into our hymnody by inclusion in *The Fellowship Hymn Book*, a fine collection used by the Adult School movement. This is *The dear glad spring returns to earth*, verses rich in poetry and devotion by Nikolai Grundtvig, and translated by Mrs. Ella Armitage. It is of special interest as the author was the founder of the Danish High Schools, a movement for Adult Education in Denmark, which has earned the enthusiastic approval of Sir Richard Livingstone, in his plea for the development of similar enterprise in England. Grundtvig compiled for use in the Danish churches, a collection of hymns designed to relate the hymnody of Denmark to its national history and literature. He once said, "Like a bird in the greenwood I sing for the country folk. It will be my greatest happiness if I can write songs that will make legs skip in the street at the sound of them. That shall be called my best poem which is the greatest favourite in the Danish harvest fields".

One Danish hymn, well known to English congregations and sung frequently, is the familiar *Through the night of doubt and sorrow*, translated by S. Baring-Gould. The original was the work of Bernard S. Ingemann, a Danish poet, and Baring-Gould found it in a supplement to *High-mass Hymns*, issued in 1842, a collection Ingemann had published in 1825, designed to provide hymns for each festival of the Church. Baring-Gould translated it for the Sunday School children at Horbury Bridge church, when he was curate there.

Ingemann was a Danish writer of historical romances, influenced very strongly by the works of Walter Scott, and, in addition, he rivalled Hans Andersen as a writer for children. The children of Denmark expressed their gratitude by raising a halfpenny subscription fund, by means of which they presented Ingemann with a golden horn, adorned with figures from his poetry.

Treasures of Translation:
Greek and Latin

NO richer treasure has been brought to modern English hymnody than the recovery and translation of some of the great hymns of the Greek and Latin Churches. Although a number of translators have worked on this material, one name stands out and dominates all others. This is John Mason Neale, a remarkable Anglican priest of the nineteenth century.

Neale's work in translation was abundant and distinguished, but in many ways the man was even more remarkable than his work. Always delicate in health, he passed away at the early age of forty-eight, but had accomplished in his short life an amazing volume of work. In 1843 he was presented to the living of the parish of Crawley, Sussex, but never took up his duties there owing to lung trouble, which compelled him to go to Madeira for a while.

He used this period of enforced seclusion to read widely, and to store his mind with a fund of material for later books. Neale was an extreme and uncompromising 'High Church-man' in a day when views such as he held were unpopular with most Anglicans. He was a profound student of medieval religious life and thought; an ardent admirer and friend of the Eastern Orthodox Church, and author of a noteworthy *History of the Holy Eastern Church*. He was a Fellow of Downing College, Cambridge, and one of the founders of the Cambridge Camden Society for the study of ecclesiology. In 1846 Neale was appointed Warden of Sackville College, East Grinstead, a refuge for indigent aged men. There, in an obscure almshouse, with a salary which did not exceed twenty-seven pounds a year, this frail man spent the rest of his life, but with a fruitful activity of his manifold interests and abilities that has left a lasting inheritance in English hymnody, and an enduring influence in developments which he fostered and encouraged in the Church by his learning, zeal, and devotion. His literary output was substantial, and one of his most important acts the formation of the Sisterhood of St. Margaret at East Grinstead, an effort which won for him at the time the bitterest opposition and abuse from his critics.

But this by no means exhausted Neale's wide and varied interests. He was a pioneer of Christian reunion, a social reformer, and antiquary, whose zeal for our ancient churches led the way in the movements for their preservation. He was deeply interested in psychical research, and above all a sensitive poet and mystic, with a true discernment of the wealth of splendour latent in Greek and Latin hymnody. To Neale more than to any other we are indebted for the treasures now included in all our hymnals from these early sources. *Art thou weary, art thou languid?* is one of our best-known hymns, but many who sing it fail to know that it is a translation from Greek sources by this remarkable man. The same thought applies when we sing the familiar and beloved Christmas carol, *Good King Wenceslas*. This popular carol is a delightful example of Neale's creative imagination.

Neale restored in the translation of Greek hymns which he made the ancient treasures of over a thousand years ago. One or two examples may be mentioned out of the vast mass of hymnody created by the Greek Church. Neale computed that of the five thousand quarto pages of which the Greek office books consist, four thousand are poetry. One of the translations is the well-known evening hymn, included in most English hymnals, *The day is past and over*. It is a hymn, adapted by Neale, from the early Greek hymn known as the *Lamplighting or Candlelight Hymn*. In the primitive churches of the East, it was, in earlier times, a common act of Christian hospitality for members of the congregation who could do so

to give a supper on Sunday evenings to their poor friends and
visitors from a distance. It was a deeply significant act,
expressing the oneness of Christian believers. As darkness fell
it was the duty of the deacon to light the lamps, and while this
was being done the little company would unite in a hymn of
thanksgiving to the Lord, Who is the Light of life. This hymn
was as early as the fourth century. In course of time, as services became more elaborated, this simple hymn developed
into an antiphonal anthem, sung in procession in the church,
and forming part of an "After-Supper Service", during which
lighted torches were carried. Our hymn, *The day is past and
over*, is taken from this After-Supper ceremony. As an example
of how its verses reflect the original text, one verse may be
cited. In the early version one response is:

> The day is passing away; I glorify Thee, O Master;
> that the evening with the night may be offenceless, I
> beseech: Grant to me, Saviour, and save me.

Now observe how Neale renders this:

> The joys of day are over;
> We lift our hearts to Thee,
> And ask Thee that offenceless
> The hours of dark may be:
> O Jesu, make their darkness light,
> And guard us through the coming night.

A verse is now usually omitted from most hymnals, indicative
of the weakening in the modern mind of belief in a personal
agency of evil. Yet it expresses a realistic sense of conflict
with this evil, which our own generation may be wise to
recognise:

> Lighten mine eyes, O Saviour,
> Or sleep in death shall I
> And he, my wakeful tempter,
> Triumphantly shall cry:
> "He could not make their darkness light,
> Nor guard them through the hours of night."

155

The authorship of the original is not certain, but it is usually attributed to a Greek saint, Anatolius, in the eight century. Neale said that in our own day, "It is to the scattered hamlets of Chios and Mitylene what Ken's evening hymn is to the villages of our own land".

Probably the most popular and well-known of all Neale's Greek translations is *Art thou weary, art thou languid*, although it contains so little that is from the Greek that it would seem to be rather a hymn of Neale's own composition, inspired by a poem written by an Eastern monk, Stephen the Sabaite, a title derived from his attachment to the monastery of Mar Saba, situated on the rocky heights overhanging the gorge of the brook Kedron, about ten miles from Jerusalem. Stephen went to this monastery when a boy of ten, and remained there for sixty years. In the same monastery were two other highly gifted hymn writers, both relatives of Stephen. One was the famous St. John of Damascus, and St. Cosmas, who was also an accomplished ecclesiastical poet. It will be noted that this familiar hymn is written in antiphonal form, a mode of singing much in vogue in the primitive Christian Church, as early as the second century. It is a device which one wonders is not more widely used. Wesley found it very effective in deepening the appeal of a hymn to the people.

Even at the risk of digression a defence of this hymn must be made in view of the tendency of critics to-day to disparage it. It is, for example, omitted from *Songs of Praise*. One wonders what are the grounds of objection? Are we never weary; never tired? Or if we are, why are we ashamed to confess it? There seems a tendency on the part of a somewhat "let's all be jolly" school of modern religious thought to ignore the distresses of sick souls, of whom there are so many in this nerve-strained world. It leads to a superficial view of spiritual experience that leaves aside the more profound pathos and stress of life. So far as this limited outlook relates to the present hymn it may be assumed that the objection is mainly to the opening line. It seems singular to ignore the obvious beauty of some subsequent verses, which must come to mind when the hymn is mentioned:

Is there diadem as Monarch,
That His brow adorns?
'Yea, a crown in very surety:
But of thorns.'

If I ask Him to receive me
Will He say me nay?
'Not till earth and not till heaven
Pass away!'

And the triumphant note of the last verse:

Finding, following, keeping, struggling,
Is He sure to bless?
Saints, apostles, prophets, martyrs,
Answer, 'Yes'.

In the great monastery of the Stadium, at Constantinople, another famous group of hymn writers resided. One of the most distinguished was known as Joseph the Hymnographer. A native of Sicily, he had fled from there when the Mahommedans invaded the land. For a while he was in Constantinople, but again became an exile owing to persecution. Captured by pirates, he was made a slave, and in this position converted many of the other slaves to the Christian faith. He was able to return after a time to Constantinople, and founded a monastery there, but once more became a fugitive during a period of intense religious dispute and intolerance. It is easy to understand how such experiences prompted the thought to Neale of the lines contained in his hymn *O happy band of pilgrims*. Again, as is true of the previous hymn mentioned, the words of this familiar hymn are Neale's, but its sentiment was, doubtless, the outcome of his reflections on the life of Joseph the Hymnographer.

Other hymns suggested by Greek originals, or translations of them made by Neale, include a fine Christmas hymn, beginning:

157

A great and mighty wonder,
A full and blessed cure!
The Rose has come to blossom
Which shall for aye endure.

The original of this was by Germanus, a seventh-century Patriarch of Constantinople. One of the greatest of the Greek hymns, which we have in a faithful translation by Neale, is the glorious Easter hymn, *Come, ye faithful, raise the strain,* and another equally inspiring for the same season, *The Day of Resurrection.* Both are from the masterpiece of the most noted Greek hymn writer, John of Damascus, and form part of the "Golden Canon" for Easter, a composition of eight odes. A graphic account has been given of its use at Athens, and if, in imagination, we follow the scene, as enacted in the picturesque ceremonial of the Eastern Church, we shall feel the impact of the poetry more intensely. It is the report of a traveller, quoted by Neale in his *Hymns of the Eastern Church*:

As midnight approached, the Archbishop with his priests, accompanied by the King and Queen, left the church, and stationed themselves on the platform, which was raised considerably from the ground, so that they were distinctly seen by the people. Everyone now remained in breathless expectation, holding their unlighted tapers in readiness when the glad moment should arrive, while the priests still continued murmuring their melancholy chant in a low half-whisper. Suddenly, a single report of a cannon announced that twelve o'clock had struck, and that Easter Day had begun. Then the Archbishop, elevating the cross, exclaimed in a loud, exultant tone: *Christos anesti!* (Christ is risen) and instantly every single individual of all that host took up the cry and dispelled the mournful silence with one spontaneous shout of indescribable joy and triumph, "Christ is risen! Christ is risen!" At the same moment the oppressive darkness was dispersed by a blaze of light from thousands of tapers, which, communicating one from another, seemed to send streams of fire in all directions, rendering the minutest objects distinctly visible, and casting a vivid glow on the expressive faces of the rejoicing crowd. The bands of music struck up their gayest strains; the roll of the drum through the town, and further on the pealing of the cannon, announced far and near these 'glad tidings of great joy', while from hill and plain, from the sea-shore and the far off olive grove, rocket after rocket, ascending to the clear sky, answer back with their mute eloquence that Christ is risen indeed ... everywhere men clasped each other's hands, and congratulated one another, and embraced with faces beaming with delight, as though to each one separately some wonderful happiness had been proclaimed, while the priests were chanting forth a glorious old hymn of victory, to tell the world how "Christ is risen from the dead, having trampled death beneath His feet".

Against this background, we can feel the passionate assurance of the climax-verse of the hymn:

> Now let the heavens be joyful,
>   And earth her song begin,
> The round world keep high triumph,
>   And all that is therein;
> Let all things seen and unseen
>   Their notes of gladness blend,
> For Christ the Lord hath risen,
>   Our joy that hath no end.

The eighth ode in the "Golden Canon" was also translated by Neale, and is the Easter hymn beginning:

> Thou hallowed chosen dawn of praise,
>   That best and greatest shinest:
> Fair Easter, queen of all the days,
>   Of seasons best, divinest!
> On thee our praises Christ adore
>   For ever and for evermore.

These are a few examples of the treasures contained in early Greek hymnody, made available for English congregations by the skilful and devoted work of Neale.

Another source of enrichment has been found in the abundant treasury of Latin religious verse. Many of the treasures from this field of hymnody have now become familiar and beloved in our English tongue. The greatest of all is, undoubtedly, the *Te Deum laudamus*. It belongs to the earliest period of Latin hymnody, but remains one of its greatest achievements. The general view now is that it was written by Niceta, who was missionary bishop of Remesiana, in Dacia, at the end of the fourth century, although some scholars hold that the first part of this famous hymn belongs to a much earlier date. The first evidence we have of its use is in the Rule of St. Benedict in the first half of the sixth century. It is true to say that the *Te Deum* remains the masterpiece in the hymnody of the Christian Church. It is, in every way, a model of what a perfect hymn should be. It opens with a note of pure adoration, and brings to this adoration of God the whole of the earthly and heavenly order. It emphasises the glorious apostolic tradition of the Church, and the witness and ministry of prophets and martyrs. It centres the thought of the worshipper on the Incarnation of God in Christ, expressing the Eternal facts in a few lines of amazing beauty, and matchless economy of form and expression. There is, as the conclusion is reached, a note of intercession for the whole Church and Christian Fellowship, while the last note of all is the prayer for personal salvation. This wonderful gem of devotion remains without a rival, and is a link between Christians throughout the world.

The use of metrical hymnody in the services of the Western Church is usually attributed for its origin to St. Ambrose, Bishop of Milan in the fourth century. There is one sense in which a comparison can be made between Ambrose and Isaac Watts—although Watts was not a bishop! Both were instrumental in breaking down an irrational prejudice against hymnody. This was a task Ambrose shared with the monastic leaders, Benedict and Caesarius, of a somewhat later period.

The hymnody of Ambrose attained such popularity that his critics accused him of having bewitched the people. He was an amazing personality, who wielded his episcopal authority without regard to fear or favour. It was he who refused to admit to communion the Emperor Theodosius, until he had made penance for the massacre of a multitude of innocent persons at Thessalonica. From the movement in hymnody which Ambrose inaugurated something like a hundred examples have come down to us, and as they are more akin to our Western modes of thought they achieved an earlier popularity in our midst than those from the Eastern or Greek Church. The hymns of this school are, for the most part, marked by a terse simplicity, and an austere severity of expression. They lack the picturesque imagery of many of the Eastern hymns, but gain in power by the simple precision of style which they present, and mainly monosyllabic structure. One of the best examples is the hymn *Deus creator omnium*, of which it is certain Ambrose himself was the author. It is now included in several modern hymnals.

> Creator of the earth and sky,
> Ruling the firmament on high,
> Clothing the day with robes of light,
> Blessing with gracious sleep the night.
>
> That rest may comfort weary men,
> And brace to useful toil again,
> And soothe awhile the harassed mind,
> And sorrow's heavy load unbind:
>
> Day sinks; we thank thee for thy gift;
> Night comes; and once again we lift
> Our prayer and vows and hymns that we
> Against all ills may shielded be.
>
> Thee let the secret heart acclaim,
> Thee let our tuneful voices name,
> Round thee our chaste affections cling,
> Thee sober reason own as King.

That when dark blackness closes day,
And shadows thicken round our way,
Faith may no darkness know, and night
From faith's clear beam may borrow light.

Rest not, my heaven-born mind and will;
Rest, all ye thoughts and deeds of ill;
May faith its watch unwearied keep,
And cool the dreaming warmth of sleep.

From cheats of sense, Lord, keep me free,
And let my heart's depth dream of thee;
Let not my envious foe draw near,
To break my rest with any fear.

Augustine was a disciple of Ambrose, and he mentioned how the above hymn had been a comfort to him on the death of his mother, Monica. The translation given here was made by the late Dr. Charles Bigg, a former Regius Professor of Ecclesiastical History at Oxford.

The hymns of Ambrose and his followers were soon widely used, and found a place in the breviaries of every locality in Western Christendom. It is certain that Ambrose did for the Western Church of his time what Watts and Wesley did for the Protestant Church at a later date. The Ambrosian hymnody was designed to be popular. It employed plain and simple tunes which all could learn easily. Ambrose encouraged the congregations to take part in the singing, though not without some measure of opposition, it may be assumed. Certain of the Early Fathers objected to women having a share in the singing, though one suggested that this objection might be met if the women would sing so softly that no one could hear them! But the good St. Ambrose was not a man to suffer opposition. That he did not shrink from conflict is well illustrated by the famous incident of his refusal to allow the young Emperor Valentinian II to use the principal church in Milan for heretical worship. "The Emperor", he said, "has his palaces; let him leave the churches to the bishop". Violence resulted, and street fighting began, and again the rare spirit of Ambrose was shown in the offer which he made to give his own life if it would prevent bloodshed; an action which so deeply impressed the soldiers that some of them joined the Christians, saying that they would pray rather than fight. In this period of struggle some of the Christians locked themselves in the church, and there sang for their comfort and assurance the hymns they had been taught by the saintly Ambrose.

The Latin hymns of Ambrose and his successors held possession of the Western Church for twelve hundred years. They reached the highest point of excellence in the *Veni Creator* and the *Veni Sancte Spiritus*. Yet, notwithstanding their manifest merit and beauty, there was a strong opposition to their general use in worship, so much so that it called for the decision of a Council to give this innovation the status of official authority and approval. In the seventh century the Council of Toledo threatened with excommunication all in Spain or France who resisted the use of hymns in divine worship. One of the losses of the Reformation was the failure to give English congregations the rich wealth of hymnody provided by the Latin store. Granted that many of these hymns expressed doctrine contrary to the Reformed outlook, yet others were gems of pure devotion, and their recovery through subsequent translation has enabled us to understand our indebtedness to the scholarly and devoted translators who have restored these treasures to us in the vernacular. The Tractarian movement in the Anglican Church did an admirable work in fostering the recovery of the great Latin hymns, and it is certain that they have become increasingly appreciated in the Reformed Churches during the past few decades. *The Westminster Hymnal*, the official hymn book of the Roman Communion in this country, contains an ample number of these ancient Latin, and medieval hymns, and this collection should be studied by all who are desirous of judging for themselves the strength and beauty of these distinctive verses.

A remarkable work which is the source of several very familiar hymns, now found in all our standard hymnals, is the poem *De contemptu mundi* (On Contempt of the World), a massive and remarkable production by a monk of Cluny called Bernard of Morval (or Morlaas) in the twelfth century. The original work is a lengthy poem of three thousand lines, and again it is to J. M. Neale we owe the translation of the sections which constitute four very well-known hymns— namely, *Brief life is here our portion*: *The world is very evil*: *For thee, O dear, dear, country*, and, best known of all, *Jerusalem the golden*. It may be a surprise to many who know and value these popular hymns to learn that the long poem, of which they form a part, was really written as a bitter satire on the corruptions and worldliness of the great monastery at Cluny when Bernard was an occupant. At the time Cluny was the most powerful and wealthy religious establishment in France, and it is not surprising to know that its prosperity bred a spirit of worldliness and spiritual declension. Within its walls were jealousy, scandal, and strife. Bernard, one of the four hundred and fifty brethren dwelling there, felt his spirit torn by the rampant worldliness he found in this great centre of religion. His distress found expression in this bitter satire, in which he castigated the contentions and follies which were corrupting the life of this house of Cluny:

> 'Tis fury, ill and scandal,
> 'Tis peaceless peace below.

From the spectacle of these present distresses he turns his thought, wistfully and longingly, to a realm where such evils will be banished, and pure worship and unsullied love will order all:

> The home of fadeless splendour,
> Of flowers that fear no thorn,
> Where they shall dwell as children
> Who here as exiles mourn.

If we sing the hymns taken from this poem with its background in our mind, we shall feel how the words spring up

with a new life. We can imagine the distressed and weary
Bernard picturing a realm of goodness where these present
evils would be no more:

> There is the throne of David,
>   And there, from care released,
> The shout of them that triumph,
>   The song of them that feast:
> And they, who with their leader
>   Have conquer'd in the fight,
> For ever and for ever
>   Are clad in robes of white.
>
> O sweet and blessed country,
>   The home of God's elect!
> O sweet and blessed country
>   That eager hearts expect!
> Jesu, in mercy bring us
>   To that dear land of rest:
> Who art, with God the Father
>   And Spirit, ever blest.

No hymn lights up more clearly the value of having in mind
the historical background when it is sung. It is given in this
way new significance and depth, and this is true of a great
many other hymns.

Another hymn, dating from a period a little earlier than the
above work of Bernard, the monk of Cluny, is one which has
found an assured place in Anglican hymnals. This is the hymn
beginning:

> Oh, what the joy and the glory must be,
> Those endless Sabbaths the blessed ones see;
> Crown for the valiant, to weary ones rest;
> God shall be All and in all ever Blest.

This hymn is another of Neale's translations and the original
was the work of one of the most remarkable men in medieval

religious history—Pierre Abelard, an eminent philosopher and theologian of his time in the great University of Paris. The hymn is selected from a number which he wrote in compiling a hymn book for the Abbey of the Paraclete, of which his beloved Heloise was abbess, and it was designed for use at Vespers on Saturday evening. The collection was dedicated to Heloise, "to my dear sister, dear while in the world, but more dear now in Christ".

To the eleventh century belongs another hymn which has become a favourite in the worship of all Christian communions. This is *Jesu dulcis memoria.*

> Jesu, the very thought of thee
> With sweetness fills my breast;
> But sweeter far thy face to see,
> And in thy presence rest.

This hymn was once regarded as the work of Bernard of Clairvaux (not to be confused with Bernard of Cluny, mentioned above), but the discovery of a MS. of the eleventh century has compelled a revision of this belief. The MS. contains the verses and ascribes them to a Benedictine abbess. There is additional interest in the fact that the beautiful, and widely popular hymn was written by a woman.

Mention cannot be omitted of the translation of the hymns by the famous author of the *Imitation of Christ*; Thomas à Kempis. Even in translation one can appreciate the distinctive quality of thought and phrase in these verses, marked as they are by clarity, beauty, and an eternal accent of devotion by which they are lifted above the changing vogues and modes of time. The best known are *O Love, how deep! how broad! how high*, a masterly epitome in seven brief verses of the Christian creed and faith, and *Again the Lord's own day is here*, a fine hymn for the opening of Sunday morning worship, uttering joyously the glorious fact of the Resurrection of our Lord. Set to J. W. Elliott's inspiring tune "Church Triumphant" there are few more worthy or uplifting hymns at the beginning of congregational worship. Less well-known, but an example

of perfect felicity in thought and expression is the hymn of
Thomas à Kempis beginning:

> If there be that skills to reckon
>   All the number of the blest,
> He perchance can weigh the gladness
>   Of the everlasting rest,
> Which, their earthly exile finished,
>   They by merit have possessed.

Observe, too, in this hymn the gracious thought set forth in
the third verse:

> There the gifts of each and single
>   All in common right possess;
> There each member hath his portion
>   In the body's blessedness;
> So that he, the least in merits,
>   Shares the guerdon none the less.

Mark how these splendid hymns of Thomas à Kempis
declare the faith and conviction of the Risen Life, and how the
dignified and lovely symbols of the heavenly world leave
nothing that the changing thought of the years can wish to
alter. This is typified in the uplifting hymn,

> Light's abode, celestial Salem,
>   Vision whence true peace doth spring,
> Brighter than the heart can fancy,
>   Mansion of the Highest King;
> Oh, how glorious are the praises
>   Which of thee the prophets sing.

How finely suggestive is the thought in the fourth verse:

> Oh, how glorious and resplendent,
>   Fragile body, shalt thou be,
> When endued with so much beauty,
>   Full of health, and strong and free,
> Full of vigour, full of pleasure
>   That shall last eternally.

One is grateful to the compilers of *The English Hymnal* for including another hymn ascribed to Thomas à Kempis— *Our Father's home eternal*, a worthy hymn, once more expressing the radiant conviction of the intense reality of the heavenly world; a theme so constant and congenial to the age of Thomas à Kempis, and one inseparably linked with the Christian outlook.

It is impossible in the limited space available to give many examples of these splendid Latin hymns, but this brief outline may suffice to indicate what a rich store of devotional verse has been unlocked by such treasures of translation. Their strong objectivity makes them essentially suitable for congregational worship, while the virile, clear conviction vibrant in them is a tonic in an age of vagueness and nebulous creeds. Further, they exhibit a simplicity of expression, and healthy sincerity of utterance, delivering them from any suspicion of affectation or sentimentality. This is made clear by the morning hymn, ascribed to St. Gregory, of the sixth century. It is a model of its kind:

Father, we praise thee, now the night is over,
    Active and watchful, stand we all before thee;
Singing we offer prayer and meditation:
            Thus we adore thee.

Monarch of all things, fit us for thy mansions;
    Banish our weakness, health and wholeness sending;
Bring us to heaven, where thy saints united
            Joy without ending.

All-holy Father, Son and equal Spirit,
    Trinity blessed, send us thy salvation;
This is the glory, gleaming and resounding
            Through all creation.

11

A Century of Development

IT will now be clear that by the middle of the nineteenth
century a rich and varied store of hymnody had grown up
in the English Churches. The main sources have been indicated. Watts and the Wesleys had contributed a generous
measure of verse destined to occupy a permanent and prominent place in all later hymnals of the Protestant Churches.
At the middle of the nineteenth century, however, their hymns
were mainly confined to Nonconformist circles. The Anglican
Church had been slow to respond to the innovation of congregational hymn singing, and as late as 1854 a bishop objected
to the singing of the Passiontide hymn *Jesu, meek and lowly* on
the ground that it was "contrary to the spirit of the Book of
Common Prayer". But the impetus given by the Tractarians,
the treasures discovered by translation, and the resultant
approval of congregational hymnody by the more Catholic
section of the Anglican Church led rapidly to the popularity
of hymn singing in the Established Churches. No longer was
it what it had been for many years, almost a monopoly of
Nonconformity, and then of the Evangelical wing of the
Establishment.

At the same time the divergent sources of hymnody failed to
coalesce in a common stream. Watts and the Wesleys, and
their followers among the hymn writers, were excluded from
the hymn collections of Anglicanism, except the more extreme
Evangelical section, while hymns of Catholic origin were
banned in Dissenting circles. Although modern hymnals are
vastly more eclectic in their composition, the influence of the

early prejudice and exclusiveness still lingers. It is surprising to discover what a number of fine hymns of Nonconformist origin are missing from the leading Anglican books in use, while the otherwise admirable Free Church compilations are strangely shy of hymns expressive of a true Catholicism. A conspicuous example of the latter is the omission from Nonconformist hymnals (and *Songs of Praise*, it should be added) of the splendid hymn by Dean Plumptre, *Thy Hand, O God, has guided*. Yet this hymn can present no difficulty to a modern Free Churchman, who is jealous to claim that his own particular communion is a valid branch of the Holy Catholic Church. It is a glorious hymn, and one of the finest written in the second half of the nineteenth century:

> Thy hand, O God, has guided
> Thy flock, from age to age;
> The wondrous tale is written,
> Full clear, on every page;
> Our fathers owned thy goodness,
> And we their deeds record;
> And both of this bear witness,
> One Church, one Faith, One Lord.

Again, the third verse is a timely reminder of a fact which should be a tonic in our confused days:

> Through many a day of darkness,
> Through many a scene of strife,
> The faithful few fought bravely
> To guard the nation's life.
> Their gospel of redemption,
> Sin pardoned, man restored,
> Was all in this enfolded,
> One Church, one Faith, one Lord.

It was my privilege to share in a service at the time of the first Amsterdam Conference of World Churches, when this hymn was sung as sincerely and fervently by the Nonconformists present as by their Anglican neighbours.

If we look back a century we shall find the custom of congregational hymn singing firmly established in both the Anglican and Nonconformist Churches. One natural result followed. The writing of hymns increased enormously. The rising tide became a flood. The growing demand stimulated an unfailing supply. The result was the production of a vast quantity of poor and mediocre verse. Not a little of it was banal and absurd, and merely served to indicate how a sense of humour is frequently absent from good religious folk. The winnowing fan of time has disposed of much of this chaff, although a proportion of it survives in modern hymnals, due to the timidity of compilers. Some of this feeble verse is a deposit from the revivalist mission hymns which had an extensive vogue in the second half of the nineteenth century, and the earlier years of the present one. This is not to suggest that religious revivals have not produced great hymns. The Methodist revival is an instance to the contrary. But Charles Wesley was a poet of genius, and had his gifts been devoted to secular verse instead of the purpose to which they were consecrated he would have ranked as one of the greatest English poets.

Again, although in a different category, and far inferior to the wonderful hymns of Methodism, the collection used by the famous revivalists, Sankey and Moody, contained a few hymns marked by a simple poetic beauty, and genuine spiritual appeal. An example is the hymn which for many years had a wide vogue in more Evangelical circles, Elizabeth C. Clephane's verses, *There were ninety-and-nine that safely lay*. There is no doubt that sung by Ira D. Sankey it touched the emotions, and awakened a response in thousands of hearts. Times have changed, and this hymn would probably make little appeal to a modern congregation. Hymns of this character definitely 'date' and so differ from the truly great hymns of the Church, which enshrine eternal vitality, remaining fresh and appealing in every age.

The success of the revivalist hymns was due largely to the easy and 'catchy' tunes to which they were usually linked. In circles where they are still favoured this remains true. They frequently employ the device of the chorus, simple, easily remembered and with a lilting tune. Very often the words seem written for the music, and the chorus in which ordinary folk can readily join becomes the excuse for the verbal shortcomings. Mr. Sankey himself was aware of this for he once said, "I find it much more difficult to get good words than good music. Our best words come from England; the music which best suits our purposes comes from America".

The danger of the revivalist hymn is that it easily degenerates into crude nonsense, as, for example:

> The Devil and me, we can't agree,
> I hate him and he hates me;
> He had me once, but let me go,
> He wants me again but I will not go.

As no true religious revival can be 'organized', so no good hymn can be written merely to exploit emotion. Here is the subtle difficulty in the writing of a good hymn. It must have an emotional appeal. If it is only a philosophical reflection, or theological statement clothed in rhymed sentences, it will not be a good hymn. Yet it must touch the whole personality, the reason and the will. The less worthy revivalist hymn aims crudely at an emotional response, so far touching the will, but ignoring the reason, and easily slipping into banal nonsense. One recalls many instances of this in a collection imported from America, but familiar in this country in the early years of the century; the hymns of the Torrey-Alexander mission. Many may remember the 'Glory Song' with its jingling tune, and cheap appeal. There is no need to give further examples, but this class of hymn presents one of the peculiar features of religious life in the past century, in England, and America.

It would be impossible within the modest limits of this volume to survey fully the vast output of hymnody which marked the nineteenth century. Such a survey would be largely a catalogue of names, many of which are now forgotten, and of hymns which no longer find a place in our standard hymnals. The more important task is to outline the contributions made which have had permanent influence and have served to supply a substantial number of the hymns now in general favour. It is interesting to recall that although the Anglican Church was slow to respond to the growing movement for the adoption of congregational hymn singing, when it did so it proved fertile in the supply of hymn writers. Meanwhile, important new influences were coming from the Nonconformist side, and among those that call for mention, because of the abiding value of their work, is the name of Josiah Conder (1789-1855) both for the merit of the hymns he wrote, and for his editorial work in the sphere of hymnody, which helped to elevate the standard of good taste.

Conder was one of the most important influences from the Free Church side, and under his editorship the *Congregational Hymn Book* published in 1836 marked a distinct advance. It was intended to be used as a supplement to Dr. Watts' *Psalms and Hymns*. It is significant that it was only possible to offer this new collection as a supplement to the latter work. Dr. Watts had by that date secured a veneration among the Independents similar to the regard once given exclusively to the Psalter, while Methodist hymnody at the time was confined almost entirely to the verses of Charles Wesley. Conder's supplement was a sign of the times, and it prepared the way for the more eclectic and selective hymnals in the Congregational and Baptist Churches which are in use to-day. To this supplement Conder contributed fifty-six hymns from his own pen, too large an output of his own work, and not all of equal quality. This was a common failing. Many other writers then and later were capable of a few good hymns, but frequently wrote too many, with the result that much work of inferior merit was produced. All the same the general level of Conder's work was high, and it is a cause for question why they are not more widely known and used beyond the boundaries of the denominations named. It is a further example, possibly, of the suspicion that still mars the free and generous welcome of good hymns by the various Churches, without regard for the particular sectarian attachments of the writers. It is remarkable that Conder's hymns have been given so little attention in even the most recent Anglican hymnals. There is only one in *The English Hymnal*, and two in *Songs of Praise*. Probably unknown, therefore, to most Anglican congregations is the fine hymn of worship:

> The Lord is King: lift up thy voice,
> O earth, and all ye heavens rejoice:
> From world to world the joy shall ring,
> The Lord Omnipotent is King.

> One Lord, one empire, all secures:
> He reigns,—and life and death are yours.
> Through earth and heaven one song shall ring,
> The Lord Omnipotent is King.

Somewhat better known, but still almost completely neglected outside Nonconformist circles, is the truly beautiful hymn *Beyond, beyond that boundless sea*, possibly the finest Conder wrote. It is reproduced here to illustrate not only a hymn that should be better known and more widely used to-day, but also to indicate that hymns of merit were being written in this earlier Victorian period, when so much mediocre and pedestrian religious verse was produced. The merit of the following hymn is obvious.

> Beyond, beyond that boundless sea,
>   Above that dome of sky,
> Farther than thought itself can flee,
>   Thy dwelling is on high;
> Yet dear the awful thought to me,
>   That Thou my God art nigh;—

> Art nigh, and yet my labouring mind
>   Feels after Thee in vain,
> Thee in these works of power to find,
>   Or to Thy seat attain;
> Thy messenger the stormy wind;
>   Thy path, the trackless main.

These speak of Thee with loud acclaim,
    They thunder forth Thy praise,
The glorious honour of Thy name,
    The wonders of Thy ways:
But Thou art not in tempest-flame,
    Nor in day's glorious blaze.

We hear Thy voice, when thunders roll
    Through the wide fields of air:
The waves obey Thy dread control;
    Yet still Thou art not there.
Where shall I find Him, O my soul,
    Who yet is everywhere?

O! not in circling depth or height,
    But in the conscious breast,
Present to faith, though veiled from sight,
    There doth His Spirit rest.
O come, Thou Presence Infinite:
    And make Thy creature blest.

One further example demands quotation, inasmuch as it was written over a century ago, when the present ecumenical movement in the Church would have seemed a dream remote. It reveals the truly Catholic mind of Conder, and his anticipation of our growing aspiration for unity. The hymn is also an admirable example of simplicity and economy of expression, contained, as it is, in three brief stanzas:

Head of the Church, our risen Lord,
Who by Thy Spirit doth preside
O'er the whole body; by whose word
They all are ruled and sanctified:

Our prayers and intercessions hear
For all Thy family at large,
That each in his appointed sphere,
His proper service may discharge.

175

So, through the grace derived from Thee,
In Whom all fulness dwells above,
May Thy whole Church united be,
And edify itself in love.

Again, the tendency to keep hymnody within the water-tight compartments of sectarian and denominational boundaries, is further illustrated by the neglect of the splendid hymns of T. T. Lynch. Like Conder, his name is almost completely unknown in Anglican circles. There is only one of his hymns in *The English Hymnal*, although three have been included in *Songs of Praise*. Once more we owe it to the unfailing good judgment of Garrett Horder, that Lynch's beautiful hymns have been rescued from oblivion, and one ventures to predict that they will find a larger place in the hymnals of the future. Garrett Horder placed fourteen of them in *Worship Song*, a treasure house of so many worthy discoveries, while eleven had previously appeared in an earlier collection, *Congregational Hymns*, edited by Dr. Horder in 1884. Lynch was himself a remarkable personality, who fulfilled one of those distinctive, lonely, individual ministries that from time to time add a unique contribution to the life of the Church. A man of frail health and physique, he began his career as usher in a school, but later entered the Congregational ministry. In 1855 he published *The Rivulet: Hymns for Heart and Voice*. It was the occasion for a tremendous outbreak of theological fury in Free Church circles. This was due to a fact which makes Lynch's work of special significance in the history of English hymnody. *The Rivulet* was creative. It was a reaction against the intensely dogmatic type of hymn which had become increasingly dominant, particularly in Nonconformity. It ventured to base hymns on themes inspired by the contemplation of the sights and sounds of nature. It also served to emphasise another fact, then largely forgotten but destined to be recovered more fully as the century went on, that although a poem is not necessarily a hymn; a hymn should be a poem. This may sound to us a commonplace, although it is far from being clearly understood, but at the time when Lynch wrote his hymns, the prevailing demand was for rhymed dogma, and theology in verse. Hymns could express the great dogmas of Christian faith; this was well demonstrated by the Ambrosian, and earlier classical hymns of the Church, but once the hymn had become deliberately subordinated to didactic and doctrinal purposes, it tended to become formal, stilted, often unreal and sometimes patently absurd. The wise words of another distinguished hymnologist of the nineteenth century, Canon Ellerton (himself the author of a number of notable hymns) need to be borne in mind:

Hymns may express adoration, thanksgiving, commemoration of God's mercies; they may be prayers, penitential, supplicatory, intercessory; they may be devout aspirations after God; but in any case they must be forms of worship. It is not enough that they *suggest* devotion, they must be capable of expressing it. The observance of this rule would clear the ground at once of much irrelevant matter with which the hymn books of every Church and sect are at present encumbered. The whole multitude of didactic and hortatory verses, the addresses to sinners and saints, the paraphrases of Scripture prophecies, promises and warnings, the descriptions of heaven and hell, the elaborate elucidations of the anatomy and pathology of the soul; all these . . . ought utterly and for ever to be banished from the choir.

It seems strange and singular that a Church which held the Word made Flesh as one of the pillars of its faith should be heedless of the presence of God in nature, or with such an exquisite model of nature-poetry as the *Benedicite* should disregard the work of a poet who laboured in this tradition. But so it was, and Lynch was attacked from pulpits and denounced in articles. Spurgeon joined in the onslaught, complaining of "the non-doctrine scheme" into which "carnal preachers" were leading the people. From the pulpit of Mornington Church, London, which had been built for him, Lynch bore witness to Christian truth, marked by a generous charity, deep devotion and enlightened Christian

M 177

thought, which he carried on until his early death at the age of fifty-three in 1871. Much more should be known of the quiet, but truly creative work and ministry of this remarkable man. Allied to a noble charity of spirit, and a discernment of outlook far in advance of his time, he had a delightful sense of humour. This is evident from the only reply which the storm of criticism provoked. He published another work called *Songs Controversial, by Silent Long.* As these will be unknown to most readers, one may be quoted, called *A Negative Affair*, a satire addressed to those who spurned his hymns as lacking in the positive dogmas which they demanded in all their verses:

When sugar in the lump I see
  I know that it is there;
Melt it, and then I soon suspect
  A negative affair;
Where is the sugar, Sir? I say,
  Let me both touch and see;
Sweetness instead of sugar, Sir,
  You'll not palm off on me.

Don't tell me that the sugar-lumps
  When dropt in water clear,
That they to make the water sweet,
  Themselves must disappear:
For commonsense, Sir, such as mine,
  The lumps themselves must see;
Sweetness instead of sugar, Sir,
  You'll not palm off on me.

For instance, Sir, in every hymn
  Sound doctrine you should state
As clearly as a dead man's name
  Upon a coffin-plate.
Religion, Sir, is only fudge—
  Let's have theology;
Sweetness instead of sugar, Sir,
  You'll not palm off on me.

The attack on Lynch did little credit to his critics, and was one more instance of the bigotry which has far too often stained and blotted the pages of Church history, but the best reply was Lynch's own spirit of charity and large-heartedness. It was with prophetic insight that he wrote: "The air will be all the clearer for this storm . . . . men will have more liberty to love one another, notwithstanding their differences". And again: "We must conquer our foes by suffering them to crucify us, rather than by threatening them with crucifixion".

One or two examples of Lynch's hymns will enable us to appreciate their merit, and set against the prevailing standard of the time when they were written we can see what an advance they marked.

> Where is thy God, my soul?
>   Is He within thy heart;
> Or ruler of a distant realm
>   In which thou hast no part?
>
> Where is thy God, my soul?
>   Only in stars and sun;
> Or have the holy words of truth
>   His light in every one?
>
> Where is thy God, my soul?
>   Confined to Scripture's page;
> Or does His Spirit check and guide
>   The spirit of each age?
>
> O Ruler of the sky,
>   Rule Thou within my heart:
> O great Adorner of the world,
>   The light of life impart.
>
> Giver of holy words,
>   Bestow Thy holy power,
> And aid me, whether work or thought
>   Engage the varying hour.

In Thee have I my help,
  As all my fathers had;
I'll trust Thee when I'm sorrowful,
  And serve Thee when I'm glad.

What prayer for Christian service could be more beautifully expressed than the following:

Dismiss me not Thy service, Lord,
  But train me for Thy will;
That even I, in fields so broad,
  Some duties may fulfil;
And I will ask for no reward,
  Except to serve Thee still.

How many serve, how many more
  May to the service come;
To tend the vines, the grapes to store,
  Thou dost appoint for some,
Thou hast Thy young men at the war,
  Thy little ones at home.

All works are good, and each is best
  As most it pleases Thee;
Each worker pleases when the rest
  He serves in charity;
And neither man nor work unblest
  Wilt Thou permit to be.

O ye who serve, remember One,
  The worker's way Who trod;
He served as man, but now His throne
  It is the throne of God;
The sceptre he hath to us shown
  Is like a blossoming rod.

Our Master all the work hath done
   He asks of us to-day;
Sharing His service, every one
   Share too His Sonship may;
Lord, I would serve, and be a son;
   Dismiss me not, I pray.

Lynch was the author of an evening hymn of genuine poetic beauty, strangely little known and used, yet of a quality deserving to rank with the best of hymns for the evening hour. One may hope that it will be more generally included in hymnals of the future, and widely used, linked with Dr. Mann's appropriate tune, "St. Asaph".

How calmly the evening once more is descending
   As kind as a promise, as still as a prayer;
O wing of the Lord, in Thy shelter befriending,
   May we and our households continue to share.

The sky, like the kingdom of heaven, is open;
   O enter, my soul, at the glorious gates;
The silence and smile of His love are the token,
   Who now for all comers invitingly waits.

We come to be soothed with Thy merciful healing;
   The dews of the night cure the wounds of the day;
We come, our life's work and its brevity feeling,
   With thanks for the past, for the future we pray.

Lord save us from folly; be with us in sorrow;
   Sustain us in work till the time of our rest;
When earth's day is over, may heaven's to-morrow
   Dawn on us, of homes long expected possest.

The new tide of English hymnody was flowing with Lynch. To-day the viewpoint of his critics seems an echo of the past. We regard a flower service on a summer's day as almost a commonplace, but when Lynch, one Sunday morning, took a bunch of flowers into the pulpit, and made it the theme of his sermon, it provoked something of a scandal among many of his ministerial brethren. Yet one of the features of the new hymnody was to be the increasing recognition and praise of God in His works. The year Lynch died there was published another 'nature' hymn which has attained wide popularity—Bishop W. Walsham How's, *Summer suns are glowing*. The recognition assigned to this type of hymn was further marked by the publication of Garrett Horder's *Congregational Hymns* in 1884, when one special section, headed "Nature", set an example for future hymnals, and, together with hymns for the seasons and for flower services, embraced twenty-two excellent hymns, exclusive of others devoted to thanksgiving for harvest. One is glad to see this feature repeated, with an admirable choice of hymns for the purpose, in *Songs of Praise*.

Not only was Lynch's brave witness and example to bear fruit in the recognition of this special type of hymn, but it did much to emancipate Nonconformist hymnody from the cramping limitations imposed upon it by the survival of a narrow Puritan outlook. As a result, together with the fruitful efforts of Conder, which have already been noticed, a new spirit was developing slowly in Free Church circles. It received an enormous impetus through the splendid pioneer work of Garrett Horder, to whom frequent reference has been made already. Garrett Horder has not yet received the generous recognition his work deserves. He takes rank as one of our great hymnologists. At this distance of time (for his first pioneer collection appeared in 1884) we may fail to assess the value of his achievement, now that so many of the fine hymns he introduced have been included in various modern hymnals. But another leader in hymnology, Percy Dearmer, warmly acknowledged the debt due to Garrett Horder by all compilers of recent hymnals, in these words:

Many of the finest, most manly and noblest of the hymns, which are now sung everywhere to-day, and give their character to our twentieth century hymnals, would never have become known but for the learning and discernment of Garrett Horder in his *Worship Song*, and other collections, which struck a new note, and began a new era.

Garrett Horder was for many years a distinguished Congregational minister, holding pastorates in Yorkshire, Wood Green, and, later, at Ealing, where his fruitful work won for him a distinction which will not be forgotten. Preacher, scholar, poet, mystic and writer, he was a man of exceptional endowments and an unusual combination of gifts. He realized to the full the vital place of hymns in the public worship of God, and laboured unceasingly to improve standards of taste and judgment, and to eliminate the shoddy and mediocre. Garrett Horder had made a special study of American religious poetry, and published the best selection of verse we have from this source. His lectures on hymnology were much valued and appreciated in America, and it was part of his unique contribution to English hymnody that he brought some of the great American hymns to this country for the first time. Formerly, most hymns from the other side of the Atlantic had been of the sensational revivalist type, and American friends owe it to Garrett Horder (which they undoubtedly acknowledge) that he introduced to English Churches a different and vastly better type of American hymnody, to which further reference will be made.

Possibly only the student of hymnology can now appreciate all that Garrett Horder did, for it is by a comparison of *Congregational Hymns* (1884) with the books then in use that one can see clearly what a complete transformation was wrought by his discernment, and fearless discrimination. A vast amount of doggerel and poor verse had been discarded, and new treasures brought for the first time to the use of English Churches. The collection was later revised, and issued as *Worship Song*, a wise departure from denominational titles which should have assured its wide adoption by Churches irrespective of sect although it is doubtful if this result was achieved. It would need a separate volume to detail in full the new wealth of hymnody made available by Garrett Horder's pioneer work, but the statement by Percy Dearmer quoted above is a tribute to the fact that a foundation was laid on which others have since built. Apart from the American hymn writers, whose verses were included in *Congregational Hymns*, and, later, in *Worship Song*, there were a number of British hymn writers, whose work was brought into use as a new gift for English hymnody. One was Dr. George Matheson, whose magnificent hymn *O Love that wilt not let me go*, has become more widely known and enjoyed through its frequent inclusion in religious broadcasts.

Matheson was a close friend of Garrett Horder, and it was the latter who had the privilege of introducing his friend's truly choice hymns to English congregations. They are still far too little known. Dr. Matheson was not an extensive hymn writer, but the few hymns of which he was author are marked by a mystical power, spacious charity, and luminous vision which justify their place with the very best hymns in our tongue. It is to *Worship Song* we owe the exquisite hymn *Three Doors there are in the temple*:

> Three doors there are in the temple
> Where men go up to pray,
> And they that wait at the outer gate
> May enter by either way.
>
> O Father give each his answer—
> Each in his kindred way;
> Adapt Thy light to his form of night,
> And grant him his needed day.
>
> O give to the yearning spirits,
> That only Thy rest desire,
> The power to bask in the peace they ask,
> And feel the warmth of Thy fire.
>
> Give to the soul that seeketh,
> 'Mid cloud, and doubt and storm,
> The glad surprise of the straining eyes
> To see on the waves Thy form.

Give to the heart that knocketh
At the doors of earthly care,
The strength to tread in the pathway spread
By the flowers Thou hast planted there.

For the middle wall shall be broken,
And the light expand its ray,
When the burdened of brain and the soother of pain
Shall be ranked with the men that pray.

It is in Garrett Horder's *Worship Song* also that we find the great prayer of unity by George Matheson, *Gather us in, Thou love that fillest all*, another hymn that deserves to be much more widely known and valued.

Garrett Horder also anticipated another modern development in the compilation of hymns. He recognized the value as hymns of certain religious poems, written originally as devotional verse, but without being intended for congregational use. His wide sympathy, and independence of sectarian bias prompted him to select such verses from writers of varying schools of religious thought, Papist and Protestant alike, and to recognise clearly the invaluable contribution made by women writers. Thus, he gave prominence to some of the sensitive and lovely verses of Adelaide Anne Procter. This lady was the eldest daughter of Bryan Waller Procter, better known as "Barry Cornwall" under which *nom de plume* he gained reputation as a poet and dramatist, accomplishments additional to his work as a barrister. He was an intimate friend of Charles Lamb, Leigh Hunt and Charles Dickens, so we can imagine that the daughter was not a little influenced and inspired by the great men in her father's circle of friendship. An interesting fact is that under the name of "Mary Berwick" Miss Proctor contributed verse to *Household Words*, the weekly journal edited by Dickens, the merit and distinction of which at once attracted his notice, although he had no idea of the real identity of the contributor. So excellent was the work, however, that she was invited to contribute more verse, which became a regular feature of the journal. It was only later that Dickens learned that "Miss Berwick"

185

was no other than his friend's daughter, Adelaide Anne
Proctor. Of the songs she wrote one that achieved great
popularity was *The Lost Chord*. Miss Proctor joined the Church
of Rome in 1851, when she was twenty-six years of age.
Garrett Horder incorporated a number of the poems in *Congregational Hymns*, retaining them later in *Worship Song*, and
adding one fine evening hymn, beginning as its first verse:

> The shadows of the evening hours
> Fall from the darkening sky;
> Upon the fragrance of the flowers
> The dews of evening lie:
> Before Thy throne, O Lord of Heaven,
> We kneel at close of day;
> Look on Thy children from on high,
> And hear us while we pray.

Another hymn, increasingly well known by its general
inclusion now in Free Church hymnals, and in *Songs of Praise*,
is the poem *Thankfulness* which now forms the hymn *My God
I thank Thee, who hast made the earth so bright,* and also a tender
and lovely hymn *We ask for Peace, O Lord!* The value of the
work done by Garrett Horder can best be judged by the
provision of such verses for congregational use, at a time when
hymns of this calibre were all too rare. The only limitation
is that these poems are very often so personal and intimate as
to be rather unsuitable for the different level of congregational
singing. Garrett Horder recognized this, particularly in
relation to the beautiful verses *I do not ask, O Lord, that life
may be a pleasant road,* but wisely included them in his collection.
It is a hymn that might be used more appropriately by a small
devotional group, or "Quiet Day", but as it may be little
known it is reproduced, as a typical example of the finely
sensitive thought of this gifted writer.

> I do not ask, O Lord, that life may be
> A pleasant road;
> I do not ask that Thou wouldst take from me
> Aught of its load.

I do not ask that flowers should always spring
   Beneath my feet;
I know too well the poison and the sting
   Of things too sweet.

For one thing only, Lord, dear Lord, I plead:
   Lead me aright,
Though strength should falter, and though heart
   Through Peace to Light. [should bleed,

I do not ask, O Lord, that Thou shouldst shed
   Full radiance here;
Give but a ray of peace, that I may tread
   Without a fear.

I do not ask my cross to understand,
   My way to see;
Better in darkness just to feel Thy hand
   And follow Thee.

Joy is like restless day: but peace divine
   Like quiet night;
Lead me, O Lord, till perfect day shall shine
   Through Peace to Light.

It would not be easy to find verses marked by deeper
mystical understanding, or a purer devotion than these.

Although Garrett Horder was officially a Congregationalist,
he belonged to the truly catholic minded souls who cannot be
confined within any denominational boundaries. Those who
know his delightful anthologies of prose will quickly recognize
his eclectic taste and capacious sympathies. It is natural, therefore, that we find him selecting hymns of merit irrespective of
the particular communion to which the writer belonged. He
was particularly attracted by the hymns of Faber (which have
been considered in earlier pages) and does not allow the fact
that Faber was a Papist to stand in the way of his appreciation. In like manner he was the first to introduce into his

compilation many of the verses of the American poet, Whittier, with his Quaker background. For this reason *Worship Song* became a model of hymnody which editors of the future may study with profit for their guidance.

It was, for example, from the hymnody of the Roman communion that Garrett Horder selected a gem that is little known (possibly little known to Roman Catholic congregations), but verses enshrining such gracious wisdom that they should become more familiar. The following is the original version taken from the Roman book *The Westminster Hymnal*. In *Worship Song* the verses are abbreviated and revised, and somewhat weakened. They were written by Sister M. Xavier, a Religious of the nineteenth century:

> Lord, for to-morrow and its needs
> I do not pray;
> Keep me, my God, from stain of sin,
> Just for to-day.
>
> Let me both diligently work
> And duly pray;
> Let me be kind in word and deed,
> Just for to-day.
>
> Let me be slow to do my will,
> Prompt to obey;
> Help me to mortify my flesh,
> Just for to-day.
>
> Let me no wrong or idle word
> Unthinking say;
> Set Thou a seal upon my lips,
> Just for to-day.
>
> Let me in season, Lord, be grave,
> In season, gay;
> Let me be faithful to Thy grace,
> Just for to-day.

XIV Sir John Bowring, distinguished scholar and diplomat and Unitarian writer of hymns. Author of *In the Cross of Christ I glory*.

XIII John Greenleaf Whittier, American Quaker poet. Extracts from his poems now appear in our standard hymn books.

XVI OLIVER WENDELL HOLMES, celebrated American man of letters and author of *Lord of all being! throned afar.*

XV HARRIET BEECHER STOWE, famous American author of *Uncle Tom's Cabin* and writer of hymns of rare mystical beauty.

And if to-day my tide of life
    Should ebb away,
Give me Thy sacraments divine,
    Sweet Lord, to-day.

In Purgatory's cleansing fires
    Brief be my stay,
Oh, bid me, if to-day I die,
    Go home to-day.

So, for to-morrow and its needs
    I do not pray;
But keep me, guide me, love me, Lord,
    Just for to-day.

In the same way, without hesitation, Garrett Horder selected verses of merit from more heterodox sources. Unitarian writers find inclusion with hymns of distinction, and it is to be regretted that this example has not been followed with the same generosity in more recent collections. It is difficult, for example, to understand how the latter could omit the following two hymns for evening worship. They were written by the Reverend Ambrose Blatchford, a saintly and devoted man, with a genius for friendship, who was beloved by members of all religious communions during a remarkable ministry of over forty years at the Lewins Mead Unitarian Meeting-House, Bristol. The hymns, as will be seen, are marked by a tenderness and gentleness, very appealing in hymns for the late hours of the day:

Softly the silent night
    Falleth from God,
On weary wanderers
    Over life's road;
And as the stars on high
Light up the darkening sky,
Lord, unto Thee we cry—
    Father above!

Slowly on failing wing
  Daylight has passed;
Sleep, like an angel kind,
  Folds us at last.
Peace be our lot this night,
Safe be our slumber light,
Watched by Thine angels bright,
  Father above!

And when the gleam of morn
  Touches our eyes,
And the returning day
  Bids us arise,
Happy beneath Thy will,
Steadfast in joy or ill,
Lord, may we serve Thee still,
  Father above!

Another evening hymn by the same writer is included, in
which, again, there is a simple devotion, with no conscious
straining after effect. It is a natural, quiet mood of meditation
and prayer:

Peacefully round us the shadows are falling,
  Glad be our praises and trustful our prayer!
Hear us, O Lord! on Thy providence calling,
  Lighten our darkness, and banish our care!

Hushed are the sheep-bells afar on the moorland,
  O'er the still meadows the night breezes sweep,
Faint fall the footsteps in city and hamlet,
  Safely the children are folded to sleep.

Softly may weary ones rest from their duty,
  Bright be the dreams of the troubled and worn!
While through the shade beam the stars in their beauty
  Watching the world till the breaking of morn.

> Lord of the night! let Thine angels befriend us!
> Sunshine and gloom are alike unto Thee.
> Lord of the day! let Thy Spirit attend us,
> Bless us and keep us wherever we be!

Members of the Unitarian communion contribute other hymns which have been included in this representative collection. Sir John Bowring's noble hymn *In the Cross of Christ I glory*, although written by a Unitarian, is now in several modern hymnals, including, for the Anglican Church, *The English Hymnal*. Yet for long there was a nervous dread of adopting these fine verses, although they express a faith as real as any Evangelical Christian could wish or express. Other Unitarian hymn writers of merit find space in *Worship Song*. It seems clear the test question of all acceptance was, "Is this a good hymn?" and not "To what particular type of religious thought does the writer belong?" This is certainly the only criterion that should be applied.

But it must not be inferred that Garrett Horder's sole concern was to give prominence to new and unknown hymns. Like the wise householder in the parable, he was careful to bring out of his treasure things old, as well as new. It is, indeed, particularly interesting to mark the older hymns included, for in the main they are the hymns that have features of enduring merit, and are a further tribute to the compiler's judgment. There is only space to refer to one or two, but they will be representative of others. A Victorian hymn writer whose verses have shown true 'survival-value', a member of the Free Church of Scotland, and one whose hymns retain a wide appeal, irrespective of church or party, is Dr. Horatius Bonar. His hymns will be found in every standard book of both Anglican and Nonconformist Churches. There are nine in *Hymns Ancient and Modern*; six in *The English Hymnal*; thirteen in *The Methodist Hymn Book*. In *Worship Song*, Garrett Horder used no less than twenty, a number only exceeded by one other hymn writer—the American Quaker, J. G. Whittier.

One of the best known and most widely sung of Bonar's hymns is *I heard the voice of Jesus say*. It is not altogether easy

191

to explain the abiding and widespread popularity of his hymns. One would think that, *A few more years shall roll, I was a wandering sheep*, and *I lay my sins on Jesus*, may not rank first in favour with the present generation of church goers, and, also, it may be said that Dr. Bonar's best-known and most popular hymns are not his best work. Some of his verses are, indeed, devotional gems. One of the best, yet a marvel of brevity, is the following:

> Beloved, let us love: love is of God;
> In God alone hath love its true abode.
>
> Beloved, let us love: for they who love,
> They only, are His sons, born from above.
>
> Beloved, let us love: for love is rest,
> And he who loveth not abides unblest.
>
> Beloved, let us love: for love is light,
> And he who loveth not dwelleth in night.
>
> Beloved, let us love: for only thus
> Shall we behold that God Who loveth us.

On the same level of excellence is the splendid hymn, *O Love of God, how strong and true*. His productions included several hymns for Holy Communion, which rank with the best for this service. Dr. Bonar passed away in 1889 at the age of eighty-one, so that he can be regarded as essentially a Victorian hymn writer, and an example of what the period could offer at its best.

Another Victorian hymn writer, this time an Anglican, to whom Garrett Horder gave extensive space in his collection, is J. S. B. Monsell, who lived from 1811 to 1875, and at the time of his death was Vicar of Guildford. Dr. Monsell published several volumes of hymns, and his verses are marked by poetic grace, and at times, distinction. He wrote nearly three hundred hymns, and a few have secured permanent place in most of the hymnals now in use. The best known of his hymns is beyond question *Fight the good fight with all thy might*—due, no doubt, to its widespread use in school hymnals, but one of the most poetic and worthy is *O Worship the Lord in the beauty of holiness*. Although Monsell was an Anglican, this hymn is strangely absent from *Hymns Ancient and Modern*, but by its inclusion in later Anglican collections it is now becoming more widely known in the Church of England. Its verses are of genuine beauty, of which this one is typical:

> Fear not to enter His courts in the slenderness
> Of the poor wealth thou wouldst reckon as thine:
> Truth in its beauty, and love in its tenderness,
> These are the offerings to lay on his shrine.

Worship Song is dealt with extensively because it marked a new era in Free Church hymnody. Its eulogy does not overlook the fact that it was not as comprehensive as it aimed to be. There were big omissions from the Catholic sources, and for this reason the book was confined to Nonconformist, and mainly Congregational churches. Its enduring value lies in the fine work it achieved in revealing the store of excellent hymns available, many of which hitherto had been ignored. But it was not a complete book, nor indeed, did it claim to be. It was the need for a richer provision of hymnody more in line with traditional Catholicism which prompted the production of *The English Hymnal*, in 1906, edited by Percy Dearmer.

This latter publication is of particular interest as showing how difficult it is to devise a hymn book which is not to become the monopoly of some party, or special movement within the Church. From the more Catholic side the aim of *The English Hymnal* was as eclectic as that of *Worship Song*. The following words occur in the preface:

> *The English Hymnal* is a collection of the best hymns in the English language. . . . It is not a party book expressing this or that phase of negation or excess, but an attempt to combine in one volume the worthiest expressions of all that

N   193

lies within the Christian Creed, from those "ancient Fathers" who were the earliest hymn writers down to contemporary exponents of modern aspirations and ideals. . . .

Thus we have endeavoured to produce a book that shall suit the needs of learned and simple alike, and shall at the same time exhibit the characteristic virtue of hymnody—its witness, namely, to the fact that in the worship of God, Christians are drawn closer together as they are drawn more closely to the one Lord. In Christian song Churches have forgotten their quarrels and men have lost their limitations, because they have reached the higher ground where the soul is content to affirm and to adore. The hymns of Christendom show more clearly than anything else that there is even now such a thing as the unity of the Spirit.

The truth enunciated in the above should be beyond dispute. The aspiration to find in hymnody a common link with Christians of all the various Churches is entirely right. Its fulfilment is hindered by the persistent demand that a hymn shall be made the vehicle of a particular doctrine. It is the insistence on the *theological* hymn, or the nervous effort to detect the real, or imagined dogmatic bias latent in a hymn, that is the stumbling block. There is no evading the fact that the ambition of the compilers of *The English Hymnal* was not realised. To-day, the three major hymnals of the Anglican Church have acquired partizan associations, for to detect the green covers of *The English Hymnal* is ground for expecting a distinct Catholic emphasis in the church in which it is used, employing the accommodating word "Catholic" in a rather free and easy way. Again, the light blue of *Songs of Praise* promises a Liberal Evangelical, or somewhat Modernist outlook, while the decorous dark blue of *Hymns Ancient and Modern* usually suggests a firm resolve to tread the middle road, together also with a discreet decision not to demand too much of the congregation in the way of unfamiliar tunes!

The present variety, and to some extent rivalry, of hymnals in the Church of England, is a reflection of the conflicting types of thought to be found within this historic communion. Moreover, it suggests the well nigh impossible task of providing a book which shall be acceptable to all Christians, and so fulfil the aspiration of the compilers of *The English Hymnal*. There is at least one Anglican church at the present time (possibly unique) where *Worship Song* and *Hymns Ancient and Modern* are both in use. There is a resultant sense of increased scope inasmuch as the deficences of the one are supplied by the other, and the combination helps the congregation to appreciate better the two streams of hymnody, Anglican and Nonconformist, which meeting together in this way create a generous and varied river of song. It may be hoped it is a promise of future hymnals which will transcend the prejudice which until now has tended to limit and impoverish our store of praise and devotion.

At this stage it will be necessary to go back a little in point of time to indicate something of the background against which the modern Anglican hymn books appeared. It has already been observed that by the middle of the nineteenth century congregational hymn singing had taken firm hold on the Church of England, where it had been resisted for so long. The Evangelical section of this Church had been the first to encourage it, by admitting a generous number of Charles Wesley's hymns, and a smaller selection of Isaac Watts' verses, together with a goodly and increasing number written by Evangelical Anglicans. Then, as already described, the Tractarians adopted the practice in congregational worship, and this was rapidly encouraged by the wealth of material translation provided. In consequence of these developments numerous collections were produced for parochial use, until the appearance of the first edition of *Hymns Ancient and Modern* in 1861. By this date, so popular and widespread had hymn singing become in the hitherto reluctant Established Church that the number of hymn books had become well-nigh countless. Dr. Julian enumerates at least seventy-eight as having appeared, differing vastly in their degrees of merit, between 1820 and 1850. Many of the clergy who could afford it compiled collections for their own congregations, and often it was impossible to find two churches in a town using the same book. The singing, for the most part, was equally deplorable. The hymns, given out by the clerk, were mainly restricted to four verses, with the organist (where an organ existed) playing an interlude between each verse. In the hope of correcting such general confusion the Society for Promoting Christian Knowledge published a small collection in 1852, and three years later it was issued in an enlarged form as *Psalms and Hymns*, to which after the lapse of another eight years an appendix was added. But during this period there emerged the book which was destined to occupy the foremost place in Anglican hymnody. This was *Hymns Ancient and Modern*, first published in 1861, and followed by an appendix in 1868. But it was by no means certain at the time that this now popular compilation would win first place in Anglican usage. Other books of importance and merit appeared. One was *Church Hymns*, for which Canon John Ellerton was largely responsible, and another *The Church of England Hymn-Book*, compiled by Prebendary Godfrey Thring. These efforts are of little more than historic interest, except that both editors have left for our use hymns which have proved increasingly popular. Thring was the author of the familiar hymns *From the Eastern mountains, Fierce raged the tempest o'er the deep*, and the beautiful hymn for evening, *The radiant morn hath passed away*, while a number of other hymns by this gifted writer, although less known, are marked by the fine literary quality which is a conspicuous feature of Thring's verses. Canon John Ellerton ranks as a leading hymnologist of the English Church. In editing, revising, and translating he was one of the most potent influences in Anglican hymnody in the nineteenth century. In addition, his own hymns are some of the best in our present collections. One is the widely popular evening hymn, *The day Thou gavest, Lord, is ended*, while another of his evening hymns, *Saviour again to Thy dear name we raise*, is equally well known and treasured. His hymn for the morning, *This is the day of light*, is another example of his truly excellent work. A national hymn of outstanding merit by the same author is *Praise to our God whose bounteous hand*. He was equally gifted in the task of translation, and we have some choice hymns at our disposal from Ellerton's labours in this field. One of the finest is the hymn usually sung at the evening hour:

> O strength and stay upholding all creation,
> Who ever dost Thyself unmoved abide,
> Yet day by day the light in due gradation
> From hour to hour through all its changes guide.

Furthermore, Ellerton was a critic in the sphere of hymnody whose clear insight, sound values and informed judgment did much to raise the whole standard of Anglican hymnals. He shared with Thring a sensitive awareness of excellence, and both did much to discourage the merely showy and shoddy, and to impart to English hymnody a more refined and elevated standard.

The reason why a number of books competed for favour must be found in the party spirit which existed, and still persists, in the Church of England. For one section, *Hymns Ancient and Modern* was too 'Catholic', while for another it was not sufficiently so. To-day it represents the moderate outlook, but it was not always so regarded. Yet it forged ahead, although for a time *Church Hymns*, largely compiled by Ellerton, competed for favour. It appealed to the taste of great numbers of church people, including, as it did, not only Ellerton's splendid hymns, but others which have remained general favourites. These comprised the rousing stanzas of *Onward Christian Soldiers*, written by the Rev. S. Baring-Gould, for which Sir Arthur Sullivan contributed the marching-tune, "St. Gertrude" which fastidious modern choirs are prone to ban as being vulgar. Those who object to hymn and tune, as beneath the dignity of the Anglican service, should remember its origin. Anyhow, they were ingredients in the popularity of *Church Hymns*, and the persisting love for the hymns mentioned will explain it.

There is no need here to review much of the subsequent history of various Anglican hymnals, or to trace the growing ascendance of *Hymns Ancient and Modern*. The publication later of supplements, which now form part of the existing book, did much to widen the scope of this familiar hymnal, and to bring into its orbit a goodly number of excellent hymns, many of which deserve to be far more widely known than they are at present.

In this brief survey of a century of development in English hymnody, the important fact to observe is that over a long stretch of years, the differing schools of thought, and various parties in the Church, tended to foster and encourage hymns of a type favoured by their own votaries. Thus, the more Catholic section viewed with disfavour the hymns of Watts and Wesley, while, on the other hand, the Evangelicals approved the verses of these two writers, and for long tended to restrict their choice to them, rejecting the translations of the older hymns which began to appear and find favour in Catholic circles. It is against this background that we can understand the aspiration of Percy Dearmer and his co-workers to produce a further hymn book wide enough in its scope to meet the needs of both wings of the Church of England. Percy Dearmer is another name which must be added to the ranks of illustrious hymnologists represented in the century under review. He was a man of versatile and brilliant gifts; artist, poet, preacher, writer and social reformer, and a scholarly exponent of liturgical history. Many will remember his distinguished and original ministry at Primrose Hill, and later his influential work as Canon of Westminster, together with his fearless advocacy of social reform, in the work of the Christian Social Union. His reforming zeal was nowhere more in evidence than in his anxiety to improve still further the hymnody of the Anglican Church, and its congregational singing. He was as zealous in this as Ellerton and Thring had been in their own day. Dearmer had a wide outlook and eclectic sympathies, and was not one whose mind could be restricted within the prescribed limits of any party. The tribute he paid to Garrett Horder, already cited, found reflection in his own generous mind. His desire was to bring to the worship of God all that was best in hymns, ceremonial music and architecture. Most certainly this is an aspiration which must be shared by all who long to worship God in the beauty of holiness. The effort to realize this worthy end prompted Dearmer to bring to a new hymnody treasures from past and present; from all lands and climes. It may be that zeal in an effort so ambitious led sometimes to results which reflection will qualify, but beyond question his work will remain as one of the important landmarks in the evolution of English hymnody.

Dearmer's further efforts in the realm of hymnody led to the publication of *Songs of Praise* in 1925, and it has now taken its place among the standard hymnals of the Anglican Church, and is, indeed, finding increasing favour with the Free Churches, and is widely used in schools. This was the intention, expressed in the preface:

Songs of Praise is intended to be national, in the sense of including a full expression of that faith which is common to the English-speaking peoples to-day, both in the British Commonwealth and in the United States.

While, in the introduction to *Songs of Praise Discussed*, it is stated that the book is "for all the Churches . . . for the forward-looking people of every communion", again, the ideal has not been fully realized. The party spirit still persists. The book has been attacked, sometimes in high places, from both Evangelical and Catholic quarters. It is not flawless. Amendments and revisions have been made in certain hymns, together with omission of verses, which may easily be made ground for dispute. But the book is a further sign of the movement towards a hymnody that will embrace the thought and worship of Christians in all communions, and no collection of hymns in the future can be regarded as satisfactory which does not seek the same comprehensive goal. To quote again from the above *Introduction*:

We are reaching the time when denominational hymn books will be recognized as an anachronism and a hindrance to the unity of the Spirit. Why should we thus emphasise and perpetuate our peculiarities? The hymns themselves show how catholic we have become in spite of ourselves . . . . the ideal for all the Churches is to use the same books, so that the distinction will not be between one denomination and another, but merely the still natural as inevitable one between those who are lingering behind, and those who go forward.

Dearmer himself wrote a number of hymns, some of real distinction, twenty-three of which find inclusion in *Songs of Praise*. The book is mentioned here, not in order to give it detailed study, which has already been fully done in *Songs of Praise Discussed*, but because it is a sign of the times. It indicates and incorporates the conspicuous features of modern hymnody, namely, the more generous use of verses written originally as poems, but not as hymns; the transformation in the character of hymns written for children; the substantial proportion of American hymns, and the prominence given to hymns relating to social reform and what might be called Christian humanism. Most significant of all is the effort to transcend denominational and sectarian limitations. It is a cause for some astonishment that the various denominations should continue to issue books bearing their own distinctive labels, yet including in large measure the same hymns. It seems a tedious desire to perpetuate denominational names. Here, at least, the new hymnody points a better way.

Note. Since this book was prepared for the press a new edition of *Hymns Ancient and Modern* has been published (April 1950). It should be understood that the references contained here relate to the 1916 edition, which may remain in widespread use for a considerable period.

12

Hymns for Children

WHEN comparing modern English hymn books with those in use half a century ago, no change is more striking than the transformation wrought in the section devoted to children's hymns. It is, in fact, little short of a revolutionary change. When we look at the older hymnals it is well nigh beyond belief that some of the sentiments and dogmas expressed could have been imposed on children, and it is clear that no serious effort was made to provide them with suitable hymns. In earlier pages a few examples from Puritan sources have already been quoted, and also the fact was mentioned that neither Isaac Watts, nor Charles Wesley, masters of English hymnody as they were, have left much of value for the use of children in worship. To-day it is astonishing to think of the author of *Our God, our help in ages past* writing for a child such lines as the following:

> What if the Lord grow wroth, and swear,
> While I refuse to read and pray,
> That He'll refuse to lend an ear
> To all my groans another day?
> What if His dreadful anger burn
> While I refuse His offered grace,
> And all His love to anger turn,
> And strike me dead upon the place?
> 'Tis dangerous to provoke a God!
> His power and vengeance none can tell:
> One stroke of His almighty rod
> Shall send young sinners quick to hell.

It seems a persistent weakness of this older type of children's verse that although the author, when writing for adults, could rise into more noble and spacious realms of imagination and poetry, when writing for children the whole outlook was cramped and twisted by the harsh, unlovely theology of the period.

At moments Watts could do better. There is wholesome instruction and sound sentiment in the following:

> Should I e'er be rich or great,
>   Others shall partake my goodness,
> I'll supply the poor with meat,
>   Never showing scorn nor rudeness.
>
> Where I see the blind or lame,
>   Deaf or dumb, I'll kindly treat them . . .

And also when he turns the young eyes to nature:

> Lord, how Thy wonders are displayed,
>   Where'er I turn mine eyes . . .
>
> There's not a plant or flower below,
>   But makes Thy glories known.

There was a glimpse, here, of better lines of appeal, like a ray of light breaking through a sky marked for the most part by sombre gloom. Fear and terror were the great instructors of youth. A children's hymn book in the Middle Ages meant a collection of the usual office hymns and sequences, with notes and helps in construing—a school book for the choristers' schools, and so designed only for the boys. One such is preserved in a Cheshire church, with a grim frontispiece representing three little boys seated on a low bench before a stern ecclesiastic, who wields a formidable birch-rod—a good illustration of the method then in vogue of teaching a child to be good! For the most part one looks in vain for hymns in this early period which would now serve the needs of young people.

Even in some of the standard hymnals of our own day there are queer survivals, and the "children's section" still calls for revision and pruning. Thus *Hymns Ancient and Modern* continues to offer the following verses:

> Within the churchyard, side by side,
>   Are many long low graves;
> And some have stones set over them,
>   On some the green grass waves.
>
> Full many a little Christian child,
>   Woman, and man, lies there;
> And we pass near them every time
>   When we go in to prayer.
>
> They cannot hear our footsteps come,
>   They do not see us pass;
> They cannot feel the warm bright sun
>   That shines upon the grass.
>
> They do not hear when the great bell
>   Is ringing overhead;
> They cannot rise and come to Church
>   With us, for they are dead.
>
> But we believe a day shall come
>   When all the dead will rise,
> When they who sleep down in the grave
>   Will ope again their eyes.

Apart from the misleading thought quoted in the last two lines of the above, the morbidity of the verses is clearly quite unsuitable for either children or adults. It is only fair to add that this hymn, written by Mrs. Alexander in the middle of the nineteenth century, is not a good example of her gift as a writer of hymns. She was the author of many excellent verses including two other hymns for children which remain deservedly popular—namely, *Once in royal David's city* and *All things bright and beautiful.*

But signs of the new era in children's hymnody began to appear in the early part of the last century. An instance of this is the delightful hymn *I think when I read that sweet story of old*. Jemima Luke wrote it in a stage coach, for use in a village school near Bath, where her father resided. It is singular that the writer of such a fine hymn does not appear to have attempted others. Another splendid hymn for children, written in the middle of the century, was the work of a Presbyterian, James Drummond Burns. It is the well known, and ever popular hymn:

> Hushed was the evening hymn
> The temple courts were dark;
> The lamp was burning dim
> Before the sacred ark;
> When suddenly a Voice Divine
> Rang through the silence of the shrine.

Another admirable example of a hymn for the young is provided by Emily Miller's verses; an instance of the change of outlook in children's hymnody which marked the second half of the last century.

> I love to hear the story
>   Which angel voices tell,
> How once the King of glory
>   Came down on earth to dwell.
> I am both weak and sinful,
>   But this I surely know,
> The Lord came down to save me,
>   Because He loved me so.

> I'm glad my blessed Saviour
>   Was once a child like me,
> To show how pure and holy
>   His little ones might be:
> And if I try to follow
>   His footsteps here below,
> He never will forsake me,
>   Because he loves me so.

To sing His love and mercy
My sweetest songs I'll raise;
And though I cannot see Him
I know He hears my praise;
For He has kindly promised
That even I may go
To sing among His angels,
Because He loves me so.

A great improvement this, and one notes the emphasis placed upon the divine love, rather than the appeal to fear and terror. Another pioneer in creating the better type of children's hymns, in the same later Victorian period, was Benjamin Waugh. A lover of children, he did much for their protection. The provision of a good hymn for children demands a combination of the concrete and abstract in thought. Naturally, the child mind grasps the concrete, but religious thought must involve a measure of the abstract. The blend of the two is most happily illustrated in Benjamin Waugh's beautiful hymn, which should be much more widely known:

Where is Jesus, little children?
Is He up in Heaven?
Has God taken back the present
Which of old was given?

Where is Jesus, little children?
Is He in a book?
Has He ceased to talk to people,
And on them to look?

Where is Jesus, little children?
With us evermore
He is here, and we may find Him
Shut within this door.

Jesus is a lovely spirit,
Lowly, pure and kind;
Feeling in the hearts of people,
Thinking in their mind.

Self-forgetting, gentle mercy,
  Love that will not die,
These reveal the heart of Jesus,
  Tell us He is nigh.

Shut within the souls of children,
  Jesus makes His home;
Where the heart has heard him knocking,
  And has bid Him come.

Jesus, make in us Thy dwelling;
  Come with us to live;
And to each and all our doings
  Thy dear beauty give.

Another conspicuous example of the new era in hymns for the young, is the fine hymn *The wise may bring their learning*, which appeared first in the *Congregational Church Hymnal*, in 1887, by an unknown author. It will be marked how a stronger and more healthy note begins to emerge. It is a hymn phrased in a manner designed to touch the life and thought of the average child:

The wise may bring their learning,
  The rich may bring their wealth,
And some may bring their greatness,
  And some their strength and health:
We, too, would bring our treasures
  To offer to the King;
We have no wealth or learning—
  What shall we children bring?

We'll bring the many duties
  We have to do each day;
We'll try our best to please Him,
  At home, at school, at play:
And better are these treasures
  To offer to our King
Than richer gifts without them;
  Yet these a child may bring.

We'll bring Him hearts that love Him,
  We'll bring Him thankful praise,
And young souls meekly striving
  To walk in holy ways.
And these shall be the treasures
  We offer to the King,
And these are gifts that even
  The poorest child may bring.

It seems strange that many writers of children's hymns appear to have had what one can only term 'the lamb obsession'. 'Lambs' appear, over and over again, while "little lambkin" is not unknown, as the title employed for the child in the language of worship. It is extremely doubtful if any child finds the term agreeable. In the same way, it was long before hymns, deliberately written for the young, could be cleared of the constant, and quite untrue suggestion, that the child's constant concern was with the thought of heaven and the life hereafter. The persistence of these features has tended to impair many otherwise good hymns, and a glance at popular hymnals still in use will confirm this criticism. It is, therefore, worth noting one or two examples of the better movement in juvenile hymnody, in addition to the earlier types above cited, which are admirable in their sober strength, and yet ring with beauty and sincerity of a quality which must appeal to all children.

One such example is the splendid modern version of the Franciscan Canticle of the Creatures, written by the Reverend W. H. Draper, when rector of a Yorkshire parish, for a Whitsuntide festival of school children at Leeds. It is a glorious hymn of worship for both young people and adults, and an outstanding instance of the more promising type of hymn for the young:

All creatures of our God and King,
Lift up your voice and with us sing
  Alleluya, alleluya!

Thou burning sun with golden beam,
Thou silver moon with softer gleam:
   O praise Him, O praise Him,
   Alleluya, alleluya, alleluya!

Thou rushing wind that art so strong,
Ye clouds that sail in heaven along,
  O praise Him, alleluya!
Thou rising morn, in praise rejoice,
Ye lights of evening, find a voice:
   O praise Him, etc.

Thou flowing water, pure and clear,
Make music for thy Lord to hear,
  Alleluya, alleluya!
Thou fire so masterful and bright,
That givest man both warmth and light:
   O praise Him, etc.

Dear mother earth, who day by day
Unfoldest blessings on our way,
  O praise Him, alleluya!
The flowers and fruits that in thee grow,
Let them His glory also show.
   O praise Him, etc.

And all ye men of tender heart,
Forgiving others, take your part,
  O sing ye, alleluya!
Ye who long pain and sorrow bear,
Praise God and on him cast your care:
   O praise Him, etc.

And thou most kind and gentle death,
Waiting to hush our latest breath,
  O praise Him, alleluya!
Thou leadest home the child of God,
And Christ our Lord the way hath trod:
   O praise Him, etc.

Let all things their Creator bless,
And worship Him in humbleness,
    O praise Him, alleluya!
Praise, praise the Father, praise the Son,
And praise the Spirit, Three in One.
    O praise Him, etc.

The above hymn is of value, also, in indicating the wisdom of reaching the mind of the child through the appeal to Nature. It is the abiding appeal of the Franciscan Canticle, as it is of another great hymn of the Church, the *Benedicite*.

A further illustration is a delightful little hymn based on the toil of the fisherman. It is suggestive of another line of thought, fertile in stimulating the imagination of the child, based on the everyday work of the world, and helping to link vividly life and worship. The following hymn would certainly appeal to children in our fishing-ports, but it is of value to the inland child, reminding him of the toil of those who go down to the sea in ships—an activity always stirring to the young imagination:

When lamps are lighted in the town,
    The boats sail out to sea;
The fishers watch when night comes down,
    They work for you and me.

We little children go to rest;
    Before we sleep, we pray
That God will bless the fishermen
    And bring them back at day.

The boats come in at early dawn,
    When children wake in bed;
Upon the beach the boats are drawn,
    And all the nets are spread.

God hath watched o'er the fishermen
    Far on the deep dark sea,
And brought them safely home again,
    Where they are glad to be.

An example of a happy blend of the concrete and abstract in thought is found in the following modern hymn by Percy Dearmer. It merits inclusion with the best of recent hymns written for the young; though equally suitable for older folk:

> Jesus, good above all other,
> Gentle child of gentle mother,
> In a stable born our brother,
>   Give us grace to persevere.
>
> Jesus, cradled in a manger,
> For us facing every danger,
> Living as a homeless stranger,
>   Make we Thee our King most dear.
>
> Jesus, for Thy people dying,
> Risen Master, death defying,
> Lord in heaven, Thy grace supplying,
>   Keep us to Thy presence near.
>
> Jesus, who our sorrows bearest,
> All our thoughts and hopes Thou sharest,
> Thou to man the truth declarest;
>   Help us all Thy truth to hear.
>
> Lord, in all our doings guide us;
> Pride and hate shall ne'er divide us;
> We'll go on with Thee beside us;
>   And with joy we'll persevere!

Here, with a fine economy of expression is included the historic episodes in our Lord's life, resurrection and ascension, in relation to our own earthly need and experience. The hymn is fortunate in being linked with a tune of beautiful cadence; "Quem pastores laudavere", a version by Vaughan Williams of a German carol melody.

The modern transformation wrought in children's hymnody has received enormous impetus by the greater care given to it in our public schools, and in education generally. Children's hymnals now form a worthy section of the Church's order of worship, and in them will be found much that is best in modern hymn-writing. There is no excuse to-day for careless and unsuitable choice of hymns for young people. It is certain that no such carelessness can be excused, for two things now, and in the future, of the most vital influence in training the child in worship, are the hymn and the film. Productive difficulties may still hamper the efficient use of the latter in the religious teaching of children (though vastly more might be done) but with a wealth of fine material at our disposal there is no reason to be content with anything shoddy in the hymnody we offer children. Much more space could be given to worthy examples of hymns of the present era, but one final instance shall stand as representing the quality that is available. It is a splendid hymn, written by a distinguished Congregational minister, the Reverend Charter Piggott:

> In our work and in our play,
>   Jesus be Thou ever near;
> Guarding, guiding all the day,
>   Keep us in Thy presence dear.

> Thou, who at Thy mother's knee
>   Learned to hearken and obey,
> Then, work done, ran happily
>   With the children to their play;

> And by Joseph's bench did stand,
>   Holding his edged tools, as he
> Guiding them with skilful hand,
>   Made a carpenter of thee.

> Help us, that with eager mind
>   We may learn both fact and rule,
> Patient, diligent and kind
>   In the comradeship of school.

211

Help us, too, in sport and game
  Gallantly to play our part;
Win or lose, to keep the same
  Dauntless spirit and brave heart.

May we grow like Him in grace,
  True in mind and pure of soul,
Meeting life with steadfast face,
  Run its race and reach the goal.

13

Poets' Corner

AN important feature marking the development of modern hymnody is the increasing use made of verses from the poets. It is the growing recognition that although not all poems are hymns, a good hymn should be true poetry. For long failure to perceive this led to the production of dreadful doggerel which one regrets found place in hymnals. That the accomplished religious poets of the seventeenth century did not employ their gift in the production of worthy hymns is explained by the exclusion of hymns from public worship by both the Established Church and the dissenting communities. It is certain that the inspired religious poets of the period, Donne, Vaughan, Traherne, Herbert, and others, would have given to the hymnody of the Church gems of enduring value. It has been left for later compilers to survey this rich mine of poetry, and to take from it verses which now form some of our choicest hymns.

Reference has been made to John Donne in an earlier chapter, together with a reproduction of his moving verses, *Wilt Thou forgive that sin where I begun.* George Herbert stands out as the best-known religious poet of the time, and one whose beautiful life and ministry, although brief, have left a fragrance and power that it is safe to predict will not diminish. At least seven hymns, derived from Herbert's poems, have found a welcome place in more recent hymnals. One of the best known is *Teach me, my God and King,* and another, now close in favour, is the inspiring *Let all the world in every corner sing*. Deserving to be more widely known and used is the brief but beautiful hymn:

> Come, my way, my truth, my life;
>   Such a way as gives us breath,
> Such a truth as ends all strife,
>   Such a life as killeth death.
>
> Come, my light, my feast, my strength;
>   Such a light as shows a feast,
> Such a feast as mends in length,
>   Such a strength as makes his guest.
>
> Come my joy, my love, my heart;
>   Such a joy as none can move,
> Such a love as none can part,
>   Such a heart as joys in love.

Another hymn of Herbert's, exquisite in thought and expression is the following:

> Sweet day, so cool, so calm, so bright,
>   The bridal of the earth and sky,
> The dew shall weep thy fall to-night;
>   For thou must die.
>
> Sweet rose, whose hue, angry and brave,
>   Bids the rash gazer wipe his eye,
> Thy root is ever in its grave,
>   And thou must die.
>
> Sweet spring, full of sweet days and roses,
>   A box where sweets compacted lie,
> My music shows you have your closes,
>   And all must die.
>
> Only a sweet and virtuous soul,
>   Like seasoned timber, never gives;
> But, though the whole world turn to coal,
>   Then chiefly lives.

A moment's reflection on these lines will indicate their poetic quality. Each word, and each line is made to yield suggestion clothed in delicate beauty of thought.

A very different personality from George Herbert, but one whose humanity and whimsical humour still reach to us across the years, was Robert Herrick, the parson of the little Devon parish of Dean Prior. We are told that this country parson never lost his nostalgia for the London he loved, but his delightful poems are fragrant with the air of the countryside, and reflect its sights and sounds. He was an original man. We are told that on one occasion when his congregation was very inattentive he threw his sermon at their heads. He used his poetry to instruct his little flock, and sometimes made epigrams on Master Midge, or Prickles, or Mistress Bridget, or other folk who troubled him. During the Commonwealth he was ejected from his living, and lived in Westminster until the Restoration, when he was reinstated in his Devon parish, where it is good to know he lived to be eighty-three, and spent the evening of his days in quietness and peace. He is now rightly regarded as one of the greatest of English lyric poets. Those who know Herrick's verses will recall that they are by no means confined to religious themes. He wrote quaint and dainty love lyrics, and delightful nature poems. But there was more serious material also. His *Noble Numbers*, published in 1647, contained some hymns which were sung, so it is said, before the first Charles in Whitehall. There is a gentle spirit expressed in the hymn *In the hour of my distress*.

> In the hour of my distress,
> When temptations me oppress,
> And when I my sins confess,
>   Sweet Spirit, comfort me.
>
> When I lie within my bed,
> Sick in heart, and sick in head,
> And with doubts discomforted,
>   Sweet Spirit, comfort me.

When the house doth sigh and weep,
And the world is drowned in sleep,
Yet mine eyes the watch do keep,
Sweet Spirit, comfort me.

When God knows I'm tossed about,
Either with despair or doubt,
Yet before the glass be out,
Sweet Spirit, comfort me.

When the tempter me pursu'th
With the sins of all my youth,
And condemns me for untruth,
Sweet Spirit, comfort me.

When the judgment is revealed,
And that opened which was sealed;
When to Thee I have appealed,
Sweet Spirit, comfort me.

Two verses are, however, omitted from the published versions of this hymn, in deference rightly to the noble profession of medicine:

When the artless doctor sees
No one hope, but of his fees,
And his skill runs on the lees,
Sweet Spirit, comfort me.

When his potion and his pill
Has, or none, or little skill,
Meet for nothing but to kill,
Sweet Spirit, comfort me.

The major difficulty with Herrick's poetry, as with much other religious verse, is that it was written in a metre not suited to hymnic use. Had there been a demand for hymns

216

in his day, we may be sure that Herrick would have been one
of the foremost writers. We can imagine the inspired verse
which would have come from a pen that could write such
lines as:

> We see Him come, and know Him ours,
> Who, with His sunshine and His showers,
> Turns all the patient ground to flowers.

In the same century we meet the inspired verses of Henry
Vaughan, the Welsh physician, and one of the greatest meta-
physical poets of the period. It is remarkable that his poems
were practically forgotten for two centuries, until Henry
Francis Lyte (author of *Abide with me*) edited an edition of
Vaughan's works in 1847. One of the poems which has found
a place in several modern hymnals is the now familiar hymn
My soul, there is a country:

> My soul, there is a country
>   Far beyond the stars,
> Where stands a winged sentry
>   All skilful in the wars:
>
> There above noise, and danger,
>   Sweet peace sits crowned with smiles,
> And one born in a manger
>   Commands the beauteous files.
>
> He is thy gracious friend,
>   And—O my soul, awake!—
> Did in pure love descend,
>   To die here for thy sake.
>
> If thou canst get but thither,
>   There grows the flower of peace,
> The rose that cannot wither,
>   Thy fortress and thy ease.

Leave then thy foolish ranges,
    For none can thee secure
But one, who never changes,
    Thy God, thy life, thy cure.

The depth and power of Vaughan's sublime verse find striking expression in another hymn, less known, but one of the finest. It is certain that the profound feeling of the spirit in contemplation of the life beyond death can never find more luminous utterance:

They are all gone into the world of light,
    And I alone sit lingering here;
Their very memory is fair and bright,
    And my sad thoughts doth clear.

I see them walking in an air of glory,
    Whose light doth trample on my days;
My days, which are at best but dull and hoary,
    Mere glimmering and decays.

Dear beauteous death! the jewel of the just,
    Shining nowhere but in the dark;
What mysteries do lie beyond thy dust,
    Could man outlook that mark.

And yet as angels in some brighter dreams
    Call to the soul when man doth sleep;
So some strange thoughts transcend our wonted
    And into glory peep.   [themes,

O Father of eternal life, and all
    Created glories under Thee,
Resume Thy Spirit from this world of thrall
    Into true liberty.

Another member of this famous group of poets, of whom Isaak Walton was the human link and friendly centre, was

218

Sir Henry Wotton. A little poem, marked by delightful strength and simplicity, is the following, which has rightly found place in most of our hymnals at the present time. It breathes a spirit of personal integrity and virility which has a pertinent message for an age when true individuality is threatened by mass-pressure:

> How happy is he born and taught,
>   That serveth not another's will;
> Whose armour is his honest thought,
>   And simple truth his utmost skill;
>
> Whose passions not his masters are;
>   Whose soul is still prepared for death,
> Untied unto the world by care
>   Of public fame or private breath;
>
> Who God doth late and early pray
>   More of his grace than goods to lend;
> And walks with man from day to day
>   As with a brother and a friend.
>
> This man is freed from servile bands
>   Of hope to rise or fear to fall;
> Lord of himself, though not of lands;
>   And having nothing, yet hath all.

The House of Commons is not, normally, an emotional assembly, but it was rarely and deeply moved when it listened to Mr. Asquith's recital of these lines, in his oration of tribute at the time of Sir Henry Campbell-Bannerman's decease. The poem is one of the finest portraits in words of a true gentleman. Although the critic may rightly hold that it is not strictly a hymn, yet we feel it is essentially right that it should be so employed.

Mention has been made already of others belonging to the same period to whom we owe hymns of abiding merit. Ken has been noted, and also Richard Baxter. It is in the nineteenth century we find the source of the next group of examples. The eighteenth century offers little material in this field, not because it was deficient in religious verse, but because it marked the rise of hymnody proper, and the great creative work of Watts and the Wesleys. One poet of this century, who wrote hymns as distinct from his poetical works, was William Cowper, whose contributions to the *Olney Hymns* have been described. Coleridge links the eighteenth and nineteenth centuries, and Geoffrey Dearmer has made a modern adaptation of some lines from *The Ancient Mariner*, which form the following delightful hymn:

> O sweeter than the marriage-feast,
>   'Tis sweeter far to me,
> To walk together to the kirk
>   With a goodly company;
>
> To walk together to the kirk,
>   And all together pray:
> Old men and babes and loving friends
>   And youths and maidens gay.
>
> He prayeth well, who loveth well
>   Both man and bird and beast;
> And he that loveth all God made
>   That man he prayeth best.
>
> He prayeth best, who loveth best
>   All things both great and small;
> For the dear God who loveth us
>   He made and loveth all.

Looking at the nineteenth century, which was an age of great poets, it will be recognized that few of them wrote hymns. The verses which now appear linked with their names are, for the most part, derived from the poems. This absence of hymn writing on their part was not due to a lack of Christian faith and conviction. Wordsworth, Tennyson, and Browning were

all gifted with deep spiritual insight, and informed by a profound faith in God and His providence. In these troubled,
confused times we can return to their outlook and message
with unfailing advantage. Tennyson seems to have felt the
special difficulty of hymn writing, for not long before the end
of his life the poet remarked to Dr. Warren, President of
Magdalen: "A good hymn is the most difficult thing in the
world to write. In a good hymn you have to be commonplace
and poetical. The moment you cease to be commonplace and
put in any expression at all out of the common, it ceases to be
a hymn". With all deference to the opinion of a great poet,
this is a wrong view, but as Dr. Dearmer rightly said: "That
was a Victorian idea; and it partly accounts for the bad
hymnody of the time". Yet Tennyson, if he did not write
hymns, provided poetry from which have been gleaned verses
happily contained in our present hymnals, and certain to find
an abiding place in the future. A beautiful example is the
hymn:

> Sunset and evening star,
>   And one clear call for me!
> And may there be no moaning of the bar,
>   When I put out to sea.
>
> But such a tide as moving seems asleep,
>   Too full for sound and foam,
> When that which drew from out the boundless
>   Turns again home.   [deep
>
> Twilight and evening bell,
>   And after that the dark!
> And may there be no sadness of farewell,
>   When I embark;
>
> For though from out our bourne of time and place
>   The flood may bear me far,
> I hope to see my Pilot face to face
>   When I have crost the bar.

These verses are now always printed at the end of the collected poems, and concerning them Tennyson's son wrote:

Crossing the Bar was written in my Father's eighty-first year, on a day in October [1889] when we came from Aldworth to Farringford [the home of Tennyson in the Isle of Wight]. Before reaching Farringford he had the moaning of the bar in his mind, and after dinner he showed me this poem written out. I said 'That is the crown of your life's work.' He answered; 'It came in a moment.' He explained the 'Pilot' as 'that Divine and Unseen who is always guiding us.' . . . A few days before my father's end [1892] he said to me, 'Mind you put *Crossing the Bar* at the end of all my poems.'

It is interesting to recall how the district of the Solent, and the Isle of Wight, has suggested more than one famous hymn. Isaac Watts found in the distant vista from his home in Southampton, the inspiration for the thoughts contained in his familiar hymn *There is a land of pure delight*, while it was the spectacle of the wide expanse of starlit sky over the Island, seen from his manse in Newport, that gave to the Congregational minister, Dr. Thomas Binney, the thoughts expressed in his noble hymn:

> Eternal Light! Eternal Light!
>   How pure the soul must be,
> When, placed within Thy searching sight
> It shrinks not, but, with calm delight
>   Can live, and look on Thee!

Tennyson's masterpiece, *In Memoriam*, is the source of two hymns which have become increasingly used in recent years; the opening stanzas, beginning "Strong Son of God, immortal Love", and the verses relating to the dawn of the New Year, "Ring-out, wild bells, to the wild sky." A stanza in the former merits reflection here, as it is indicative of the modern spirit, which finds such eloquent expression in the whole of this magnificent poem, and is the key to its understanding. This is the spirit created by the conflict of faith with doubt; the struggle of the human soul to find certitude beyond the dissolving forms and symbols of changing types of thought. It is mirrored in the lines:

> We have but faith: we cannot know;
> For knowledge is of things we see;
> And yet we trust it comes from Thee;
> A beam in darkness: let it grow.

> Let knowledge grow from more to more,
> But more of reverence in us dwell;
> That mind and soul, according well,
> May make one music as before.

This is the definite accent of our modern era. It is a great change from the confidence that rings in the jubilant hymns of Isaac Watts, and the glowing affirmations of Charles Wesley. The poetry of the nineteenth century which has formed the basis of some truly beautiful modern hymns, reflects a faith won through conflict, a wistful longing for fuller light. Two other examples serve to make this clear. One is the very lovely hymn *And didst Thou love the race that loved not Thee?* It is not nearly as well known as it should be, although it appeared in the *Congregational Church Hymnal* as early as 1887. It is from the poems of Jean Ingelow, first published in 1860. In addition to being the author of poetry of genuine distinction, she was also a novelist and writer of fairy tales. A poem entitled *The Love of Christ* provides the verses which constitute the following hymn:

> And didst Thou love the race that loved not Thee?
> And did Thou take to heaven a human brow?
> Dost plead with man's voice by the marvellous sea?
> Art Thou his kinsman now?

O God, O kinsman loved, but not enough,
 O Man, with eyes majestic after death,
Whose feet have toiled along our pathways rough,
 Whose lips drawn human breath:

By that one likeness which is ours and Thine,
 By that one nature which doth hold us kin,
By that high heaven, where, sinless, Thou dost shine
 To draw us sinners in:

By that last silence in the judgment hall,
 By long foreknowledge of the deadly tree,
By darkness, by the wormwood and the gall,
 I pray Thee visit me.

Come, lest this heart should, cold and cast away,
 Die ere the guest adored she entertain:
Lest eyes which never saw Thine earthly day
 Should miss Thy heavenly reign.

For yet further example mention must be made of verses by Francis Turner Palgrave, compiler of the famous anthology of poetry, *The Golden Treasury*. Palgrave was for a while Gladstone's secretary, following which he held several important educational appointments, and became Professor of Poetry at Oxford in 1885. The following hymn has a note of wistful intensity of longing, expressive of the mood of the age:

Thou say'st, 'Take up thy cross,
 O man, and follow Me';
The night is black, the feet are slack,
 Yet we would follow Thee.

But, O dear Lord, we cry,
 That we Thy face could see!
Thy blessed face one moment's space—
 Then might we follow Thee.

Dim tracts of time divide
Those golden days from me;
Thy voice comes strange o'er years of change;
How can we follow Thee?

Comes faint and far Thy voice
From vales of Galilee;
Thy vision fades in ancient shades;
How should we follow Thee?

O heavy cross of faith
In what we cannot see!
As once of yore Thyself restore
And help to follow Thee!

Ah, sense-bound heart and blind
Is nought but what we see?
Can time undo what once was true?
Can we not follow Thee?

If not as once Thou cam'st
In true humanity,
Come yet as guest within the breast
That burns to follow Thee.

Within our heart of hearts
In nearest nearness be;
Set up Thy throne within Thine own:
Go, Lord: we follow Thee.

Mark in the above lines how the wistful longing and struggling faith emerge in the resolute and active decision of the
last line: "Go, Lord: we follow Thee". The religious mood
of the changing century is here. Faith is present, but it is a
faith that has to be won through struggle.

One of the minor poets of the century was Dorothy Frances
Gurney, who published two volumes of her works, and wrote
one hymn, which has become most popular for use at

weddings: *O perfect Love, all human thought transcending*. It is interesting to recall that she was also the writer of a delightful song which has grown in favour, containing the lines:

> The kiss of the sun for pardon,
> The song of the birds for mirth,
> One is nearer God's heart in a garden,
> Than anywhere else on earth.

The verses were composed after viewing the gardens of Hammerfield, Penshurst, Kent. She wrote it in the visitors' book.

The use of poems or selections from them as hymns is a task not without its own peculiar limitations. One essential feature of a hymn is that it shall have a metre which is singable. While there is no need to construct every hymn within the strictly limited metres of former days, yet it is clear that some regard must be paid to metrical form if it is likely to make a suitable hymn. The zeal for employing as hymns the devotional thought enshrined in much of our poetry is a marked and admirable feature of *Songs of Praise*. In this respect the book has set an example which is bound to influence the compilers of all future hymnals. But one feels that at times the zeal has been excessive, and the metrical limitation has occasionally been ignored. Added to this, it is doubtful if the material is always of a nature appropriate to congregational worship. Thus it is not easy to employ the following (contained in *Songs of Praise*) for congregational use: It is Pippa's song, from Browning's *Pippa Passes*:

> The year's at the spring,
> And day's at the morn;
> Morning's at seven;
> The hill-side's dew pearled;
> The lark's on the wing;
> The snail's on the thorn;
> God's in His heaven—
> All's right with the world.

226

The most ardent students of Browning will undoubtedly admit that, apart from the unusual and difficult metre of much of his verse, his complex and intensely condensed thought calls for quiet, reflective reading, and is by no means suitable for hymnody. Nothing but excessive zeal could have induced the compilers to include as a hymn in *Songs of Praise* the verses of Browning from *Rabbi Ben Ezra*, beginning:

> Then welcome each rebuff
> That turns earth's smoothness rough,
> Each sting that bids nor sit nor stand but go!
> Be our joy three parts pain!
> Strive and hold cheap the strain;
> Learn, nor account the pang; dare, never grudge the
> [throe.

> Yet gifts should prove their use;
> I own the past profuse
> Of power each side, perfection every turn:
> Eyes, ears took in their dole,
> Brain treasured up the whole;
> Should not the heart beat once 'How good to live and
> [learn!'

Magnificent as a poem, it is plainly unsuitable as a hymn. The same must be said of the use as a hymn of Shakespeare's sonnet, *Poor Soul, the centre of my sinful earth*. These instances should once more point the truth that while every hymn should be a poem, every poem is not a hymn, and, for congregational singing, at least, the distinction must be kept clear.

One conspicuous triumph is found in the use of Blake's *Jerusalem*, where a poem has become one of the most popular modern hymns. This is in large measure due to Sir Hubert Parry's inspired tune, which was written on the suggestion of Dr. Robert Bridges, and given to Sir Walford Davies, when it quickly became widely used and appreciated. Equally happy, too, has been the inclusion as a hymn of another of Blake's poems—*The Divine Image*, from *Songs of Innocence*:

To Mercy, Pity, Peace and Love
  All pray in their distress,
And to these virtues of delight
  Return their thankfulness.

For Mercy, Pity, Peace and Love
  Is God our Father dear;
And Mercy, Pity, Peace and Love
  Is Man, his child and care.

For Mercy has a human heart,
  Pity, a human face,
And Love, the human form divine,
  And Peace, the human dress.

Then every man, of every clime,
  That prays in his distress,
Prays to the human form divine,
  Love, Mercy, Pity, Peace.

Another welcome addition to our modern collection of
hymns derived from poetic sources, is George Macdonald's
They all were looking for a king. There are three short verses of
rare beauty and simplicity:

They all were looking for a king
  To slay their foes, and lift them high:
Thou cam'st a little baby thing
  That made a woman cry.

O Son of Man, to right my lot
  Nought by Thy presence can avail;
Yet on the road Thy wheels are not,
  Nor on the sea Thy sail!

My fancied ways why should'st Thou heed?
  Thou com'st down Thine own secret stair;
Com'st down to answer all my need,
  Yea, every bygone prayer.

A little jewel of poetry, in a few brief lines, is Matthew Arnold's *Calm Soul of all things*, which, thanks again to Garrett Horder, is happily included as a hymn in *Worship Song*. It is strange that it has not found a place in any other modern hymnal, an omission which it may be hoped will be rectified in future editions.

Matthew Arnold wrote the verses while resting in the quiet beauty of Kensington Gardens, impressed by the sudden hush so closely adjacent to the noise and bustle of London's traffic:

> Calm Soul of all things! make it mine
> To feel, amid the city's jar,
> That there abides a peace of Thine
> Man did not make, and cannot mar!
>
> The will to neither strive nor cry,
> The power to feel with others give!
> Calm, calm me more! nor let me die
> Before I have begun to live.

Possibly no hymn by a modern English poet is better known, or used more frequently than Kipling's famous Recessional, *God of our fathers, known of old*, written for Queen Victoria's Diamond Jubilee in 1897. It is of interest to observe that Kipling corrected a proof of this hymn, submitted to him by Garrett Horder, by deleting the term "National" in relation to its use, and insisting on "Recessional", that is, a hymn to be sung by clergy and choir when leaving the church.

A modern, and most highly gifted poet, who has done unique and creative work for English hymnody, is Robert Bridges. No reference to the influence of the poets in this sphere could be complete without generous tribute to his work. In 1899 he published his *Yattendon Hymnal*, containing "100 hymns with their music, chosen for a village choir". It was an ambitious venture, far ahead of its time. In style and production, as well as in contents, it was a work of distinction. Dr. Bridges, with both a sensitive ear and poetic genius, grasped the sound principle that there is an intimate and real

NATIONAL HYMN.

1240 *"I have trodden the wine-press alone."*—Isa. lxiii. 3. Irr.

m Mine eyes have seen the glory of the
  coming of the Lord :
  He is trampling out the vintage where
  the grapes of wrath are stored ;
f He hath loosed the fatal lightning of His
  terrible, swift sword :
  His truth is marching on.

He hath sounded forth the trumpet that
  shall never call retreat ;
m He is sifting out the hearts of men before His judgment seat :
  Oh, be swift, my soul! to answer Him ;
  be jubilant, my feet !
f Our God is marching on.

p In the beauty of the lilies Christ was
  born, across the sea,
m With a glory in His bosom that trans-
  figures you and me :
p As He died to make men holy, let us
  live to make men free !
f While God is marching on.

  Julia Ward Howe.

1241 *"The world also is stablished."* Psalm xciii. 1. 8.7.5.

m Who will say the world is dying?
  Who will say our prime is past ?
f Sparks from Heaven within us lying,
  Flash, and will flash till the last.
m Fools ! who fancy Christ mistaken ;
  Man a tool to buy and sell ;
  Earth a failure, God forsaken,
  Anteroom of Hell.

f Still the race of Hero-spirits
  Pass the lamp from hand to hand ;
m Age from age the Words inherits,
  'Wife and Child and Fatherland' ;
f Still the youthful hunter gathers
  Fiery joy from wold and wood ;
  He will dare as dared his fathers,
  Give him cause as good.

m While a slave bewails his fetters ;
  While an orphan pleads in vain ;
  While an infant lisps his letters,
  Heir of all the ages' gain ;
  While a hope awaits the morrow,
p While a moan from man is wrung ;
m Know, by every joy and sorrow,
f That the world is young.

  C. Kingsley.

A Covenant Hymn.

1242 *"The brotherly covenant."* Amos i. 9. L.M.D.

m We covenant with hand and heart
  Ever to follow Christ our Lord ;
  With world and sin and self to part,
  And thus obey His sacred word :
  To love each other heartily,
  In truth and in sincerity,
p And under cross, reproach, and shame,
m To glorify His holy name.

  S. T. Benade.

~~National Hymn~~ Recessional ≡

1243 *"Some trust in chariots, and some in horses: but we will remember the name of the Lord our God."*—Psalm xx. 7. 8s.

f God of our fathers, known of old,
  Lord of our far-flung battle-line,
m Beneath whose awful hand we hold
  Dominion over palm and pine,—
  Lord God of hosts, be with us yet,
p Lest we forget—lest we forget !

m The tumult and the shouting dies,
  The captains and the kings depart,
  Still stands Thine ancient sacrifice,
  An humble and a contrite heart.
  Lord God of hosts, be with us yet,
p Lest we forget—lest we forget !

m Far-called, our navies melt away,
  On dune and headland sinks the fire
  Lo, all our pomp of yesterday
  Is one with Nineveh and Tyre !
p Judge of the nations, spare us yet
  Lest we forget—lest we forget !

m If, drunk with sight of power, we loose
  Wild tongues that have not Thee in awe,
  Such boasting as the Gentiles use,
  Or lesser breeds without the Law,—
  Lord God of hosts, be with us yet,
p Lest we forget—lest we forget !

m For heathen heart that puts her trust
  In reeking tube and iron shard,
  All valiant dust that builds on dust,
  And guarding calls not Thee to guard,
· For frantic boast and foolish word,
p Thy mercy on Thy people, Lord !

  Rudyard Kipling.

53

This is not a national hymn : and it is better to keep to the title under which [I know] it.

Correction made by Kipling in
a proof page of *Worship Song,*
containing his Recessional hymn

230

relation between the significance of the words, and the tune employed to convey their sense. He rightly felt that hymns should be jewels of beauty offered to God, and that in such a sublime act as worship, nothing is, indeed, good enough. But Dr. Bridges' achievement went far beyond the present standard of the average congregation and in extenuation of the latter it must be allowed that the *Yattendon Hymnal* was far too limited in scope. It was a drastic elimination of the shoddy and mediocre, but far too drastic, and in the process omitted a wealth of hymnody that has come to be treasured, and justly so, by all congregations. There is no doubt it was only offered as a sample for the guidance of future compilers, and those who engage in this task will do well to study it with care.

Apart from the *Yattendon Hymnal*, Dr. Bridges is one of the few great English poets who wrote hymns for congregational singing. He has left some very real treasures. One of the best known, and a model of what a 'national' hymn should be, is *Rejoice, O land, in God thy might*:

> Rejoice, O land, in God thy might;
> His will obey, Him serve aright;
> For thee the saints uplift their voice:
> Fear not, O land, in God rejoice.
>
> Glad shalt thou be, with blessing crowned,
> With joy and peace thou shalt abound;
> Yea, love with thee shall make his home
> Until thou see God's kingdom come.
>
> He shall forgive thy sins untold:
> Remember thou His love of old;
> Walk in His way, his word adore,
> And keep His truth for evermore.

It would be difficult to think of a finer example of perfect felicity of thought, expressed with such masterly economy in three brief verses.

231

Another hymn by this gifted poet, and one of singular grace and vision is *Thee will I love, my God and King.* It remains to be far more widely known and used, though its unusual metre, together with an intimate and closely woven thought, make it more suitable to a small group of worshippers, or for private devotion:

> Thee will I love, my God and King,
>   Thee will I sing,
>   My strength and tower:
> For evermore Thee will I trust,
>   O God most just
>   Of truth and power;
>   Who all things hast
>   In order placed—
> Yea, for Thy pleasure hast created;
>   And on Thy throne
>   Unseen, unknown,
>   Reignest alone
>   In glory seated.
>
> Set in my heart Thy love I find;
>   My wandering mind
>   To Thee Thou leadest:
> My trembling hope, my strong desire
>   With heavenly fire
>   Thou kindly feedest.
>   Lo, all things fair
>   Thy path prepare,
> Thy beauty to my spirit calleth,
>   Thine to remain
>   In joy or pain,
>   And count it gain
>   Whate'er befalleth.
>
> O more and more Thy love extend,
>   My life befriend
>   With heavenly pleasure;

That I may win Thy paradise,
Thy pearl of price,
Thy countless treasure;
Since but in Thee
I can go free
From earthly care and vain oppression,
This prayer I make
For Jesus' sake
That Thou me take
In Thy possession.

This is a rare gem of modern hymnody, and makes plain what can be achieved when a poet of such mature genius as Robert Bridges lends his powers to the task of hymn creation.

It serves to confirm and justify the view of Sir Arthur Quiller-Couch, that, "To theology, poetry is her wisest, eldest, ever loveliest daughter, the first of her handmaidens, enjoying the first-born's share of her love". This statement, by one of the leading literary critics of modern times, can be pondered with profit. The poet and the artist are the great interpreters of the Spirit. Theologians and philosophers come, sometimes halting, behind. The first purpose of a great hymn is to make articulate the deepest emotions of the soul. Adoration, wonder, awe, the refining sense of mystery, the noble influence of compassion, the humility of a sincere faith; these are the truly creative impulses of a great hymn, and they are the source of the grandest poetry. It is a welcome recognition of this truth that has inspired the poetic movement in modern hymnody, and it is certain to find ampler expression in future compilations, and to guide more consciously the selection and use of hymns in the highest of all human activities, and the one by which all others are conditioned; the worship of God, in beauty, truth and love.

14

American Offering

A FEATURE of modern English hymnals is the inclusion of an increasing number of hymns by American writers. Here, again, tribute must be paid to the pioneer work of Garrett Horder, for *Worship Song* was the first modern English hymn book to introduce to congregations in this country many American hymns of the highest merit. Previously what acquaintance we had with hymns from across the Atlantic was confined almost exclusively to the revivalist type, popularised through the missions of Sankey and Moody. It was pardonable if English congregations regarded this as the prevailing type of American hymnody, and we have reason to be grateful to Garrett Horder for correcting this error. He was a thorough student of American religious poetry, and compiled a comprehensive anthology which amply demonstrated the quality of the numerous writers. Moreover, he was a welcome lecturer in the United States on the subject of hymnology, and was keen in his advocacy that it should be given prominence in the curricula of the English theological colleges.

The excellence of much American work in hymn writing is due to certain causes peculiar to conditions there. One of these is the absence of any Established Church with its venerable and greatly loved Liturgy, and a resultant closer attention to hymns to make good the deficiency. There is, of course, an Episcopal Church in America, which, in common

234

with the Anglican Church here, retains—though in a somewhat different form—the Book of Common Prayer in its worship. This Church, however, is not the largest, nor the most influential religious body in the United States, and the various non-episcopal religious bodies are numerically much greater. This is one reason for the important place assigned to the hymn in American Christian worship. Another is found in the custom which prevails of inviting those with poetic gifts to contribute verses for the great anniversaries in American history. In recent years this has been further stimulated and encouraged by the Hymn Society of America, founded in 1922. This is a highly developed organisation with a wide influence throughout the American Churches, and combines within its ranks men and women whose abilities as writers, poets, composers and musicians, in co-operation with ministers of all denominations, are doing fruitful and far reaching work in the development and improvement of American hymnody. It was mentioned in the previous section that in England few of our leading poets have been hymn writers. In America it is otherwise, and much of the best in existing American hymnals reflects the genius of her leading poets.

It is also of interest to mark that some of the finest American hymns have been written by women, foremost among whom is the author of a once-famous book, widely read in this country some years ago, *Uncle Tom's Cabin*. It is to Harriet Beecher Stowe that we are indebted for the following hymn, a gem of mystical poetry.

Still, still with Thee, when purple morning breaketh—
　　When the bird waketh, and the shadows flee;
Fairer than morning, lovelier than the daylight,
　　Dawns the sweet consciousness, I am with Thee.

Alone with Thee amid the mystic shadows,
　　The solemn hush of nature newly born;
Alone with Thee in beathless adoration,
　　In the calm dew and freshness of the morn.

As in the dawning o'er the waveless ocean,
  The image of the morning star doth rest,
So in this stillness Thou beholdest only
  Thine image in the waters of my breast.

Still, still with Thee, as to each new-born morning
  A fresh and solemn splendour still is given,
So doth the blessed consciousness awakening,
  Breathe each day, nearness unto Thee and heaven.

When sinks the soul, subdued by toil to slumber,
  Its closing eye looks up to Thee in prayer;
Sweet the repose beneath Thy wings o'ershadowing,
  But sweeter still to wake and find Thee there.

So shall it be at last, in that bright morning
  When the soul waketh, and life's shadows flee;
Oh! in that hour fairer than daylight's dawning,
  Shall rise the glorious thought, I am with Thee.

Other hymns by the same writer include *When winds are raging o'er the upper ocean* and *That mystic word of Thine, O sovereign Lord*, with two final verses not often equalled in devotional depth:

> Abide in me, there have been moments blest
> When I have heard Thy voice and felt Thy power;
> When evil lost its grasp, and passion hushed,
> Owned the divine enchantment of the hour.

> These were but seasons beautiful and rare;
> Abide in me and they shall ever be;
> Fulfil at once Thy precept and my prayer—
> Come, and abide in me, and I in Thee.

It may be held with reason that verses such as these have a subtle quality of thought—an almost elusive delicacy of expression—which reduces their value for ordinary congregational singing. They are, perhaps, better restricted to small groups assembled for retreat, or for personal devotional reading. This latter use of a good hymnal should not be disregarded. Every hymn included in such a compilation may not be ideal for normal congregational use, which calls for simplicity of expression combined with a large measure of objectivity. It is for this reason that the hymns of Watts and Wesley remain of particular merit. But the hymn for the small group, and for personal devotion is in quite a different category, and these verses by Harriet Beecher Stowe are examples of hymns which are rich in suggestion and power in times of private meditation, or in special devotional services.

Another accomplished American woman writer of hymns was Eliza Scudder. In some respects she may be compared with our own Christina Rossetti. She has a metrical style which makes her hymns easier for congregational use. Here is a typical example of her work; a hymn first introduced in *Worship Song*, and now included in *Songs of Praise*.

Thou long disowned, reviled, oppressed,
　　Strange friend of human kind,
Seeking through weary years a rest,
　　Within our hearts to find.

How late thy bright and awful brow
　　Breaks through these clouds of sin;
Hail! Truth divine! we know Thee now,
　　Angel of God, come in!

Come, though with purifying fire
　　And swift dividing sword,
Thou of all nations the desire,
　　Earth waits Thy cleansing word.

Struck by the lightning of Thy glance,
　　Let old oppressions die:
Before Thy cloudless countenance
　　Let fear and falsehood fly.

Anoint our eyes with healing grace,
  To see, as not before,
Our Father in our brother's face,
  Our Maker in His poor.

Flood our dark life with golden day:
  Convince, subdue, enthral;
Then to a mightier yield Thy sway,
  And Love be all in all.

The quality of the hymns written by this inspired poet, which invite inclusion in any forthcoming English hymnal (again, it is in *Worship Song*) may be judged, also, by the following superb example. Observe how the climbing thought reaches up to a crescendo of faith and victory in the last verse:

Thou Grace divine, encircling all,
  A shoreless, boundless sea,
Wherein at last our souls must fall;
  O Love of God most free.

When over dizzy heights we go,
  A soft hand blinds our eyes,
And we are guided safe and slow;
  O Love of God most wise.

And though we turn us from Thy face,
  And wander wide and long,
Thou hold'st us still in kind embrace;
  O Love of God most strong.

The saddened heart, the restless soul,
  The toil-worn frame and mind,
Alike confess Thy sweet control,
  O Love of God most kind.

But not alone Thy care we claim,
  Our wayward steps to win;
We know Thee by a dearer name;
  O Love of God within.

238

And filled and quickened by Thy breath,
   Our souls are strong and free,
To rise o'er sin, and fear and death;
   O Love of God! to Thee.

Garrett Horder has included seven of Miss Scudder's hymns in his compilation, and more might be quoted from American sources. At least one other cannot be omitted for it deals with a question that remains insistent in the human mind, the nature of the life beyond death. It is a problem which prompts many to seek definite details through psychic media, and yet a more excellent way is indicated by these verses. Again, the climax of wisdom is epitomized in the concluding two lines:

My God, I rather look to Thee
   Than to my fancy fond,
And wait till Thou reveal to me
   That fair and far beyond.

I seek not of Thine Eden-land
   The forms and hues to know
What trees in mystic order stand,
   What strange sweet waters flow.

What duties fill the heavenly day,
   What converse glad and kind;
Or how along each shining way
   The bright processions wind.

Oh, sweeter far to trust in Thee
   While all is yet unknown,
And through the death-dark cheerily
   To walk with Thee alone!

In Thee my powers, my treasures live;
   To Thee my life must tend;
Giving Thyself, Thou all dost give,
   O soul-sufficing Friend.

Hymns such as these help us to understand to what an extent the American contribution can enrich our own store. It was Miss Scudder's uncle, Edmund Hamilton Sears, a Unitarian minister, who wrote the splendid hymn for Christmas *It came upon the midnight clear*. This is now a favourite carol at Christmastide, but it is only in recent years that it has come into general use; an example of our slowness in making use of the really choice store of hymnody which American sources offer.

Alice Cary was another American hymn writer in the second half of the nineteenth century whose verses have been brought to our shores, and are a further indication of the quality available for our use. Here is one example of Miss Cary's verse, and again there is the exquisite use of words woven into inspired thoughts that gleam like lights on the facets of a jewel. It is a rare quality which seems to mark these outstanding women poets of America. The following is a hymn for Sunday morning:

O Day to sweet religious thought
　So wisely set apart,
Back to the silent strength of life
　Help Thou my wavering heart.

Nor let th' obtrusive lies of sense
　My meditations draw
From the composed, majestic realm
　Of everlasting law.

Break down whatever hindering shapes
　I see, or seem to see,
And make my soul acquainted with
　Celestial company.

Beyond the wintry waste of death
　Shine fields of heavenly light;
Let not this incident of time
　Absorb me from their sight.

I know these outward forms, wherein
So much my hopes I stay,
Are but the shadowy hints of that
Which cannot pass away.

That just outside the work-day path
By man's volition trod,
Lie the resistless issues of
The things ordained of God.

The compression of thought here is so intense that the immensity of meaning enshrined in a line may easily elude us. Here is need for the application of the sound principle of *reading* a great hymn, slowly and thoughtfully, regardless of any tune to which it is sung. Read it, until it is stored in the memory, and then, partaking as it does of an eternal quality, its rich significance will come with ever fresh impact, and with increasing understanding. A store of such poetry in the mind will be a satisfying treasure, and a source of constant refreshment.

At least one other American woman hymn writer must be mentioned. It is possible that the hymns of Lucy Larcom are as yet little known to English congregations, but her verses deserve to rank with those of the gifted writers already quoted. It is interesting to recall that Miss Larcom worked in the cotton mills of Lawrence until she was twenty-one, when she became a school teacher. A woman of gracious personality, it can be said that poetry was in her soul from childhood. "As I think back to my childhood," she once wrote, "it seems to me as if the air was full of hymns as it was of the fragrance of clover blossoms, and the songs of blue-birds and robins, and the deep undertone of the sea". Owing to the poverty of her home she became a mill-girl at twelve years of age, and in due course a spinner. Her seat at the mill was by a window, which she made into a small library of poetry, pasting its sides all over with poems which she found from time to time in local newspapers. One day she was given a copy of the poems of the American Quaker poet, Whittier, and later the poet visited the town, and she met him. Subsequently she went to the training college at Alton, and spent some years in Boston in the higher branches of the teaching profession, but she began writing poetry while still a worker in the mills. Later Miss Larcom did some writing in collaboration with Whittier.

These facts of her life will help in the appreciation of the quality of her verse. When, for example, she tells us, writing of her early years in the mill, that the girls were allowed one day's holiday in the year—the fourth of July—they would go for a country tramp, starting at four in the morning, and would return with their "aprons full of dewy wild roses" we can trace the inspiration of her thought in the following verses. She tells us that the sweet air of the woods, and the fragrance of the roses would fill their thoughts for days. It is good to know the following is now a hymn in *Songs of Praise*. It was published in America in 1885. In England it also appears in *The Fellowship Hymn Book*, a compilation used in the Adult School movement.

I learned it in the meadow path,
I learned it on the mountain stairs—
The best things any mortal hath
Are those which every mortal shares.

The air we breathe, the sky, the breeze,
The light without us and within,
Life with its unlocked treasuries,
God's riches are for all to win.

The grass is softer to my tread,
Because it rests unnumbered feet;
Sweeter to me the wild rose red,
Because she makes the whole world sweet.

And up the radiant peopled way
That opens into worlds unknown,
It will be life's delight to say,
'Heaven is not heaven for me alone'.

Wealth won by other's poverty—
  Not such be mine! Let me be blest
Only in what they share with me,
  And what I share with all the rest.

But her greatest hymn remains, undoubtedly, the following,
marked by deep thought and spacious outlook:

In Christ I feel the heart of God
  Throbbing from heaven through earth;
Life stirs again within the clod,
  Renewed in beauteous birth;
The soul springs up, a flower of prayer,
Breathing His breath out on the air.

In Christ I touch the hand of God,
  From his pure height reached down,
By blessed ways before untrod,
  To lift us to our crown;
Vict'ry that only perfect is
Through loving sacrifice like His.

Holding His hand, my steadied feet
  May walk the air, the seas;
On life and death His smile falls sweet,
  Lights up all mysteries;
Stranger nor exile can I be
In new worlds where He leadeth me.

Not my Christ only; He is ours;
  Humanity's close bond;
Key to its vast, unopened powers,
  Dream of our dreams beyond.
What yet we shall be none can tell:
  Now are we His, and all is well.

Oliver Wendell Holmes, the eminent American man of
letters, whose wise, kindly writings are treasured by many on

243

this side of the Atlantic, is the author of a few hymns of distinction which have enriched our English collections. Best known, probably, is *Lord of all being! throned afar.* But another, which deserves to be far more widely known and used, is the following, which was included in Holmes *Complete Poetical Works* as far back as 1895:

Our Father! while our hearts unlearn
    The creeds that wrong Thy name,
Still let our hallowed altars burn
    With Faith's undying flame.

Not by the lightning-gleams of wrath
    Our souls Thy face shall see;
The star of love must light the path
    That leads to heaven and Thee.

Help us to read our Master's will
    Through every darkening stain,
That clouds His sacred image still,
    And see Him once again.

The brother Man, the pitying Friend,
    Who weeps for human woes,
Whose pleading words of pardon blend
    With cries of raging foes.

If 'mid the gathering storms of doubt
    Our hearts grow faint and cold,
The strength we cannot live without
    Thy love will not withold.

Our prayers accept; our sins forgive;
    Our youthful zeal renew;
Shape for us holier lives to live,
    And nobler work to do.

A further hymn by the same writer, also contained now in several English hymnals, is the tender and beautiful hymn of trust *O Love Divine that stooped to share.*

Mentioning American hymns which for years have been well known and extensively sung in this country, we should include Ray Palmer's, *My faith looks up to Thee,* a hymn which has become known all over the world. Dr. Palmer was a leading Congregational minister in America, and one of the most notable hymn writers and translators in that particular denomination. The hymn mentioned had the singular experience of being better known here than it was in America, when first written. It has had an extraordinary distribution, having been translated into Chinese, and numerous other languages, and appears to have been carried by Christian missionaries everywhere. It has been suggested, indeed, that its circulation has been co-equal with that of the Bible. It is an instance of the unaccountable success which may attend a hymn for no very special reason. While it is a good hymn, it cannot be claimed as outstanding, but has far outstripped in universal favour hymns of greater intrinsic merit. Dr. Palmer wrote other hymns which may be thought by some to be superior. *Lord, my weak thought in vain would climb,* is richer in thought, while a very fine hymn by the same writer is the following:

> Jesus, these eyes have never seen
>   That radiant form of Thine;
> The veil of sense hangs dark between
>   Thy blessed face and mine.
>
> I see Thee not, I hear Thee not,
>   Yet art Thou oft with me;
> And earth has ne'er so dear a spot
>   As where I meet with Thee.
>
> Like some bright dream that comes unsought,
>   When slumbers o'er me roll,
> Thine image ever fills my thought,
>   And charms my ravished soul.

Yea, though I have not seen, and still
    Must rest in faith alone,
I love Thee, dearest Lord, and will,
    Unseen but not unknown.

When death these mortal eyes shall seal,
    And still this throbbing heart;
The rending veil shall Thee reveal
    All glorious as Thou art.

In addition to his achievements as a hymn writer, Dr. Palmer was the translator of numerous hymns, many of which have become familiar throughout the world. They include, from Robert II of France, *Come Holy Ghost in love*; from Bernard of Clairvaux, *Jesus, Thou joy of loving hearts*, and from anonymous Latin authors, *I give my heart to Thee* and *O bread to pilgrims given*.

An American Presbyterian, George Duffield, was the author of a hymn which has for years been one of the most popular here, particularly in Sunday School hymnals. This was *Stand up, stand up for Jesus!* It was composed by Dr. Duffield for the funeral service of a fellow minister, Dudley Atkins Tyng, who had been rector of the Church of the Epiphany, Philadelphia, and the lines had been prompted by the fact that his dying words to the Y.M.C.A. members had been, "Tell them to stand up for Jesus". It has certainly proved one of the most popular American hymns included in English collections, and this popularity has been equally shared in the land of its origin.

From another great American, Ralph Waldo Emerson, we have derived the noble hymn, beginning:

We love the venerable house
    Our fathers built to God :—
In heaven are kept their grateful vows,
    Their dust endears the sod.

246

Here holy thoughts a light have shed
From many a radiant face,
And prayers of tender hope have spread
A perfume through the place.

It would need a very substantial anthology to indicate in any
adequate measure the number, variety, and consistently high
standard of American hymns, but of those which have found,
and are finding a place in our own hymnals, another writer
who must receive mention is the Quaker poet, John Greenleaf
Whittier, who was born in 1807. He is said to have remarked
that "two hundred years of silence had taken all the 'sing'
out of the Quakers". An examination of a modern hymnal,
however, will reveal what may seem a surprising fact, that a
good percentage is of Quaker origin. This is due to the fact
that members of the Society of Friends have been among the
best writers of devotional verse, although it may not have been
designed as hymns. Whittier is an instance of this. He was one
of America's greatest poets, but he was also leader in one of
the historic crusades of modern times, the movement for the
abolition of slavery. Yet he won the friendship of all shades of
American opinion, and became one of the most respected and
beloved of her great men. He was a great Christian, simple-
hearted, sincere, a lover of all beauty, valiant for truth, and
yet with a deep humility of spirit. A rare and lovely soul, his
sensitive, mystical insight into the heart of Christian truth,
deeper than all outward forms and creeds, is seen all through
his poetry. Tribute has already been paid to the immense debt
we owe to Garrett Horder for his introduction of great American hymns, but no debt we owe to his memory is greater than
that which is due for the selections he made from the poems
of Whittier, for inclusion in *Worship Song*. His love of Whittier's
beautiful verses has been abundantly justified and repaid by
the subsequent inclusion of many of these hymns in other
collections, and by the frequency with which they are now
employed in religious broadcasts. One of the best-known, and
one of the finest hymns we have from American sources, is
Whittier's *Dear Lord and Father of mankind*, from his poem

The Brewing of Soma. As even now there are those who do not know it, it is reproduced:

> Dear Lord and Father of mankind,
>   Forgive our feverish ways,
> Reclothe us in our rightful mind;
> In purer lives, Thy service find,
>   In deeper reverence, praise.
>
> O Sabbath rest by Galilee!
>   O calm of hills above!
> Where Jesus knelt to share with Thee
> The silence of eternity
>   Interpreted by love.
>
> With that deep hush subduing all
>   Our words and works that drown
> The tender whisper of Thy call,
> As noiseless let Thy blessing fall,
>   As fell Thy manna down.
>
> Drop Thy still dews of quietness,
>   Till all our strivings cease;
> Take from our souls the strain and stress,
> And let our ordered lives confess
>   The beauty of Thy peace.
>
> Breathe through the pulses of desire
>   Thy coolness and Thy balm;
> Let sense be dumb—its heats expire;
> Speak through the earthquake, wind and fire,
>   O still small voice of calm!

This is a hymn where reflective analysis is called for in order to appreciate its essential greatness. Dwell on the deep meaning implicit in only two lines in the second verse:

> The silence of eternity
>   Interpreted by love.

There is suggestion here which opens up a very wide vista of thought.

Brief quotation will not do justice to Whittier. The best way is to read leisurely a collection of his poems. But a most lovely poem on the future life must be given here. It has been placed by Garrett Horder in his collection of hymns, and in many ways it is the most satisfying of all hymns on this great theme of the Life Beyond:

> When on my day of life the night is falling,
>   And, in the winds from unsunned spaces blown,
> I hear far voices out of darkness calling
>   My feet to paths unknown.
>
> Thou who hast made my home of life so pleasant,
>   Leave not its tenant when its walls decay;
> O Love divine, O helper ever present,
>   Be Thou my strength and stay!
>
> Be near me when all else is from me drifting—
>   Earth, sky, home's pictures, days of shade and shine,
> And kindly faces to my own uplifting
>   The love which answers mine.
>
> I have but Thee, my Father! let Thy spirit
>   Be with me then to comfort and uphold;
> No gate of pearl, no branch of palm I merit,
>   Nor street of shining gold.
>
> Suffice it if—my good and ill unreckoned,
>   And both forgiven through Thy abounding grace—
> I find myself by hands familiar beckoned
>   Unto my fitting place.
>
> Some humble door among Thy many mansions,
>   Some sheltering shade where sin and striving cease,
> And flows for ever through heaven's green expansions
>   The river of Thy peace.
>
> There, from the music round about me stealing,
>   I fain would learn the new and holy song,
> And find at last, beneath Thy trees of healing,
>   The life for which I long.

A hymn which is becoming speedily better known by its frequent use in religious broadcasts is Whittier's *Immortal Love, for ever full,* and it brings out fully all the characteristic qualities of the writer, summed up by Dr. Julian, in his *Dictionary of Hymnology,* as "rich poetic beauty, sweet tenderness, and deep sympathy with human kind". In illustration of these qualities three verses of this hymn may be recalled:

> But warm, sweet, tender even yet
> A present help is He;
> And faith has still its Olivet,
> And love its Galilee.

> The healing of His seamless dress
> Is by our beds of pain;
> We touch Him in life's throng and press,
> And we are whole again.

> Through Him the first fond prayers are said
> Our lips of childhood frame,
> The last low whispers of our dead
> Are burdened with His name.

Everywhere in Whittier the poet and the poems seem one. A beautiful character shines through them. Their warm, gracious humanity was in the heart of the man by whom they were written. Charles Kingsley said, after an interview with him, "He is a rare old saint".

Dr. Frederick Lucien Hosmer was a distinguished American Unitarian minister to whom we owe several fine hymns that are finding a place in England—again due to the vision of Garrett Horder. One hymn from Dr. Hosmer's pen which is becoming rapidly better known here is

> Thy Kingdom come! on bended knee
> The passing ages pray;
> And faithful souls have yearned to see
> On earth that Kingdom's day.

Many radio listeners will again recognize the opening verse
of a hymn which they frequently hear. Worthy of being better
known is the following hymn by Dr. Hosmer. It has an inspired
simplicity:

> O Thou in all Thy might so far,
>   In all Thy love so near,
> Beyond the range of sun and star,
>   And yet beside us here:
>
> What heart can comprehend Thy name,
>   Or searching find Thee out,
> Who art within, a quickening flame,
>   A presence round about?
>
> Yet though I know Thee but in part,
>   I ask not, Lord, for more;
> Enough for me to know Thou art,
>   To love Thee and adore.
>
> And dearer than all things I know
>   Is childlike faith to me,
> That makes the darkest way I go
>   An open path to Thee.

A collaborator with Dr. Hosmer was another Unitarian
minister, William Channing Gannett. He was a hymn writer
of merit, and some of his verses are now available for English
congregations. Here is one hymn which is typical of his work:

> The Lord is in His holy place
>   In all things near and far:
> Shekinah of the snowflake He,
>   And glory of the star,
> And secret of the April land
>   That stirs the fields to flowers,
> Whose little tabernacles rise
>   To hold him through the hours.

He hides Himself within the love
　Of those whom we love best;
The smiles and tones that make our homes
　Are shrines by Him possessed;
He tents within the lonely heart
　And shepherds every thought;
We find Him not by seeking long,
　We lose Him not, unsought.

Our art may build its Holy Place,
　Our feet on Sinai stand,
But Holiest of Holy knows
　No tread, no touch of hand;
The listening soul makes Sinai still
　Wherever we may be,
And in the vow, 'Thy will be done',
　Lies all Gethsemane.

Two splendid American hymns have come to us from the writings of Samuel Johnson, minister of a Free Christian church, who also did important work in American hymnology, in association with Samuel Longfellow. *City of God, how broad and far* is rapidly becoming better known in England, and his lesser known *Life of ages, richly poured* is another worthy hymn, instinct with fine imagination. Samuel Longfellow, with whom Johnson collaborated, was a brother of the famous poet, and wrote some excellent hymns, six of which now have a place in *Songs of Praise*. There is a spacious outlook of wide horizons, and an invigorating faith in many of these American hymns, that make them a real spiritual tonic. These qualities are focussed in the following hymn by Samuel Longfellow:

O Life that makest all things new,
　The blooming earth, the thoughts of men:
Our pilgrim feet, wet with Thy dew,
　In gladness hither turn again.

From hand to hand the greeting flows,
From eye to eye the signals run,
From heart to heart the bright hope glows;
The seekers of the light are one.

One in the freedom of the truth,
One in the joy of paths untrod,
One in the soul's perennial youth,
One in the larger thought of God.

The freer step, the fuller breath,
The wide horizon's grander view,
The sense of life that knows no death—
The life that maketh all things new.

There are clues in these lines to the peculiar ethos of American hymnody. It is a repeated sense of "the soul's perennial youth" and "the larger thought of God". It reflects the powerful influence of liberal elements in American theological thought. It is the child of the Emersonian tradition, and it is a marked feature of the American contribution to hymnody.

This spacious spirit and dynamic inspiration find expression in a hymn which has become better known in England in the past few years. It was written by Dr. W. P. Merrill, a leading New York Presbyterian minister. It has all the invigoration of the American quality:

Rise up, O men of God!
Have done with lesser things;
Give heart, and soul, and mind and strength
To serve the King of Kings.

Rise up, O men of God!
His Kingdom tarries long;
Bring in the day of brotherhood,
And end the night of wrong.

Rise up, O men of God!
  The Church for you doth wait;
  Her strength unequal to her task;
  Rise up and make her great!

Lift high the cross of Christ!
  Tread where His feet have trod,
As brothers of the Son of Man
  Rise up, O men of God!

It is also of interest to remember that America has given a
lead in a class of hymn which has found more prominence in
modern English hymnals than was hitherto the vogue. This
is the type of hymn which is related to social and civic life and
duty. It is the fresh emphasis on the prophetic element in the
Christian religion; an element frequently overlooked and
obscured. It is significant to observe how the major emphasis
in a hymn has tended to change in different periods, and to
reflect the prevailing religious outlook of the time in which it
was written. Thus, the medieval hymns, both East and West,
tended to be occupied almost exclusively with the world
beyond this, and the life after death. Then came the post-
Reformation evangelical accent, and the dominating concern
with the salvation of the individual soul. In the lesser hymns
concerned with both these emphases, the dominating viewpoint sometimes tended to expressions and excesses bordering
on the absurd and banal.

In the past few decades, an influence has been the
emergence of a new social consciousness; and, in England,
Christian Socialism, in the teaching of some great churchmen,
such as Maurice, Kingsley, Gore and Scott Holland, provided an impetus to a type of hymn concerned with national
and social righteousness. It brought into some of our later
hymnals the song of Ebenezer Elliott, written during the
agitation for the repeal of the Corn Laws: *When wilt Thou
save the people?* In America, prominence was given to the same
type of hymn by the more liberal Christian movements, and

brought into American hymnody extracts from the democratic poetry of James Russell Lowell, and others. From Lowell's poetry were derived two hymns which have passed into English collections—*Men, whose boast it is that ye* and *Once to every man and nation*. The value of these hymns is that they restore the balance, and emphasise the prophetic nature of the Christian gospel. But it is a type of hymn that calls for skilled composition, otherwise it may foster a variety of earthbound religion, which is a travesty and negation of the Christian view. Moreover, they may be hymns which reflect a passing mode of thought, and which will easily "date" in course of time. Two examples of this class of hymn in England, indicating what is demanded, and both hymns that will endure because of their firm grasp of eternal verities, are *Judge eternal, throned in splendour*, by Scott Holland, a leader of the Anglican Church and a former Canon of St. Paul's, and Robert Bridges' fine hymn *Rejoice, O land, in God thy might*. If another English example should be needed, it can be found in G. K. Chesterton's truly magnificent hymn *O God of earth and altar*.

In concluding this section, reference must be made to the recent publication of a series of hymns of this class by the Hymn Society of America. They are called *Twelve new hymns of Christian Patriotism*. They are the result of an invitation extended by the Society in 1943 to approximately a hundred poets and hymn writers, to write one or more hymns in the category mentioned. Thirty-five writers accepted the invitation, and submitted sixty-two hymns. In the following year twelve of the sixty-two hymns sent in were accepted for publication. It is stated that "It is the hope of the Hymn Society that out of this quest may emerge . . . hymns . . . expressive and interpretative of enlightened Christian thought with reference to the relationship of the individual to his country, and to his fellow men, of whatever nation, race, or creed".

Two examples are given here. They will be evidence of the existing ability to produce hymns of a quality bearing comparison with the best of the past, and significant of the further contribution which America may make to our own rich store:

God, who hast set us in this time
  Of storm and wreck and tears,
Be near, be near, that we may bear
  The burden of the years.

God, who hast set us in this land
  Of daybreak, dust and fire,
Be near, that what we do may match
  The splendour we desire.

God, who hast placed us where the roads
  Divide, the ages part,
Be near, that no low fear betray
  The high dreams of the heart.

That we, whom Thou hast made free men,
  For self or service free,
May in the hour of judgment choose
  Not mastery, but Thee.

The above hymn was contributed by Hermann Hagedorn, who is known as "Harvard's poet". He wrote a biography of Theodore Roosevelt, and is the author of more than twenty volumes of biography and poetry. Here is another example of an American man of letters who is also a leading hymn writer.

The second example, given below, from the twelve hymns published, was written by Bishop Ralph S. Cushman, and his son, Robert E. Cushman. Bishop Cushman is bishop of the Methodist Church in the area of St. Paul, Minnesota. He has written a number of books, both poetry and prose. Few hymns can give a better sense of the relevance of our Christian faith and witness to present world conditions:

God of all peoples everywhere,
We raise to Thee our burdened prayer;
  Father of all, of every race,
  Our sin obscures Thy radiant face.

Thou who dost know the secret heart
Of men and nations, whole and part,
Thou yet dost love and pardon all
Who will upon Thy mercy call.

Since Thou hast sought us ere we prove
The worthy objects of Thy love,
Our gratitude to Thee is paid
In serving men whom Thou hast made.

Make love of self give way, to heed
The broadened boundaries of need!
Thy justice, Lord, to us impart,
But let Thy mercy rule each heart.

Grant us the kindlier heart and way,
Strength both to labour and to pray;
Unveil the evil that we laud,
Bring in the Brotherhood of God.

15

"Let all the People Sing"

THE following precepts of John Wesley given for the guidance of his Methodist choirs, are of equal value to members of the congregation. The phrasing in parts may sound a little quaint to our modern ears, but this will not discount the practical value of the counsel given.

Learn the tunes.
Sing them as printed.
Sing *all* . . . Let not a slight degree of weakness or weariness hinder you. If it is a cross to you, take it up, and you will find it a blessing.
Sing *lustily* and with a good courage.
Beware of singing as if you are half dead, or half asleep, but lift up your voice with strength. Be no more afraid of your voice now, nor more ashamed of its being heard, than when you sing the songs of *Satan*.
Sing *modestly*. Do not bawl . . . strive to unite your voices together so as to make one clear melodious sound.
Sing in *time*. Do not run before or stay behind . . . and take care not to sing too slow. This drawling way naturally steals on all who are lazy; and it is high time to drive it from among us, and sing all our tunes just as quick as we did at first.
Above all, sing *spiritually*. Have an eye to God in every word you sing. Aim at pleasing Him more than yourself, or any other creature. In order to do this, attend strictly

to the sense of what you sing, and see that your heart is not carried away with the sound, but offered to God continually.

The intention of this final brief chapter is not to discuss the general subject of church music, which is done in some admirable books recommended at the end for those musical readers who may be interested to pursue the subject along more technical lines. The purpose is to stress the importance of suitable tunes, and is a plea for congregations to participate in the singing of them, as well as for choirs to assist them in doing so. The latter appeal may sound startling. "But", someone will say, "surely that is what the choir is for". This is certainly true, but it is a fact which can be forgotten. There is no aspect of public worship in which greater progress has been made in recent years than in the quality of the music provided. To the more sophisticated choirs of the present, the primitive singers portrayed in Thomas Hardy's *Under the Greenwood Tree* may provoke an indulgent smile. But the greater musical ability and knowledge of the more proficient modern choirs create one danger unless the purpose of worship is always kept in mind. It can prompt the choir to forget that they are part of the *ministry*, which means that their function is to serve the people by helping them in the worship of God. An act of public worship is not a musical recital, nor a concert. There is a place for both the latter, when it is the privilege of the people to *listen*. But in public worship the aim of the choir is (or should be) to assist the people to *sing* not to listen. The exception to this is the anthem, which it is clearly understood is restricted to the choir.

John Wesley's exhortation, "Sing all", is an appeal which remains timely. If it is to be observed then the matter of *tune* becomes highly important. This chapter is written from the standpoint of the average member of the congregation, who may have little or no musical training, and not always too good an ear. This is true of the larger part of the average congregation in England, whatever may be said of our Welsh neighbours. The first requirement of a tune, then, is that it shall have what that excellent guide in congregational singing, Dr. Walford Davies, called "the important quality of *singableness*". This does not mean that a congregation will not learn, and in time come to love a new tune, however tenaciously sentiment and custom may incline them to cling to old ones, even when inferior. But they must be helped and encouraged, and also the tune should be set within their compass. The absence of this precaution is a frequent error. Further, although such a statement may invite protest, it may be better to allow the congregation to cling to an inferior tune if it enables them to sing with more sincerity and fervour. For example, there is little question that "Aberystwyth" is musically superior to "Hollingside", as a tune for the familiar hymn, *Jesu, Lover of my soul*, but the latter tune may have gathered to itself a wealth of association in memory that will endear it to the singer, and its appeal may deepen the sense of worship when the hymn is sung. Again, is it so easy to determine what *is* a good tune? There is sometimes an amusing conflict of opinion on the part of the leaders. "St. Clement", the popular tune to *The day Thou gavest, Lord, is ended*, is frowned upon by some critics and lauded by others. Its appeal to the congregation is beyond question. Vaughan Williams' stirring tune "Sine Nomine" is blessed by Dr. C. Henry Phillips, and, speaking of the great hymn to which this tune is attached, *For all the saints*, he said: "The words have strength in their own right but Vaughan Williams' tune gives them exultation", and with this opinion choirs would undoubtedly agree. Yet B. L. Manning, in *The Hymns of Wesley and Watts*, designates it "a feeble dance tune". Thus opinions differ. "St. Gertrude", Sullivan's popular tune to *Onward Christian Soldiers*, is frequently dismissed in these days as "vulgar" and the humble, unmusical member of the congregation may wilt under such a drastic criticism, although, in silence, he will continue to like the tune all the same.

Probably the difficulty arises from the failure to place this hymn and tune in their historical setting, and to remember that they were written for a Yorkshire Sunday School procession. They are being judged by standards a little too adult, but even so who can repress a thrill of emotion at hearing the triumphant crescendo of this tune in waves of resonant echo around the dome of St. Paul's?

Dr. Walford Davies has wisely said, "In the matter of hymns, hymn-tunes, and hymn-singing, the church musician will do well to remember that the views of the more intelligent type of layman may be considered with profit, on account of the extra-musical considerations involved".

Passing vogues and fashions can be another pitfall for the compilers of hymnals with music. Of recent date there has been a tendency to dismiss impatiently much of the hymn music of the nineteenth century, and to substitute for it tunes inspired by folk-songs. Here, too, Dr. Walford Davies has uttered a note of caution:

Many of the new tunes that are too obviously influenced by folk-song and the ecclesiastical modes begin to show signs of wear; a decade or so hence they will probably be superseded either by another and more natural type of new tune, or (perhaps even more likely) by a reinstatement of the best of the nineteenth century tunes they were intended to displace . . . . The folk-tune vogue will pass in hymnals, as already it has almost passed in composition; and it is becoming plain that many of the new tunes are less good than they appeared to be, and that certain of the old ones are less bad than we were led to believe.

This is wise counsel that one may hope will have a moderating influence on the impulsive disposition sometimes shown to jettison old and familiar tunes in favour of others unknown and uncongenial to the average congregation. Allied to the above, Dr. Harvey Grace has added the following sound judgment:

The chooser of hymns, as of every kind of music for popular use, needs to remind himself constantly that there are many kinds of good music; that in some of them the goodness is discernible only by the trained musician; in others by some sort of specialist; in yet others by the crowd—but only on thorough acquaintance. Finally, and happily, there is the kind of musical goodness that makes instant appeal to the untrained no less than to the trained musician. The music of which this may be said is truly universal; it is enormous in quantity, and it embraces every type from the symphony to the simple organ voluntary, from the oratorio to the Anglican chant. Parsons and organists with a taste for medieval melodies, Genevan psalm tunes, and German chorales are apt to forget that their liking for such things is usually the result of long familiarity or of special study. They must not expect their congregations to share their delight at once—if ever.

It is Dr. Walford Davies who gives three rules for the guidance of those in charge of congregational music (and this includes the selection of hymn tunes) which seem to sum up the whole matter with plain common sense:

1. It must be such music as is intelligible to the congregation present.
2. It must be such as can enhance the significance of the words to the worshippers.
3. It must be within the power of those who sing it.

The second rule, which aims to make the music emphasize the words, suggests the fact, not easily analysed, of the subtle link between sense and sound. There are certain hymn tunes that the average listener, as well as the more musically accomplished, will feel at once are essentially right. Thus, for example, no one will question that "St. Anne", now always set for *Our God, our help in ages past*, is the right tune. If another familiar common metre tune, "Winchester Old", is put in its place, the incongruity will be at once apparent. The former has a stately measure, a suggestion of the majestic, and an ordered dignity, entirely consistent for conveying the strength and nobility of the glorious hymn to which it is attached. On the other hand, the light and rather tripping notes of "Winchester Old", even if it is not an ideal tune, is felt to be quite congruous with Tate's Christmas hymn *While Shepherds watched*, with which it is now inseparably associated, whereas this tune for *Our God, our help in ages past*, would be felt at once to be completely unsuitable. This may be an extreme example of the mysterious relation between sense and sound, but there are many degrees less striking, but which need to be regarded with care. The "Old Hundredth" fits perfectly the rugged beauty of *All people that on earth do dwell*, but it does not follow that it would be suitable for all hymns in the same metre. The meaning of the words must enter into the choice.

In like manner, the vigorous melody of "Truro" is ideal for *Jesus shall reign where'er the sun*, but would be quite wrong for *When I survey the wondrous cross*, where the tender notes of "Rockingham", so appropriate for the latter, lack the sustained jubilation needed for the former hymn. It can be seen how sensitive is the relation between melody and meaning. Handel clearly recognized this fact in his masterly creations. Two examples spring to mind from *The Messiah*, where constantly the music paints the picture of the words. Observe how carefully Handel makes the music emphasize the word "Surely" in the sentence, "Surely He hath borne our griefs, and carried our sorrows". Here, the resonant emphasis on this word gives rich significance to the thought. Again, in the opening of the third part, mark how, in the chorus, "I know that my Redeemer liveth" the music leaps up with decisive affirmation on the word "know" and brings home the confidence and certitude of the utterance. Manifold instances could be mentioned from the music of hymns, and it is a detail which all who are responsible for the choice of the music of worship should keep carefully in mind. Great care will often be shown in the selection of the music for chants and anthems, while there is small attention paid to the suitability of hymn tunes. Yet, to quote again Dr. Harvey Grace, who has rightly said that:

Just as the immense resources of modern hymnals are still barely tapped, so the potentialities of hymn-singing are rarely realised to the full .... A plain service containing no other music than a few fine hymns, heartily sung by all, lacks nothing of dignity or beauty. . . . . The singing of a cathedral choir is never more delightful than when it is thrown into relief by some congregational hymns. *Per contra*, a first-rate choir and a half-silent congregation may produce a chilling effect.

The truth in the latter half of this remark can be tested by reference to such a work as Stainer's "Crucifixion", where choir and congregation co-operate with happy effect, the latter joining in with such moving hymns as *Cross of Jesus*.

Let it be repeated, for it cannot be said too often, that an act of public worship is an act in which all the people should be able to share happily and sincerely. Obvious though this fact should be it is easily forgotten, and the reminder of it cannot be put into better words than the following by Dr. Walford Davies:

We would here offer a warning against the ever-threatening risk of musical over-elaborateness. Euphony is beguiling in itself. But the musician at worship must remain at all points the servant of the people at worship with him. We must refrain from elaborating either melody or harmony beyond the people's mind to accept or follow. There is, for example, an adapted Easter plainsong revived in *The English Hymnal* (presumably for use) in which more than twenty notes are set to be sung to the second syllable of the word "Passover." This may have been the sincere melodic expression of rapturous devotion by men long ago to whom twenty notes in this connection were more joyously natural than one. But a lovable ancient church tradition is not of necessity either the natural or practicable, or even adaptable vehicle of an English congregation at worship to-day. Our link with the revered past must be something more vitally akin than this. Similarly, elaborate harmonies of Victorian days and descants (of various size, compass and age) can be devout to the musical enthusiast and devastating to his congregation.

Although the suggestion may sound novel, even *posture* may enhance the significance and meaning of a hymn. There are hymns which are really sung prayers, and it would serve to stress this if these hymns could be sung kneeling. An example is *Breathe on me, breath of God*, and certainly the lovely *Veni, Creator Spiritus*.

Everything is to be welcomed which will give reality, sincerity and meaning to the act of Christian worship. It is the greatest act of life. It is the crown and climax of all else. When it is real and worthy God is glorified, and man is dignified and invested with his native nobility as a child of God. If we reflect for a moment we shall agree that we should not offer to the glory of God our second best, and our worship should be in spirit and in truth. This will mean that we sing with understanding. For this reason it is desirable to *read* hymns, as well as to sing them. The hymn book should be a manual of private devotion, as well as of public worship. This will justify the inclusion of many beautiful hymns, more intimate and subjective in character than others particularly suited to collective worship, and will restore sacred verse to its place in personal devotion. Further, it will have the immense advantage of helping the reader to detect hymns which are banal or mediocre in expression, and it may be insincere in thought.

A poor hymn is not infrequently sung because it is linked with a good tune. It may contain forms of thought which have become obsolete, and to which the intelligent singer would never dream of subscribing if they were expressed in sober prose. There is no worship of God, in spirit and in truth, if we are willing to give voice to insincerity merely because we sing it, and like the tune. The same tune can probably be attached to a hymn that embodies true sentiment and conviction. There is no shortage now of available material. In the words quoted above Dr. Harvey Grace has reminded us that "the immense resources of modern hymnals are still barely tapped". This is true, and it removes every excuse for retaining unworthy hymns merely because they provide the opportunity for singing a good tune. Let us keep the melody by all means, if it is a good one, and attach it to words which are worthy.

These are times when the sublime act of Christian worship needs to be invested with passionate sincerity, and this applies to every detail; prayers, lessons, chants, sermon and hymns. It is the latter which are too often neglected. In English hymnody we have a magnificent inheritance, enriched by the inspired devotion of many lands and ages. The treasures of medieval worship have been restored to us; the noble hymns that quickened the Reformation have been placed at our service. The gems of English poetry at its greatest moments are at our disposal. America has provided a generous offering. In our own Watts and Wesley we have a wealth of glorious verse that has gone out to all the world, and steadily the volume has grown through our gifted writers of the last century.

England has a rich treasury of Christian hymns unexcelled in any other country; a noble privilege of divine praise:

O Praise God in His holiness: praise Him in the firmament of His power.

Praise Him in His noble acts: praise Him according to His excellent greatness.

Praise Him in the sound of the trumpet: praise Him upon the lute and harp.

Praise Him in the cymbals and dances: praise Him upon the strings and pipe.

Praise Him upon the well tuned cymbals: praise Him upon the loud cymbals.

LET EVERYTHING THAT HATH BREATH :
PRAISE THE LORD.

Bibliography

HYMNS

HYMNODY PAST AND PRESENT
Dr. C. S. Phillips (S.P.C.K.) 1937
Dr. Phillips writes mainly from the Anglican standpoint, and there is little reference to Free Church and American sources. Allowing for this limitation, however, it is an admirable book by a leading authority on the Anglican liturgy and music. An excellent guide to the leading Anglican hymn books at present in use.

THE EVOLUTION OF THE ENGLISH HYMN
F. J. Gillman (Allen & Unwin) 1927
Gives more information of hymn developments from Nonconformist sources, and interesting literary information.

THE HYMNS OF METHODISM
Dr. Henry Bett (Epworth Press) 1913
A thorough and scholarly appreciation of the work in hymnody of John and Charles Wesley. Easily the best book in this branch of the subject. A masterly analysis of the qualities of Charles Wesley's hymns.

THE HYMNS OF WESLEY AND WATTS
B. L. Manning (Epworth Press) 1942
A valuable book to which full reference is made in a footnote at the end of Chapter 2.

SONGS OF PRAISE DISCUSSED
Percy Dearmer (O.U.P.) 1933
An important book, not only as an introduction to the hymns contained in *Songs of Praise*, but also as a critical and reliable summary of English hymnody.

POPULAR HYMNS AND THEIR WRITERS
Norman Mable (Independent Press) 1945
THE ROMANTIC ORIGIN OF SOME FAVOURITE HYMNS.
W. T. Keeler (Letchworth Printers Ltd.) 1945
Both these books are a collection of anecdotes and stories which have become associated with some of the more popular hymns. There are also brief biographical notes about the writers.

THE ART OF PUBLIC WORSHIP
Percy Dearmer (Mowbrays) 1919
An interesting outline of Anglican music, ceremonial and liturgy, with critical suggestions for reform, including suggestive comments on the use of hymns in worship.

ISAAC WATTS
Arthur P. Davis (Independent Press) 1948
This is a splendid book. A reprint of a recent American study of Isaac Watts. It is comprehensive and based on thorough research. The section dealing with the hymns of Isaac Watts is most valuable.

JOHN ELLERTON : LIFE AND WRITINGS ON HYMNOLOGY
H. Housman (S.P.C.K.) 1896
An excellent biography of this leading Anglican hymn writer, together with his various critical and historical papers on the subject.

Dr. JULIAN'S DICTIONARY OF HYMNOLOGY 1890
The standard work of reference. Encyclopaedic, and of great value for research. Can be found in most good reference libraries.

THE ENGLISH HYMN — Louis Benson 1915

This is an American book by an authority. It is of great value for the student who wishes to carry on further research. It will be found in the British Museum.

MUSIC

MUSIC AND WORSHIP
Walford Davies and Harvey Grace
(Eyre & Spottiswoode) 1937

This is an excellent book for the average reader. Brief, clear and with wise counsel for all concerned with the direction of church music.

THE SINGING CHURCH : AN OUTLINE OF THE MUSIC SUNG BY CHOIR AND PEOPLE
Dr. C. Henry Phillips (Faber & Faber) 1945

A thorough treatment of the subject by a competent authority. It is a little technical for the non-musical reader, although the historical portions will be found of great interest by everyone.

Index of Hymn and Tune Titles

(Names of tunes in italics)

271

275

Index of Subjects

ENGLAND'S CHURCHES

THEIR RISE AND WITNESS

by H. A. L. Jefferson

"*Highly valuable. The treatment is sympathetic and understanding. The writer clearly knows several Churches from within : he is therefore somewhat uniquely qualified to write a book of this kind. His pleasant volume will be a contribution to mutual understanding among the denominations.*" —BRITISH WEEKLY.

"*The book is beautifully written—clear, simple, forthright. No trace of party spirit mars its pages, and a vast amount of information is packed into it. I recommend it most warmly. It is just the book for Sunday School teachers and scholars, for honest inquirers, and for all who desire to get above and beyond the creeds into that realm where all creeds are one.*" —INQUIRER.

"*A unique book as far as my experience goes. Since 1871 . . . no Anglican writer that I know of has treated the history and tenets of all the Free Churches . . . . But Mr. Jefferson has done it for Anglicans, Presbyterians, Congregationalists, Baptists, Methodists, Friends, and Unitarians with an understanding and sympathy which must do good. And the nine illustrations are well chosen.*" —"ARTIFEX" IN THE MANCHESTER GUARDIAN.

"*It is soundly done, with real sympathy and a commendable concern for Christian unity.*" —CONGREGATIONAL QUARTERLY.

"*Interesting and should prove of value to the average church member of an inquiring mind.*" —BAPTIST TIMES.

"*The layman can certainly learn much here which is less easily gathered from more pretentious volumes.*" —THE FRIEND.

Cloth Crown 8vo.   9 half-tone illustrations   10s. 6d. net

JACOB BOEHME

HIS LIFE AND WORKS

by Hans Lassen Martensen

Edited by STEPHEN HOBHOUSE, M.A.

Foreword by Canon Peter Green

"... *a valuable aid to an understanding of this remarkable man and his teachings.*"—DAILY TELEGRAPH

"... *enriched as it is by its able editor's reflections it is most valuable and can be recommended to all who wish to know something of Boehme but shrink from tackling him in the raw ... The translation reads very well and makes such excellent sense.*"—THE GUARDIAN

"*One can only say that the editor of this book has put us all in his debt.*"
—THE FRIEND

"*The authority of utter originality is there ... Stephen Hobhouse comments most illuminatingly.*"—THE WAYFARER

"*The work could not have been put in better hands. A disciple and interpreter of William Law, he is singularly well qualified to reintroduce students to Law's master Jacob Boehme ... Stephen Hobhouse's labour of love in this new revised edition of Martensen's book should promote a right understanding of Scripture as well as a renewed appreciation of a great mystic.*"—JOURNAL OF THEOLOGICAL STUDIES

Cloth Demy 8vo   Frontispiece of Boehme's handwriting

21s net

SELECTED MYSTICAL WRITINGS
OF WILLIAM LAW

*Edited with Notes and twenty-four studies
in the Mystical Theology of
William Law and Jacob Boehme*
by STEPHEN HOBHOUSE, M.A.

SECOND EDITION, REVISED WITH ADDITIONAL NOTES,
INCLUDING AN ENQUIRY INTO THE INFLUENCE OF JACOB
BOEHME ON ISAAC NEWTON, AND A FOREWORD BY
ALDOUS HUXLEY

*"A noble anthology. These papers give us a wonderful idea of a
noble Christian whose prose style, homely wit and deep religion represent
Anglican piety at its highest level."*
—CHURCH OF ENGLAND NEWS.

*"It only remains to commend Mr. Hobhouse's book to my readers
not only as containing matter of abundant interest, but for the admirable
temper in which it deals with matters of theological controversy."*
—HIBBERT JOURNAL.

*"This book is the fruit of profound study, wise selection and great
research . . . . deserves a wide circulation."* —THE FRIEND.

*"There is, of course, much more than the writings of William Law
within these pages and the permanent value of the volume may lie in what
Mr. Hobhouse himself contributes as much as in the reproduction of Law's
most characteristic passages. The purpose of this excellently produced
book is 'to promote both a more living worship of God and a better
understanding of the Christian faith.' "*
—WESLEY HISTORICAL SOCIETY.

"This carefully and copiously annotated anthology."
—CHURCH TIMES.

"This invaluable and scholarly selection." —RECONCILIATION.

"This admirable volume." —THE INQUIRER.

"An important book." —THE GUARDIAN (Book of the Week).

"The book contains much valuable material and repays reading."
—PEACE NEWS.

*"Finely produced volume. All will find the book deeply interesting
and rewarding."* —THE CHRISTIAN WORLD.

*"Law writes the most beautiful and translucent English, at once
imaginative and serene."*—THE TIMES LITERARY SUPPLEMENT.

Cloth, Demy 8vo.   *Frontispiece of Law's handwriting*   25s. *net.*

WILLIAM LAW

A STUDY IN LITERARY CRAFTSMANSHIP

by Henri Talon

"This extraordinarily concentrated study of William Law . . . . introduces us to the complete Law. It is exceedingly salutary to find at last a study of this remarkable man in his entire person."
—LIFE OF THE SPIRIT

"A valuable introduction to the study of one of the greatest English mystics . . . . M. Talon writes as a discerning critic." —INQUIRER.

"This excellent little book . . . There is no padding . . . . all is clear and concise. The criticism is shrewd, objective, illuminating and percipient."
—CHURCH TIMES.

"Written with knowledge, love and vigour."
—CHRISTIAN WORLD.

"To those who care for words and the mystery of style, this account of the developing relationship between Law's spiritual powers and mode of expression must be fascinating." —THE WAYFARER.

"A gifted young Frenchman has produced this impressive little work in admirable English."
—THE FRIEND.

"A very attractive and readable book."
—SCIENCE OF THOUGHT REVIEW.

"A valuable and timely introduction which will be a help both to the student and to the general reader."
—THE GUARDIAN

Cloth Cr. 8vo   with index and bibliography   8s. 6d. net.

EXISTENTIALIST PHILOSOPHIES

AN INTRODUCTION

by Emmanuel Mounier

Translated by Eric Blow

"The best general introduction to the whole movement . . . . excellently translated."
—CHURCH TIMES.

"An able assessment of a remarkable movement . . . marked by learning and penetrating flashes of insight."
—THE GUARDIAN.

"Very comprehensive and 'deep-digging.' "
—SCIENCE OF THOUGHT REVIEW.

"All through this vivid and stimulating analysis of existentialism, M. Mounier reminds us that it is not a philosophy but a faith and a mysticism . . . Mr. Blow must be congratulated on his courage and success in handling a self-made idiom."
—TIMES LITERARY SUPPLEMENT.

Cloth Demy 8vo.   15s. net